A Guide to

Diversity and Inclusion

in the 21st Century Workplace

Second Edition

Professor Michael L. Fox

New York State Bar Association publications are intended to provide current and accurate information to help attorneys maintain their professional competence. Publications are distributed with the understanding that NYSBA does not render any legal, accounting or other professional service. Attorneys using publications or orally conveyed information in dealing with a specific client's or their own legal matters should also research original sources of authority.

We consider the publication of any NYSBA practice book as the beginning of a dialogue with our readers. Periodic updates to this book will give us the opportunity to incorporate your suggestions regarding additions or corrections. Please send your comments to: Publications Director, New York State Bar Association, One Elk Street, Albany, NY 12207.

ISBN: 978-1-57969-027-4
Product Number: 415820

Dedication

To my family, friends and colleagues—
particularly my parents, Hon. Mark D. and Jean Amatucci Fox—
for their never-ending support and encouragement in this ongoing labor of love.

And to the New York State Bar Association:
the mission is vital, the calling unequaled, never tire.

TABLE OF CONTENTS

FOREWORD

When I attended law school in the 1970s, the term "diversity" was understood to mean a basis for the exercise of subject matter jurisdiction in federal court. At that time, there was little reason for law students to think about "diversity" and "inclusion" in any other context.

However, the modern dictionary defines "diversity" as "the inclusion of diverse people (as people of different races or cultures) in a group or organization" (Merriam-Webster's Collegiate Dictionary, 11th ed. (2014)).

There is little doubt that contemporary law has incorporated and dramatically expanded the dictionary definition, elevating "diversity" and "inclusion" to the level of cognizable legal rights prescribed by statute, regulation and case law. Nowhere are these rights more evident—and more hotly contested—than in the workplace.

The importance of "diversity" and "inclusion" has not been lost on the New York State Bar Association. The Association—through its Committee on Diversity and Inclusion so ably co-chaired by Mirna Santiago and Violet Samuels—is dedicated to promoting and advancing the full and equal participation of attorneys of color and other diverse attorneys in the Association and in all sectors and at every level of the legal profession through research, education, fostering involvement and leadership development in NYSBA. The Committee is also charged with promoting knowledge of and respect for the profession in communities that historically have been excluded from the practice of law.

Another example of the Association's unwavering commitment to "diversity" and "inclusion" is its publication of this volume: *A Guide to Diversity and Inclusion in the 21st Century Workplace* by Professor Michael L. Fox.

As aptly described by the author, Professor Fox, in the Introduction to his work, "[T]he purpose of this book is to provide attorneys, judges, businesspeople, and students in those relevant fields, with a hand-held, ready reference guide on the major issues of Diversity and Inclusion . . . Rather than provide a voluminous, exhaustive treatise—which already exists—this text is intended to allow the reader, following a few hours of study, to become conversant in the laws, cases and regulations governing diversity and inclusion matters for the workplace, as well as have the ability to identify and locate seminal cases or statutes with relative ease."

My perusal of the book confirms this description, and I am confident that other readers will come to the same conclusion. My confidence is based—in no small measure—on my long-time friendship with the author. I have known Michael—who I am in the habit of calling "the Professor"—as a practicing lawyer and, more recently, as a teacher of the law.

Throughout, I have known him as a bar leader *par excellence.* We have served together on the Executive Committee and House of Delegates of the New York State Bar Association, and the House of Delegates of the American Bar Association as well. He is fiercely dedicated to the missions of these Associations and approaches each issue—no matter how thorny and complex—with intellect, creativity and passion. Of course, his skills as an author—his ability to organize and write with scholarship and great clarity—will be evident to the reader.

It is a privilege to serve as President of the New York State Bar Association, the largest voluntary state bar association in the nation. That privilege is enhanced because, during my term in office, our Association is publishing the latest volume of the Professor's work, and I have been given the opportunity to author this foreword. I have great confidence and little doubt that *A Guide to Diversity and Inclusion in the 21st Century Workplace* will provide an invaluable resource to my colleagues in the profession who are called upon to address the issues of diversity and inclusion. For that, we owe the Professor a collective debt of gratitude.

Scott M. Karson
President, New York State Bar Association

How NYSBA is Putting Words Into Action on Diversity

In keeping with President Hank Greenberg's stated goal of increasing diversity within the legal profession, NYSBA's Committee on Diversity and Inclusion has committed itself to fostering these objectives by adopting the following Mission Statement:

The objectives of the Committee on Diversity and Inclusion are to promote and advance the full and equal participation of attorneys of color and other diverse attorneys in the New York State Bar Association and in all sectors and at every level of the legal profession through research, education, fostering involvement and leadership development in NYSBA and other professional activities, and to promote knowledge of and respect for the profession in communities that historically have been excluded from the practice of law.

The Committee shall also foster the development of, monitor progress of and report on diversity initiatives of the Association, as well as partner with the Sections to continue to pursue enhanced diversity and inclusion in the Association, including among the leadership of the Association.

In conducting its work, the Committee shall consult with and engage Association leaders, other entities and individuals, including Sections of the New York State Bar Association; the New York State Conference of Bar Leaders; the Committee on Leadership Development; the Committee on Women in the Law; the Committee on Civil Rights; the Committee on Disability Rights; the Committee on LGBT People and the Law; the Law, Youth & Citizenship Program; minority and women's bar associations; and others with an interest in the Committee's mission and activities.

Mirna M. Santiago, Esq. Chair	Violet E. Samuels, Esq. Chair

INTRODUCTION

The test of our progress is not whether we add more to the abundance of those who have much; it is whether we provide enough for those who have too little.[1]

Do these words of President Franklin Roosevelt refer solely to financial means? Could we interpret them to mean an abundance in any one of a number of "effects," including rights and freedoms? Perhaps they can be understood more broadly as applying to privileges and protections under law that now serve to free those who were once historically voiceless—those disadvantaged, disregarded or discarded due to their race, gender, age, disability or other such characteristic often beyond their control. That is the realm in which this book exists: evaluating employment and anti-discrimination laws in the United States as a method of analyzing diversity, inclusion and elimination of bias in society.[2]

Employment law, human resources, employee relations—whatever you call it, the field is rapidly becoming one of the most time-consuming areas of focus for business owners, executives and managers. The laws, regulations and cases are legion; the ground is ever-shifting; the topic is of the utmost importance for both a productive workforce and a liability-free business endeavor. Attorneys, or other employers, with *one* employee, 20 employees, or 1,000 employees, should remember what they have read here.

Lest you think, in this highly charged political era, that this text is unnecessary, that we live in a nation already all too conscious about diversity, and that this topic is the subject of hyper-focus, one simple example emphasizes there is always time to learn more. Take a situation in Oklahoma, where—***in the year 2019***—a Caucasian female news anchor, reporting on the story of a young gorilla at a local zoo, stated in a joking

1 Hon. Franklin Delano Roosevelt, 32nd President of the United States, Second Inaugural Address (Jan. 20, 1937). Franklin Roosevelt and his cousin President Theodore Roosevelt are alumni of Columbia University School of Law, *see* https://www.law.columbia.edu/media_inquiries/news_events/2008/september2008/roosevelt_jds; http://c250.columbia.edu/c250_celebrates/remarkable_columbians/franklin_delano_roosevelt.html.

2 *See* Montrece McNeill Ransom, *'Belongingness' Is Important to Diversity and Inclusion in the Workplace*, ABA Journal, May 2, 2019, http://www.abajournal.com/voice/article/belongingness-important-to-diversity-and-inclusion-in-the-workplace.

manner, on air, that the gorilla resembled her African-American co-host.[3] Yes, you read that correctly.

Thus, the purpose of this book is to provide attorneys, judges, businesspeople, and students in those relevant fields, with a hand-held, ready reference guide on the major issues of Diversity and Inclusion in the early

---

3 Tara Law, *White News Anchor Apologizes After Saying Black Co-Host Looks Like Gorilla*, Time, Aug. 27, 2019, https://time.com/5662957/news-anchor-says-black-cohost-looks-like-gorilla; Mallory Simon, *TV Anchor Apologizes After Comparing Black Cohost to a Gorilla*, CNN.com, Aug. 28, 2019, https://www.cnn.com/2019/08/27/us/oklahoma-tv-anchor-apologizes-racist-comments-soh/index.html. Granted, response from the public was swift and certain, condemning the statement, and the Caucasian co-host apologized, tearfully, on air the next day. *Id.* But the incident still occurred. Sadly, this is not the only modern example. In 2020, a McDonald's restaurant in Guangzhou, China banned African-Americans from entering the premises – via a sign posted at the door. It appears that the issue concerned fears over the spread of COVID-19, not that such would be a justification for any blanket ban of a race of people. Although, it should be noted that McDonald's corporate headquarters issued an apology and a statement that the actions of the restaurant franchise were "not representative of [their] inclusive values", and stated training would take place. *See* Joshua Bote, *McDonald's Issues Apology After China Restaurant Bans Black People*, USA Today, Apr. 14, 2020, https://www.usatoday.com/story/money/business/2020/04/14/mcdonalds-apologizes-after-china-restaurant-bans-black-people/2991341001/. Also in 2020, a justice on a California appeals court (and former federal magistrate judge) was ordered removed from the bench following multiple allegations of sexual harassment and touching, by several women including another justice, over a multi-year period. At the time of this writing, attorneys for the justice stated the removal order of the California Commission on Judicial Performance would be appealed. *See* Debra Cassens Weiss, *California Appeals Judge Is Removed From Bench for Sexual Harassment and Unwanted Touching*, ABA Journal, June 3, 2020, https://www.abajournal.com/news/article/california-appeals-judge-is-removed-from-bench-for-sexual-harassment-and-unwanted-touching; Debra Cassens Weiss, *State Justice Accused of Sexual Harassment That Started When He Was Federal Magistrate Judge*, ABA Journal, Jan. 16, 2019, https://www.abajournal.com/news/article/state-appeals-judge-is-accused-of-sexual-harassment-that-began-when-he-was-a-federal-magistrate. Finally, in 2019, an allegation was made against the Washington State Bar Association that its Board of Governors allowed a hostile work environment because of the alleged mishandling of sexual harassment complaints by an employee against a Board member. Multiple employees lodged concerns, including several dozen who contacted the state's Supreme Court. The former Chief Justice appointed an independent attorney to investigate, and the resulting report found: "the Board of Governors did not have in place, or hold itself accountable to, any anti-harassment policies and procedures dictating clear expectations of behavior and processes for handling complaints of inappropriate behavior against a Governor.... Finally, the Board failed to take any preventive or remedial action to address that situation thus failing to maintain a working environment for the WSBA staff employees free from intimidation, ridicule and insult in accordance with EEOC Guidance Policy". Lyle Moran, *Washington Bar's Board Mishandled Employee's Sexual Harassment Complaint, Report Finds*, ABA Journal, May 21, 2020, https://www.abajournal.com/web/article/washington-state-bars-board-mishandled-employees-harassment-complaint-report-finds; Attorney Beth Van Moppes, *Summary of Investigation, Washington State Bar Association Board of Governors*, Dec. 31, 2019, https://www.abajournal.com/files/Van_Moppes_Report.pdf (cited in L. Moran, *Washington Bar's Board Mishandled, supra*). The Supreme Court's new Chief Justice thereafter, in 2020, appointed an ombudsperson for the Bar Association's staff issues, and requested periodic reports from the Bar's Board regarding relationships with Bar leadership and staff. *See* L. Moran, *Washington Bar's Board Mishandled, supra*.

21st Century. Rather than provide a voluminous, exhaustive treatise—which already exists—this text is intended to allow the reader, following a few hours of study, to become conversant in the laws, cases and regulations governing diversity and inclusion matters for the workplace, as well as have the ability to identify and locate seminal cases or statutes with relative ease. This is accomplished by addressing respect for variances amongst peoples through evaluation of the federal and New York State laws and regulations that protect against discrimination, retaliation and harassment in employment. By so doing, an employer avoiding violations of law will in turn be showing respect for diversity and differences, and providing opportunities for inclusion of all races, genders, religious faiths, ages, disabilities, and other classes of employees.

Attorneys can utilize this text to familiarize themselves with the requirements of the laws, as well as ethical obligations regarding non-discrimination (NYRPC 8.4(g), (h)), and advise business clients concerning employee relations. Business professionals, particularly in human resource management of concerns large and small, can utilize this text to become informed consumers of legal advice, recognizing obligations, and understanding what they need to discuss with counsel.

In Chapter 1, we will review the provisions of the main federal and New York State laws concerning provisions of anti-discrimination, anti-harassment and anti-retaliation. The discussion will specifically include amendments of the New York State laws by the Senate and Assembly, and signed into law by the Governor, in the summer of 2019. In Chapter 2, we address protection for sexual orientation and the groundbreaking *Bostock v. Clayton County* decision of the Supreme Court of the United States issued in 2020, which eliminated the differences that had previously existed between the protections for sexual orientation and gender identity under federal law and New York State law, and which also resolved the differences in application that previously existed between the federal circuits. Chapter 3 will discuss the issue of equal pay, while Chapter 4 addresses the current status of the federal Equal Rights Amendment that has been pending since the 1970s and which was ratified in 2020 by the required 38th state (Virginia), despite the long-past expiration of the deadlines set by Congress. Chapter 5 provides information concerning administrative proceedings before the federal Equal Employment Opportunity Commission and the New York State Division of Human Rights, and encourages employers to understand the importance of clear policies & concurrent paperwork. In Chapter 6 we will return to federal law, by evaluating the Americans with Disabilities Act, as well as provisions under the federal Family Medical Leave Act (FMLA) and New York State Paid Leave. Chapter 7 examines the law as it pertains to the accessibility of websites for those with qualifying disabilities. The book concludes with Chapter 8, containing specific scenarios and hypotheticals for analysis, all involving concepts addressed in the preceding chapters. Throughout the text effort is also made to mention or address effects of the COVID-19 pandemic if it had an impact on law, employment practices, or specific groups of persons.

As always, an informed citizenry, knowledgeable of the laws and regulations governing their actions, is a defense against losses and legal woes. Further, when we consider the protections now afforded to those who for much of history had no recourse when subjected to harassment, discrimination or retaliation in the very workplace providing their means of sustenance and existence, we are reminded of the words of one of Ancient Rome's greatest statesmen, orators, attorneys, and last champions of the Republic, Marcus Tullius Cicero: "*Salus populi suprema est lex,*" which among its many different translations means "the welfare of the people is the highest law," "the good of the people is the highest law," or "the good of the people is the greatest law."[4]

---

4 Marcus Tullius Cicero (Roman Republic, 106-43 B.C.E.), De Legibus (*On Laws*) begun 52 B.C.E. For more, see https://www.britannica.com/biography/Cicero. This quote, translated into English as "The people's good is the highest law," is found inscribed on the wall above the Great Hall in the New York State Bar Association's Bar Center, Albany, New York, in which its governing House of Delegates meets several times each year.

CHAPTER ONE

THE LANDSCAPE OF FEDERAL AND NEW YORK STATE ANTI-DISCRIMINATION LAWS

[1.0] I. INTRODUCTION TO THE RELEVANT LAW

To begin, let us establish a baseline in one particular realm: employment. In New York and other states sharing similar provisions of law, one should recognize that employees are what are referred to as "at will," meaning "[w]here there is no defined term of employment, it is considered 'to be a hiring . . . which may be freely terminated by either party at any time for any reason or even for no reason.'"[1] That can include an employer's careless or thoughtless termination of an employee (so long as not discriminatory).[2] This "at will" status can be amended or changed by a contract between employer and employee or a labor union collective bargaining agreement, and must also yield to public policies and law (i.e., an employee cannot be terminated because the employer dislikes one or more of the employee's characteristics that places them within a recognized class protected by law).[3]

Now we will move on from that background to discuss protections as related to the creation of a more diverse and inclusive society. Regarding protected classes in employment, housing, education and places of public accommodation, the State of New York has established virtually all of the protections in the New York State Executive Law (the Human Rights Law) at § 290, *et seq*. Other protections can be found in the New York State Civil Rights Law, such as in Articles 4, 4-B and 4-C.[4] There is, additionally, overlap with New York State Correction Law Article 23-A for those who have completed service of a sentence for a crime and are entitled to rejoin society and obtain gainful employment or licensure without fear of discrimination due to past mistakes (with certain exceptions for the consideration of facts such as, *inter alia*, "there is a direct relationship between one or more of the previous criminal offenses and the specific license or employment sought or held by the individual," or "the issuance

---

1 *Maldonado v. DiBre*, 140 A.D.3d 1501, 1505-06, 35 N.Y.S.3d 731, 736 (3d Dep't 2016); *Gaines v. Schneider Nat'l, Inc.*, 2018 WL 5282902, at *2 (E.D. Wis. Oct. 24, 2018) (Griesbach, C.J.) (citing *Tatge v. Chambers & Owen, Inc.*, 219 Wis. 2d 99, 112, 579 N.W.2d 217 (1998)).

2 *Texas Farm Bureau Mut. Ins. Companies v. Sears*, 84 S.W.3d 604 (Tex. 2002) (O'Neill, J.).

3 *See, e.g., Releford v. T. Clay Stuart, PSC*, 2006 WL 1949819 at *1 (Ky. Ct. Apps. July 14, 2006) (Schroder, J.) (plaintiff was unsuccessful only because the employer did not qualify as an "employer" because the law required a threshold of eight employees, and defendant/appellee had less than eight employees; this issue of legal thresholds based on the number of employees is discussed further below).

4 N.Y. Civil Rights Law, Article 4 ("Equal Rights in Places of Public Accommodation and Amusement"), Article 4-B ("Rights of Persons with a Disability Accompanied by Guide Dogs, Hearing Dogs or Service Dogs"), Article 4-C ("Employment of Persons with Certain Genetic Disorders").

or continuation of the license or the granting or continuation of the employment would involve an unreasonable risk to property or to the safety or welfare of specific individuals or the general public" or "[t]he bearing, if any, the criminal offense or offenses for which the person was previously convicted will have on his fitness or ability to perform one or more such duties or responsibilities").[5]

Furthermore, New York City has, as part of its Administrative Code, a Human Rights Law applicable within its five boroughs,[6] as well as a Commission on Human Rights (whose Law Enforcement Bureau is responsible for enforcing the City Human Rights Law).[7] In our ongoing discussion and analysis, we will refer mainly to the New York State Human Rights Law, with occasional reference to applicable provisions in the New York City Human Rights Law. Although the reader should be, at minimum, aware of the State Civil Rights Law and Correction Law provisions and certainly the New York City Human Rights Law (which is very similar to the State law in its expansive protections) if the employer or business/public accommodation operates within the five boroughs of New York City. Thus, their inclusion in this text.[8]

Now, before we go further you may ask, "What exactly is a protected class?" Well, "protected class" has been defined as: "A group of people with a common characteristic who are legally protected from employment

5 N.Y. Correction Law § 750 ("Definitions"), § 751 ("Applicability"), § 752 ("Unfair Discrimination Against Persons Previously Convicted of One or More Criminal Offenses Prohibited"), § 753 ("Factors to Be Considered Concerning a Previous Criminal Conviction; Presumption"), § 754 ("Written Statement upon Denial of License or Employment"), § 755 ("Enforcement"). Keep in mind, though, that aside from the quoted language from §§ 752(1), (2), and 753(1)(c) in the text above, there are other mitigating factors that must also be considered by the potential employer, such as "[t]he public policy of this state, as expressed in this act, to encourage the licensure and employment of persons previously convicted of one or more criminal offenses" (§ 753(1)(a)), "[a]ny information produced by the person, or produced on his behalf, in regard to his rehabilitation and good conduct" (§ 753(1)(g)), and "a certificate of relief from disabilities or a certificate of good conduct issued to the applicant, which certificate shall create a presumption of rehabilitation in regard to the offense or offenses specified therein" (§ 753(2)).

6 *See* N.Y.C. Admin. Code, Ch. 1, § 8-107.

7 *See* New York City Commission on Human Rights, https://www1.nyc.gov/site/cchr/about/inside-cchr.page.

8 New York City's Human Rights Law also has provisions that are, at times, more protective than state or federal law. For instance, in NYC employers can ask a job applicant about education level, professional licenses, experience and gaps in employment, BUT employers may not use an applicant's current unemployment status or past unemployment status to decide compensation, terms of employment, and the like. *See* N.Y.C. Admin. Code §8-107(21); Michele Coyne & Scott Budow, *A Message to NYC Employers: Update Your Hiring Practices*, N.Y.L.J. at p. 4, Mar. 12, 2020.

discrimination on the basis of that characteristic."[9] However, protected classes extend well beyond the employment context, into many areas of society—including housing, entertainment, education and use or utilization of places of public accommodation. Furthermore, protected classes have been expanded over the years to include a number of demographic groups, including race, gender, age and disability—which will all be discussed within this text. Additional protected classes exist, including some that are only provided under state and local laws, such as in New York State and New York City.[10] Let us now delve deeper.

[1.1] II. SPECIFIC PROVISIONS OF NEW YORK STATUTORY LAW

New York's Division of Human Rights declares that New York State

> has the proud distinction of being the first state in the nation to enact a Human Rights Law, which affords every citizen "an equal opportunity to enjoy a full and productive life." This law prohibits discrimination in employment, housing, credit, places of public accommodations, and non-sectarian educational institutions, based on age, race, national origin, sex, sexual orientation, marital status, disability, military status, and other specified classes.[11]

New York's law dates back to an early version in 1951.[12]

The New York State Human Rights Law applied to employers of four or more persons, until February 8, 2020, at which time the Amendments Act signed by the Governor on August 12, 2019, reduced the number of

9 Westlaw Practical Law, *Glossary*, https://content.next.westlaw.com/5-501-5857.

10 For instance, New York State has identified "victim of domestic violence" as a specific protected class under the State Human Rights Law, while federal law contains no such direct protection (although under the operation of certain laws, such as Title VII, the Americans with Disabilities Act or the Fair Housing Act, some protection tangentially related to domestic violence may be available). *See, e.g.*, N.Y. Executive Law § 296(22) (L.2019, c. 176, § 1, *eff.* Nov. 18, 2019) (Exec. Law).

11 *Mission Statement*, N.Y.S. Division of Human Rights, https://dhr.ny.gov/mission-statement.

12 Exec. Law § 291, et seq. (L.1951, c. 800).

employees for covered entities to one.[13] Under the old law, though, there was an exception *for cases of sexual harassment*, where all employers in New York were covered by the law, whether employers of one or more persons.[14]

The New York State Human Rights Law (Executive Law) specifically provides at § 291:

> 1. The opportunity to obtain employment without discrimination because of age, race, creed, color, national origin, sexual orientation, military status, sex, marital status, or disability, is hereby recognized as and declared to be a civil right.
>
> 2. The opportunity to obtain education, the use of places of public accommodation and the ownership, use and occupancy of housing accommodations and commercial space without discrimination because of age, race, creed, color, national origin, sexual orientation, military status, sex, marital status, or disability, as specified in section two hundred ninety six of this article, is hereby recognized as and declared to be a civil right.[15]

Furthermore, New York State Civil Rights Law § 40-c, cross-referencing Human Rights Law § 292, provides:

> 1. All persons within the jurisdiction of this state shall be entitled to the equal protection of the laws of this state or any subdivision thereof.
>
> 2. No person shall, because of race, creed, color, national origin, sex, marital status, sexual orientation, gender

13 Exec. Law (Human Rights Law) § 292(5). The Amendments Act passed by the New York State Legislature in the summer of 2019 redefined an employer as any employing one or more employees, including state and political subdivisions; however the provision did not take effect until February 8, 2020, 180 days after the Governor signed the bill into law on August 12, 2019. In addition, protection for domestic workers was extended to match the same bases for harassment claims as all other New York employees under the NYS HRL as of October 11, 2019 (60 days after the Governor signed the bill). *See* 2019 Sess. Law News of N.Y. Ch. 160 (A. 8421), 2019 Sess. Law News of N.Y. Ch. 161 (S. 6594); Howard S. Lavin & Elizabeth E. DiMichele, *Gov. Cuomo Signs Law Expanding Harassment and Discrimination Protections*, Stroock Special Bulletin, Aug. 14, 2019, https://www.stroock.com/publication/gov-cuomo-signs-law-expanding-harassment-and-discrimination-protections.

14 *See* Exec. Law (Human Rights Law) §§ 292(5), 296.

15 Exec. Law (Human Rights Law) § 291.

> identity or expression, or disability, as such term is defined in section two hundred ninety-two of the executive law, be subjected to any discrimination in his or her civil rights, or to any harassment, as defined in section 240.25 of the penal law, in the exercise thereof, by any other person or by any firm, corporation or institution, or by the state or any agency or subdivision of the state.[16]

Caselaw has made abundantly clear that if a claim by a plaintiff will satisfy and sustain a cause of action under the Human Rights Law, then the same set of alleged facts will also sustain a claim under the Civil Rights Law, and vice versa.[17]

It is also important to recognize that the provisions of the New York State Executive Law concerning human rights *do not* extend to extraterritorial violations (those taking place outside of New York State) unless they are *against a New York resident*. The relevant statutory language of § 298-a is:

> 1. The provisions of this article shall apply as hereinafter provided to an act committed outside this state against a resident of this state or against a corporation organized under the laws of this state or authorized to do business in this state, if such act would constitute an unlawful discriminatory practice if committed within this state.
>
> 2. If a resident person or domestic corporation violates any provision of this article by virtue of the provisions of this section, this article shall apply to such person or corporation in the same manner and to the same extent as such provisions would have applied had such act been committed within this state except that the penal provisions of such article shall not be applicable.[18]

However, courts have since made clear that, although a New York resident corporation could be liable for discriminatory actions outside of New York State, those actions also have to be against a New York resident.[19] Thus, if a domestic New York corporation, partnership or limited liability

16 N.Y. Civil Rights Law § 40-c.

17 *See Gordon v. PL Long Beach, LLC*, 74 A.D.3d 880, 903 N.Y.S.2d 461 (2d Dep't 2010); *Illiano v. Mineola Union Free Sch. Dist.*, 585 F.Supp.2d 341 (E.D.N.Y. 2008) (Spatt, D.J.).

18 Exec. Law § 298-a(1),(2) (emphasis added).

company, having offices in another state, acts in a discriminatory manner against a resident of that state (thus not a resident of New York) in that state, there is no claim under the New York State Human Rights Law.[20]

Both the New York State and New York City Human Rights Laws contain three-year statutes of limitations for claims to be brought in court (see Chapter Five for administrative filing deadlines).[21] Furthermore, the standard required to state a claim under the laws resembles that under federal law, as discussed in later sections of this book. As stated by then-New York State Chief Judge Judith S. Kaye, in the seminal case *Forrest v. Jewish Guild for the Blind*:[22]

> A plaintiff alleging racial discrimination in employment has the initial burden to establish a prima facie case of discrimination. To meet this burden, plaintiff must show that (1) she is a member of a protected class; (2) she was qualified to hold the position; (3) she was terminated from employment or suffered another adverse employment action; and (4) the discharge or other adverse action

---

19 *See Iwankow v. Mobil Corp.*, 150 A.D.2d 272, 273, 541 N.Y.S.2d 428, 429 (1st Dep't 1989) ("The memorandum of the Executive Director of the Law Revision Commission states that the new section [298-a] was intended 'to extend the whole article extra-territorially so that it applies to acts committed outside the state by state residents and non-residents alike *against state residents*.' (Bill Jacket, L.1975, ch. 662, § 2; Emphasis supplied.) Thus, absent an allegation that a discriminatory act was committed in New York *or* that a New York State resident was discriminated against, New York's courts have no subject matter jurisdiction over the alleged wrong"); *Beckett v. Prudential Ins. Co. of Am.*, 893 F.Supp. 234, 238 (S.D.N.Y. 1995) (Scheindlin, D.J.) ("The NYHRL does not provide a non-resident with a private cause of action for discriminatory conduct committed outside of New York by a New York corporation") (citing *Iwankow*).

20 The extraterritorial application of the statutory framework and language to the potential case of a *non-New York employer* and a *New York resident employee*, with all facts and circumstances *taking place outside of New York State*, is questionable, and may depend on those very facts and circumstances. *See, e.g., Natarajan v. CLS Bank Int'l*, 2014 WL 1745024 (D.N.J. Apr. 30, 2014) (Cecchi, D.J.).

21 *Morse v. JetBlue Airways Corp.*, 941 F.Supp.2d 274, 291 (E.D.N.Y. 2013) (Matsumoto, D.J.).

22 3 N.Y.3d 295, 391 (2004) (Kaye, C.J.).

> occurred under circumstances giving rise to an inference of discrimination."[23]

This has been deemed the standard necessary for religious discrimination and gender discrimination, as well.[24] In *McNabb v. MacAndrews & Forbes Group, Inc.*, then-Chief U.S. District Judge Charles L. Brieant of the Southern District of New York, ultimately determined that the plaintiff could not succeed in defeating a motion for summary judgment because plaintiff could not satisfy two of the four elements that hinged on the same issue: "[s]pecifically, plaintiff . . . failed to demonstrate that he was fired."[25]

Under New York State law, since the Amendments Act in the summer of 2019, a showing of "severe and pervasive" action on the part of the employer—or continuing and pervasive or severe as it was also known—is no longer required. That is in contrast to what is still required under federal law, as discussed later. An employee making a claim under New York law need now only show that they are treated less well than other employees.[26] This was previously the standard under the New York City Human Rights Law.[27]

---

23 3 N.Y.3d at 391 (citing Ferrante v. Am. Lung Assn., 90 N.Y.2d 623, 629 (1997)). *See also Gittens-Bridges v. City of N.Y.*, 2020 WL 3100213 at *14 (S.D.N.Y. June 11, 2020) (Ramos, D.J.) ("An inference of discrimination can arise from circumstances including, but not limited to, ... [an employer's] invidious comments about others in the employee's protected group; or the more favorable treatment of employees not in the protected group...."); McNabb v. MacAndrews & Forbes Group, Inc., 1991 WL 284104 at *6 (S.D.N.Y. Dec. 24, 1991) (Brieant, C.J.) (citing, *inter alia, Pena v. Brattleboro Retreat*, 702 F.2d 322 (2d Cir. 1983); *Meiri v. Dacon*, 759 F.2d 989 (2d Cir.), *cert. denied* 474 U.S. 829 (1985) (religious discrimination); *Sweeney v. Research Foundation of State Univ.*, 711 F.2d 1179 (2d Cir. 1983) (gender discrimination)).

24 *Id.* Note also that under Title VII, a plaintiff must demonstrate that membership in a protected class "was a 'substantial' or 'motivating' factor contributing to the employer's decision to take the [adverse employment] action." Accordingly, to show causation for sex discrimination under Title VII, "[i]t suffices ... to show that the motive to discriminate was one of the employer's motives, even if the employer also had other, lawful motives that were causative in the employer's decision." *Vega v. Hempstead Union Free Sch. Dist.*, 801 F.3d 72, 85 (2d Cir. 2015) (Chin, J.); *Univ. of Tx. Sw. Med. Ctr. v. Nassar*, 133 S.Ct. 2517, 2523 (2013) (Kennedy, J.). *See Vega*, 801 F.3d at 86 ("[A] plaintiff in a Title VII case need not allege 'but-for' causation.").

25 *McNabb*, 1991 WL 284104 at *6.

26 *See* Exec. Law § 296(1)(h) (eff. Nov. 18, 2019).

27 *Roberts v. United Parcel Serv., Inc.*, 115 F.Supp.3d 344, 368-69 (E.D.N.Y. 2015) (Weinstein, Senior D.J.). *See also Jamiel v. Viveros*, 2020 WL 1847566 at *4 (S.D.N.Y. Apr. 13, 2020) (Daniels, D.J.).

The reader should also be aware that, in July 2019, Governor Andrew Cuomo signed amendments to the Dignity for All Students Act,[28] making it illegal to discriminate against someone on the basis of their hairstyle both in schools and the workplace. Such provision was put into place because, oftentimes, that form of discrimination accompanies race/gender discrimination. Thus, the amendments added language to the statute section to the effect of: "9. 'Race' shall, for the purposes of this article include traits historically associated with race, including but not limited to, hair texture and protective hairstyles. 10. 'Protective hairstyles' shall include, but not be limited to, such hairstyles as braids, locks, and twists."[29] The amendment was also made to the provisions of the New York Executive Law.[30] New York was the second state, following California, to expand this protection.[31] Since February of 2019, New York City's Human Rights Commission prohibited discrimination based on hairstyles in workplaces, along with schools and public places.[32]

Additionally, as a separate matter for inclusive workplaces, employers should be aware of the provisions of New York Labor Law § 201-d. That statute provides, in pertinent part:

> 2. Unless otherwise provided by law, it shall be unlawful for any employer or employment agency to refuse to hire, employ or license, or to discharge from employment or otherwise discriminate against an individual in compensation, promotion or terms, conditions or privileges of employment because of:

---

28 Educ. Law §§ 10, *et seq. See also* D. Sharmin Arefin, *Is Hair Discrimination Race Discrimination?*, ABA Bus. Law Today, Apr. 17, 2020 (discussing CROWN (Create a Respectful and Open World for Natural Hair) acts/laws, including New York's passage of its own CROWN Act (the Dignity for All Students Act), as well as legislative action in California and New Jersey, making hair discrimination race discrimination), https://businesslawtoday.org/2020/04/hair-discrimination-race-discrimination; M. Coyne & S. Budow, *A Message to NYC Employers*, supra; Daniel Turinsky & Janeen Hall, *Guidance for Complying With NY's Prohibition on Hair, Religious Garb Discrimination*, N.Y.L.J. at p. 9, Feb. 24, 2020.

29 Educ. Law § 11, 2019 Sess. Law News of N.Y. Ch. 95 (S. 6209-A).

30 Exec. Law 292(37), (38), 2019 Sess. Law News of N.Y. Ch. 95 (S. 6209-A).

31 *See* Janelle Griffith, *New York is Second State to Ban Discrimination Based on Natural Hairstyles*, NBC News, July 15, 2019, https://www.nbcnews.com/news/nbcblk/new-york-second-state-ban-discrimination-based-natural-hairstyles-n1029931.

32 *Id. See also* Eve I. Klein, *Hairdon'ts in NYC: Race Discrimination Based on Hairstyle Is Illegal*, N.Y.L.J. at p. 4, Apr. 26, 2019.

> a. an individual's political activities outside of working hours, off of the employer's premises and without use of the employer's equipment or other property, if such activities are legal, provided, however, that this paragraph shall not apply to persons whose employment is defined in paragraph six of subdivision (a) of section seventy-nine-h of the civil rights law, and provided further that this paragraph shall not apply to persons who would otherwise be prohibited from engaging in political activity pursuant to chapter 15 of title 5 and subchapter III of chapter 73 of title 5 of the USCA;
>
> b. an individual's legal use of consumable products prior to the beginning or after the conclusion of the employee's work hours, and off of the employer's premises and without use of the employer's equipment or other property;
>
> c. an individual's legal recreational activities outside work hours, off of the employer's premises and without use of the employer's equipment or other property; or
>
> d. an individual's membership in a union or any exercise of rights granted under Title 29, USCA, Chapter 7 or under article fourteen of the civil service law.[33]

Disputes sometimes arise over what particular activities are included and protected under § 201-d. What are "recreational activities"? What are political activities? For instance, if a workplace prohibits dating or fraternization amongst the staff, is that a violation of the statute? No, according to the caselaw.[34] What about support of a political candidate or cause? For instance, if an employee is a candidate for elective office, or is a campaign manager or treasurer for a campaign, a fundraiser host, or otherwise campaigns for a candidate and is terminated because the employer supports an opposing candidate, is that a violation under the statute? Yes, again according to the caselaw on the matter.[35]

Another interesting change, based on the Amendments Act in the summer of 2019, concerns claims in New York of aiding and abetting asserted

---

33 N.Y. Labor Law § 201-d.

34 *Hudson v. Goldman Sachs & Co., Inc.*, 283 A.D.2d 246, 246-47, 725 N.Y.S.2d 318, 319 (1st Dep't 2001); *State v. Wal-Mart Stores, Inc.*, 207 A.D.2d 150, 621 N.Y.S.2d 158 (3d Dep't 1995) (Mercure, J.).

35 *Wehlage v. Quinlan*, 55 A.D.3d 1344, 864 N.Y.S.2d 630 (4th Dep't 2008) (mem.).

against a manager or supervisor, or someone else in the company who as an individual contributed to, aided or abetted the discriminatory treatment.[36] That is a claim not otherwise available under federal law[37] (however, it appears individual liability would be available against an independent contractor[38]).

The claim under state law may be asserted against an individual person, although a plaintiff must prove the underlying discrimination claim first against the employer/company, otherwise there is nothing to aid and abet as far as bias, discrimination, harassment or discrimination against the plaintiff.[39] Since the summer of 2019, the New York Human Rights Law has an added term: "private employer" including "person."[40] That change could result in individual liability for an employer or individual, in cases of discrimination, harassment or retaliation, such that a specific "aiding and abetting" claim, with a prerequisite showing of underlying liability, may no longer be necessary, although the provision still exists.

With the signing of the New York State 2019 Budget Bill by Governor Cuomo in 2018, several new laws were created, influenced by the *#MeToo* Movement.[41] That was apparently only the first step, however, since the Amendments Act signed on August 12, 2019 added additional provisions to the statutes.

First, § 201-g of the Labor Law (*eff.* Oct. 9, 2018) requires the State Department of Labor and Division of Human Rights to create and publish a model sexual harassment policy *inter alia*, to prohibit harassment, include information on statutory provisions, include a standard complaint form, and inform employees of their rights. The Department of Labor and

---

36 *See* Exec. Law § 296(6).

37 Courts have discussed aiding and abetting claims as only falling under state laws. *Grauer v. UBS Financial Services, Inc.*, 2008 WL 11398936 at *10, *15 (S.D.N.Y. Dec. 17, 2008) (Preska, D.J.); *Cullen v. Putnam Savings Bank, Inc.*, 1997 WL 280502 at *5 (D. Conn. May 17, 1997) (Nevas, D.J.) (Connecticut law; "Based on the express statutory language of Conn. Gen.Stat. § 46a–60(a)(5) and the Second Circuit's acknowledgment in *Tomka* that state anti-discrimination statutes may go further than federal laws and provide for aiding and abetting liability").

38 *See Quincy Mut. Fire Ins. Co. v. Vivint Solar Dev., LLC*, 2018 WL 3974820 at *3-*4 & n.1 (D.R.I. Aug. 20, 2018) (Burroughs, D.J.).

39 *See Haggood v. Rubin & Rothman, LLC*, 2014 WL 6473527 at *22 (E.D.N.Y. 2014) (Feuerstein, D.J.); *Forrest v. Jewish Guild for the Blind*, 3 N.Y.3d 295, 314 (2004).

40 Exec. Law § 292(37), 2019 Sess. Law News of N.Y. Ch. 160 (A. 8421).

41 *See* Labor Law § 201-g (eff. Oct. 9, 2018) (2018 Sess. Law News of N.Y. Ch. 57 (S. 7507-C)); Exec. Law § 296-d (eff. Apr. 12, 2018) (2018 Sess. Law News of N.Y. Ch. 57 (S. 7507-C)); CPLR 7515 (eff. July 11, 2018) (2018 Sess. Law News of N.Y. Ch. 57 (S. 7507-C)).

Division of Human Rights must also produce a model sexual harassment prevention training program for the workplace.[42] Employers must have written policies, and training, covering specific issues—*inter alia*, examples of conduct, remedies, standard complaint forms, procedures, and anti-retaliation provisions—either adopting the model policies, or crafting policies the same as or exceeding the government's models.[43] The 2019 Amendments Act created additional provisions concerning the languages in which the model policies must be expanded, and how they are to be made available to employees.[44]

In addition, § 296-d of the Executive Law (Human Rights Law) was created in 2018, and it expanded liability and the negligence standard for an employer to prevent or stop harassment of a non-employee (consultant, vendor or contractor) by an employee. Such requirement was not included in the law before.

> It shall be an unlawful discriminatory practice for an employer to permit sexual harassment of non-employees in its workplace. An employer may be held liable to a non-employee who is a contractor, subcontractor, vendor, consultant or other person providing services pursuant to a contract in the workplace or who is an employee of such contractor, subcontractor, vendor, consultant or other person providing services pursuant to a contract in the workplace, with respect to sexual harassment, when the employer, its agents or supervisors knew or should have known that such non-employee was subjected to sexual harassment in the employer's workplace, and the employer failed to take immediate and appropriate corrective action. In reviewing such cases involving non-employees, the extent of the employer's control and any other legal responsibility which the employer may have with respect to the conduct of the harasser shall be considered.[45]

---

42 *See* Appendices A, B and C for copies of the relevant New York State Department of Labor and Division of Human Rights policies and guidance.

43 *See* Labor Law § 201-g(a)(1).

44 *See id.*, 2019 Sess. Law News of N.Y. Ch. 160 (A. 8421).

45 *See* Exec. Law § 296-d.

With the Amendments Act of 2019, the provisions of the law have been expanded to other forms of discrimination and harassment.[46]

Finally, in 2018, a new section was added to the Civil Practice Law and Rules: 7515. That section prohibited (unless inconsistent with federal law) pre-dispute mandatory arbitration provisions that require the parties to arbitrate sexual harassment claims, as those provisions are included in written contracts entered after July 11, 2018.

> (b)(i) Prohibition. Except where inconsistent with federal law, no written contract, entered into on or after the effective date of this section shall contain a prohibited clause as defined in paragraph two of subdivision (a) of this section.
>
> (ii) Exceptions. Nothing contained in this section shall be construed to impair or prohibit an employer from incorporating a non-prohibited clause or other mandatory arbitration provision within such contract, that the parties agree upon.[47]

Agreements made after a dispute arises are not covered by the act; parties can agree to arbitrate a claim once it is made. Following the Amendments Act of 2019, the provisions of CPLR 7515 have been expanded to all harassment, discrimination and retaliation claims under Article 15 of the Executive Law (Human Rights Law).[48]

A problem exists, however, in the form of preemption under the Federal Arbitration Act (FAA). The case of *Latif v. Morgan Stanley & Co. LLC*,[49] in the Southern District of New York, was the first to directly address the application of the FAA to the new CPLR 7515. Quoting from § 2 of the FAA, the Court stated: "a written provision in . . . a contract evidencing a transaction involving commerce to settle by arbitration a controversy thereafter arising out of such contract or transaction . . . shall be valid, irrevocable, and enforceable, save upon such grounds as exist at law or in equity *for the revocation of any contract*."[50] The plaintiff in *Latif* was

46 *Id.*

47 CPLR 7515 (*eff.* July 11, 2018).

48 *See* CPLR 7515 (*eff.* Oct. 11, 2019) (2019 Sess. Law News of N.Y. Ch. 160 (A. 8421)).

49 2019 WL 2610985 (S.D.N.Y. June 26, 2019) (Cote, D.J.).

50 *Id.* at *2 (citing 9 U.S.C. § 2) (emphasis by court).

found to have a binding arbitration provision in his contract of employment, such that the state law (CPLR 7515) invalidating that agreement for a claim-specific reason, rather than grounds for revocation of any contract (such as fraud, duress or unconscionability), was held to be preempted and invalid as applied to the plaintiff's contract provision.[51] In fact, CPLR 7515 in its language states explicitly that it applies unless inconsistent with federal law, which is the FAA.[52] While *Latif* was a decision of a federal trial court, and thus is not binding precedent, one can expect this will not be the last time a court addresses this issue.[53] But, for the moment, *Latif* stands for the proposition that CPLR 7515 cannot have the impact envisioned by legislators in New York. This is a matter that deserves attention and recognition, since CPLR 7515 may be largely preempted by the FAA despite all good intentions by the New York State Legislature.

Finally, the reader should take note of the 2018 additions of CPLR 5003-b and General Obligations Law § 5-336 (GOL), which limit the use of confidentiality and non-disclosure agreements connected to resolution of sexual harassment claims in New York.[54] General Obligations Law § 5-336 provides that plaintiff employees must have 21 days to consider the provision and seven days to revoke after signing (which revokes the entire agreement), and the non-disclosure provisions must be at the plaintiff employee's option/choice.[55] The Amendments Act of 2019 extended the provisions of the laws to all forms of discrimination, harassment or retaliation under Article 15 of the Executive Law.[56] Furthermore, as of January 1, 2020, express provision must also exist to advise the employee or

51 *Id.* at *2, *4 (citing *AT&T Mobility LLC v. Concepcion*, 563 U.S. 333, 341 (2011); *Lamps Plus, Inc. v. Varela*, 139 S. Ct. 1407, 1412, 1422 (2019) (Roberts, C.J., majority opinion, and Ginsburg, J., dissenting)).

52 *Id.* at *3 (and quoting CPLR 7515).

53 *See* Frances Kulka Browne and Erika Ghaly, *Mandatory Arbitration of Sexual Harassment Claims and FAA Preemption*, N.Y.L.J. at p. 6, Aug. 20, 2019. *See also Tantaros v. Fox News Network, LLC*, 2020 WL 3050576 at *3-5 & n.6 (S.D.N.Y. June 8, 2020) (Carter, D.J.) (recognizing issue of first impression in Second Circuit—namely, does FAA preempt CPLR 7515 if there are no federal claims; mentioning that *Latif* involved federal statutory claims under Title VII and Section 1981, and even with state and city law claims the parties in *Latif* agreed that the federal court could resolve the preemption issue; granting plaintiff's motion for certificate of appealability under 28 U.S.C. § 1292(b), for interlocutory appeal for potential resolution of the matter by the Second Circuit).

54 CPLR 5003-b (eff. July 11, 2018) (2018 Sess. Law News of N.Y. Ch. 57 (S. 7507-C)); GOL § 5-336 (eff. July 11, 2018) (2018 Sess. Law News of N.Y. Ch. 57 (S. 7507-C)).

55 GOL § 5-336 (eff. July 11, 2018).

56 GOL § 5-336 (2019 Sess. Law News of N.Y. Ch. 160 (A. 8421)); CPLR 5003-b (2019 Sess. Law News of N.Y. Ch. 160 (A. 8421)).

potential employee that they are not prohibited "from speaking with law enforcement, the equal employment opportunity commission, the state division of human rights, a local commission on human rights, or an attorney retained by the employee or potential employee."[57]

"Why such changes, why such attempts at restricting arbitration and non-disclosure provisions?" you may ask. Well, consider the timing. The original statute sections, which became effective July 11, 2018, were influenced at least in part by the tumultuous time of the *#MeToo* and *#TimesUp* movements. Trials are part of an American's right to a public hearing of their legal claims, while pre-dispute mandatory arbitration clauses and settlement non-disclosure clauses specifically aim to avoid the public hearing and potential media coverage of a claim, particularly in this realm of harassment, discrimination and retaliation.

Attorney Preet Bharara, the former U.S. Attorney for the Southern District of New York under President Barack Obama, admirably stated in his book *Doing Justice, A Prosecutor's Thoughts on Crime, Punishment, and the Rule of Law*:

> Public trials in America are, I think, rightly exalted not just as exhilarating exercises for practitioners but as important expressions and guarantors of democracy for the general public. Trials, after all, are showcase moments for our legal system and for the rule of law; they fulfill the requirement that justice must not only be done but also be *seen* to be done. In many ways, trials are touchstones of our democracy, in its most direct and tactile form. When trials vanish, citizenship also suffers.[58]

Although Attorney Bharara's writings may be largely with the criminal justice system in mind, this author would posit that his words ring no less

57 GOL § 5-336(2) (eff. Oct. 11, 2019) (2019 Sess. Law News of N.Y. Ch. 160 (A. 8421)).

58 Preet Bharara, Doing Justice, A Prosecutor's Thoughts on Crime, Punishment, and the Rule of Law, at p. 263 (Knopf 2019) (emphasis in original). We will not delve into the fact, or rather concern, that trials are rapidly disappearing in the American justice system overall, in both the civil and criminal fields. *See* John Gramlich, *Only 2% of Federal Criminal Defendants Go to Trial, and Most Who Do Are Found Guilty*, Pew Research Center, June 11, 2019, https://www.pewresearch.org/fact-tank/2019/06/11/only-2-of-federal-criminal-defendants-go-to-trial-and-most-who-do-are-found-guilty (for federal criminal cases, the most recent numbers suggest 8% are dismissed, 90% plead, and 2% go to trial); Jeffrey Q. Smith and Grant R. MacQueen, *Going, Going, but Not Quite Gone, Trials Continue to Decline in Federal and State Courts. Does It Matter?*, 101 Judicature 27 (Duke Univ. Sch. of Law Winter 2017) (providing statistics on the rapid decline in trials over the last two decades).

true for the civil system. With the restriction on pre-dispute mandatory arbitration provisions in employment contracts, the system seeks to maintain the ability of plaintiffs to have their day in court if they wish—to have justice *seen* being done.

As should be very clear to the reader, New York State and New York City have been active jurisdictions in creating and amending myriad statutory provisions and rules to advance the cause of diversity, inclusion and elimination of bias in the workplace, in education, in places of public accommodation, and across society. In fact, following the tragic deaths of George Floyd, Breonna Taylor, and many others, and in the wake of the worldwide Black Lives Matter protests in the spring of 2020, Governor Cuomo signed an Executive Order, adding New York to a list of states recognizing Juneteenth in some form, and in New York as a holiday for state employees in 2020.[59] One would do well to understand the nature and extent of all the relevant laws.

[1.2] III. CLAIMS ON THE FRINGE OF THE "GENDER" PROTECTED CLASS—ATTRACTIVE EMPLOYEES

When it comes to one particular claim under the heading of gender discrimination, we find ourselves at the fringes when the claim relates to adverse employment actions (terminations) that are suffered by employees because their employers see them as "too attractive," a "distraction" or a "threat to their marriages." There is an apparent split between the holdings of courts in two states—New York and Iowa—as well as much in the way of shades of gray.

For instance, in New York, one might warn employers to be careful if they think an employee is "too cute" or "too attractive," and they terminate that employee. That happened in the case of *Edwards v. Nicolai*,[60] where plaintiff was terminated as a yoga and massage therapist at a chiropractic practice because the wife and co-owner of the business believed that the plaintiff was "too cute" and a threat to her marriage. The defen-

59 *See* Appendix D (N.Y. Executive Order 204 (2020)). "Juneteenth," celebrated on June 19, is a recognition of the day—June 19, 1865—when Union Major General Gordon Granger read General Order No. 3 in Galveston, Texas, announcing that the Civil War had ended, affirming the *Emancipation Proclamation* and the end of slavery. *See id.* In summer 2020, the N.Y.S. legislature also passed two bills—A.10628 and A.10831—recognizing Juneteenth as a public holiday as well as Abolition Commemoration Day, respectively. However, as of the date of this writing, the governor had yet to sign them into law.

60 153 A.D.3d 440, 60 N.Y.S.3d 40 (1st Dep't 2017).

dant wife was becoming jealous that the defendant husband co-owner of the business might become attracted to the plaintiff and compromise their marriage vows.[61] It is important to note that there was no allegation of actual inappropriate interaction between plaintiff and the defendant husband. The trial court dismissed plaintiff's claim, holding the New York State and New York City Human Rights Laws did not cover this scenario, since the laws speak to gender protection (among other classes), but this was not a matter directly falling under "gender." However, the Appellate Division, First Department reversed the trial court, and held the circumstance of plaintiff's firing was sufficient to raise a claim of gender discrimination under both State and City Human Rights laws.[62]

Now, in contrast, consider the case of *Nelson v. James H. Knight DDS, P.C.*[63] Ironically, the facts in *Nelson* were very similar to those in *Edwards*. Plaintiff was a dental assistant for defendant Knight. Unlike with his other female employees, in this case there did come a point in time where defendant and plaintiff began exchanging text messages outside of work. Both were married, with children, and neither objected to the messages.[64] After a time of exchanging messages, the defendant began to view plaintiff and their interaction as a potential "detriment" to his marriage. Defendant fired plaintiff after discussions with his wife, and with a pastor present, telling plaintiff that defendant believed plaintiff's firing was in the best interests of their families and marriages.[65] Plaintiff was provided one month's severance pay. Importantly, in this case, there was no allegation of an actual relationship other than a work or friend relationship between plaintiff and defendant; however, there were some alleged instances of potential flirting and some inappropriate text messages, though there was no allegation of or claim of sexual harassment. Following the termination, defendant actually hired another female assistant.[66]

The Iowa Supreme Court determined that the termination was lawful and not a violation of the state's Civil Rights Act. The perceived threat

---

61 *Id.*

62 *Id.*

63 834 N.W.2d 64 (Iowa 2013) (Mansfield, J.).

64 *Id.*

65 *Id.*

66 *Id.*

presented to the defendant's marriage was held to be a sufficient, legitimate cause not finding its roots in discriminatory animus.

The holdings of both the *Edwards* and *Nelson* courts are provided here at near full-length from the opinions, so that the reader may review them and contrast and analyze the reasoning. While there is a distinction between *Nelson* and *Edwards*, largely because it seems in *Nelson* the plaintiff and defendant did have a personal, non-sexual relationship outside of the office, the question is whether *Nelson*, from a time prior to *Edwards*, presents the majority view in states or rather a view that will become more outdated as time passes.

Edwards v. Nicolai (New York State, Appellate Division, First Department) Memorandum Decision

> Order, Supreme Court, New York County . . . entered May 13, 2016, which granted defendants' motion to dismiss the amended complaint to the extent of dismissing the causes of action for gender discrimination in violation of the New York State Human Rights Law (NYSHRL) and the New York City Human Rights Laws (NYCHRL), and denied the motion as to the cause of action for defamation, unanimously modified, on the law, to deny the motion as to the discrimination causes of action, and otherwise affirmed, without costs.
>
> . . .
>
> Defendant Charles V. Nicolai is married to defendant Stephanie Adams. Nicolai and Adams are co-owners of Wall Street Chiropractic and Wellness (WSCW). Nicolai is the head chiropractor and oversees the medical operations, while Adams is the chief operating officer. In April of 2012, Nicolai hired plaintiff, Dilek Edwards, as a yoga and massage therapist, and thereafter was her direct supervisor.
>
> The complaint alleges that the relationship between Nicolai and plaintiff was "purely professional" and that Nicolai "regularly praised Plaintiff's work performance throughout her period of employment." In June 2013, however, Nicolai allegedly "informed Plaintiff that his wife might become jealous of Plaintiff, because Plaintiff

was 'too cute.'" Approximately four months later, on October 29, 2013, at 1:31 a.m., Adams sent Edwards a text message stating, "You are NOT welcome any longer at Wall Street Chiropractic, DO NOT ever step foot in there again, and stay the [expletive] away from my husband and family!!!!!!! And remember I warned you." A few hours later, at 8:53 a.m., plaintiff allegedly received an email from Nicolai stating, "'You are fired and no longer welcome in our office. If you call or try to come back, we will call the police.'" The complaint further alleges that, on October 30, 2013, Adams filed a complaint with the New York City Police Department (NYPD) alleging—falsely—that Adams had received "threatening" phone calls from plaintiff that so frightened her as to cause her to change the locks at her home and business.

As noted, plaintiff alleges that her relationship with Nicolai was strictly professional and that she "has no idea what sparked . . . Adams' [sic] . . . suspicions" to the contrary.

Based on the foregoing factual allegations, the amended complaint asserts a cause of action for gender discrimination in violation of the NYSHRL, a cause of action for gender discrimination in violation of the NYCHRL, and a cause of action for defamation. In lieu of answering, defendants moved to dismiss under CPLR 3016(a) and 3211(a)(7). Supreme Court granted the motion to the extent of dismissing the two gender discrimination claims, but sustained the defamation claims. Both sides have appealed.

. . .

The [trial] court erred, . . . in dismissing the causes of action for gender discrimination under the NYSHRL and the NYCHRL. It is well established that adverse employment actions motivated by sexual attraction are gender-based and, therefore, constitute unlawful gender discrimination (*see, e.g., Williams v. New York City Hous. Auth.*, 61 A.D.3d 62, 75 (1st Dep't 2009), *lv. denied* 13 N.Y.3d 702 (2009) [sexual harassment is "one species of sex- or gender-based discrimination"]; *see also Oncale v. Sun-*

> *downer Offshore Services, Inc.*, 523 US 75, 80 (1998); *King v. Board of Regents of Univ. of Wis. Sys.*, 898 F.2d 533, 539 (7th Cir 1990)). Here, while plaintiff does not allege that she was ever subjected to sexual harassment at WSCW, she alleges facts from which it can be inferred that Nicolai was motivated to discharge her by his desire to appease his wife's unjustified jealousy and that Adams was motivated to discharge plaintiff by that same jealousy. Thus, each defendant's motivation to terminate plaintiff's employment was sexual in nature.
>
> Defendants' reliance on certain cases in the "spousal jealousy" context is misplaced. Because these cases involve admitted consensual sexual affairs between the employer and the employee, they are distinguishable (*see Rainer N. Mittl, Ophthalmologist, P.C. v. New York State Div. of Human Rights*, 100 N.Y.2d 326, 332 (2003); *see also Mauro v. Orville*, 259 A.D.2d 89, 92-93 (3d Dep't 1999), *lv. denied* 94 N.Y.2d 759 (2000); *Tenge v. Phillips Modern Ag Co.*, 446 F.3d 903, 910 (8th Cir. 2006)).
>
> In such cases, it was the employee's behavior—not merely the employer's attraction to the employee or the perception of such an attraction by the employer's spouse—that prompted the termination. Here, assuming the truth of the allegations of the amended complaint, as we are required to do upon a motion to dismiss, plaintiff had always behaved appropriately in interacting with Nicolai and was fired for no reason other than Adams's belief that Nicolai was sexually attracted to plaintiff. This states a cause of action for gender discrimination under the NYSHRL and the NYCHRL.

Edwards ends with the following footnote:

> While Supreme Court correctly observed that it is not necessarily unlawful for an employer to terminate an at-will employee at the urging of the employer's spouse, such a discharge is actionable if the spouse urged the discharge for unlawful, gender-related reasons. Taking plaintiff's allegations as true, what makes her discharge unlawful is not that Nicolai's wife urged him to do it, but

> the reason she urged him to do it and the reason he complied.

The New York court in *Edwards*, inexplicably, did not mention the *Nelson* case in Iowa, although it did mention the Eighth Circuit decision in *Tenge*, which is discussed at length in *Nelson, infra*.

Keeping in mind the reasoning of the *Edwards* court in 2017, we now examine the analysis of the Iowa Supreme Court, in the Court's own language, on the similar question.

> **Nelson v. James H. Knight DDS, P.C. (Iowa Supreme Court)**
> **Mansfield, Justice**
>
> Can a male employer terminate a long-time female employee because the employer's wife, due to no fault of the employee, is concerned about the nature of the relationship between the employer and the employee? This is the question we are required to answer today. For the reasons stated herein, we ultimately conclude the conduct does not amount to unlawful sex discrimination in violation of the Iowa Civil Rights Act.
>
> We emphasize the limits of our decision. The employee did not bring a sexual harassment or hostile work environment claim; we are not deciding how such a claim would have been resolved in this or any other case. Also, when an employer takes an adverse employment action against a person or persons because of a gender-specific characteristic, that can violate the civil rights laws. The record in this case, however, does not support such an allegation.
>
> **I. Facts and Procedural Background**
>
> . . . In 1999, [defendant] hired [plaintiff] to work as a dental assistant in his dental office. . . .
>
> Over the next ten-and-a-half years, [plaintiff] worked as a dental assistant for [defendant]. [Defendant] admits that [plaintiff] was a good dental assistant. [Plaintiff] in turn acknowledges that [defendant] generally treated her with

respect, and she believed him to be a person of high integrity.

On several occasions during the last year and a half when [plaintiff] worked in the office, [defendant] complained to [plaintiff] that her clothing was too tight and revealing and "distracting." [Defendant] at times asked [plaintiff] to put on her lab coat. [Defendant] later testified that he made these statements to [plaintiff] because "I don't think it's good for me to see her wearing things that accentuate her body." [Plaintiff] denies that her clothing was tight or in any way inappropriate.

During the last six months or so of [plaintiff]'s employment, [defendant] and [plaintiff] started texting each other on both work and personal matters outside the workplace. Both parties initiated texting. Neither objected to the other's texting. Both [defendant] and [plaintiff] have children, and some of the texts involved updates on the kids' activities and other relatively innocuous matters. [Plaintiff] considered [defendant] to be a friend and father figure, and she denies that she ever flirted with him or sought an intimate or sexual relationship with him. At the same time, [plaintiff] admits that a coworker was "jealous that we got along." At one point, [plaintiff] texted [defendant] that "[t]he only reason I stay is because of you."

[Defendant] acknowledges he once told [plaintiff] that if she saw his pants bulging, she would know her clothing was too revealing. On another occasion, [defendant] texted [plaintiff] saying the shirt she had worn that day was too tight. After [plaintiff] responded that she did not think he was being fair, [defendant] replied that it was a good thing [plaintiff] did not wear tight pants too because then he would get it coming and going. [Defendant] also recalls that after [plaintiff] allegedly made a statement regarding infrequency in her sex life, he responded to her, "[T]hat's like having a Lamborghini in the garage and never driving it." [Plaintiff] recalls that [defendant] once texted her to ask how often she experienced an orgasm. [Plaintiff] did not answer the text. However, [plaintiff] does not remember ever telling [defendant] not to text her or telling him that she was offended.

In late 2009, [defendant] took his children to Colorado for Christmas vacation. [Defendant]'s wife Jeanne, who was also an employee in the dental practice, stayed home. Jeanne Knight found out that her husband and [plaintiff] were texting each other during that time. When [defendant] returned home, Jeanne Knight confronted her husband and demanded that he terminate [plaintiff]'s employment. Both of them consulted with the senior pastor of their church, who agreed with the decision.

Jeanne Knight insisted that her husband terminate [plaintiff] because "she was a big threat to our marriage." According to her affidavit and her deposition testimony, she . . . thought it was strange that after being at work all day and away from her kids and husband that she would not be anxious to get home like the other [women] in the office.

At the end of the workday on January 4, 2010, [defendant] called [plaintiff] into his office. He had arranged for another pastor from the church to be present as an observer. [Defendant], reading from a prepared statement, told [plaintiff] he was firing her. The statement said, in part, that their relationship had become a detriment to [defendant]'s family and that for the best interests of both [defendant] and his family and [plaintiff] and her family, the two of them should not work together. . . .

. . . [Defendant] told Steve Nelson [plaintiff's husband] that Melissa Nelson had not done anything wrong or inappropriate and that she was the best dental assistant he ever had. However, [defendant] said he was worried he was getting too personally attached to her. [Defendant] told Steve Nelson that nothing was going on but that he feared he would try to have an affair with her down the road if he did not fire her.

[Defendant] replaced [plaintiff] with another female. Historically, all of his dental assistants have been women.

> . . . [Plaintiff]'s one-count petition alleges that [defendant] discriminated against her on the basis of sex. [Plaintiff] does not contend that her employer committed sexual harassment. . . . Her argument, rather, is that [defendant] terminated her because of her gender and would not have terminated her if she was male.
>
> . . . [T]he district court sustained [defendant's] motion [for summary judgment]. The court reasoned in part, "Ms. Nelson was fired not because of her gender but because she was a threat to the marriage of [defendant]." [Plaintiff] appeals.
>
> . . .
>
> **III. Analysis**
>
> Section 216.6(1)(a) of the Iowa Code makes it generally unlawful to discharge or otherwise discriminate against an employee because of the employee's sex. . . "When interpreting discrimination claims under Iowa Code chapter 216, we turn to federal law, including Title VII of the United States Civil Rights Act." *Deboom v. Raining Rose, Inc.*, 772 N.W.2d 1, 7 (Iowa 2009).Generally, an employer engages in unlawful sex discrimination when the employer takes adverse employment action against an employee and sex is a motivating factor in the employer's decision. *See Channon v. United Parcel Serv., Inc.*, 629 N.W.2d 835, 861 (Iowa 2001).
>
> [Plaintiff] argues that her gender was a motivating factor in her termination because she would not have lost her job if she had been a man. *See, e.g., Watson v. Se. Pa. Transp. Auth.*, 207 F.3d 207, 213, 222 (3d Cir. 2000) (affirming a jury verdict in a Title VII case because the charge, taken as a whole, adequately informed the jury that sex had to be a but-for cause of the adverse employment action). [Defendant] responds that [plaintiff] was terminated not because of her sex—after all, he only employs women—but because of the nature of their relationship and the perceived threat to [defendant]'s marriage. Yet [plaintiff] rejoins that neither the relationship

nor the alleged threat would have existed if she had not been a woman.

Several cases, including a decision of the United States Court of Appeals for the Eighth Circuit, have found that an employer does not engage in unlawful gender discrimination by discharging a female employee who is involved in a consensual relationship that has triggered personal jealousy. This is true even though the relationship and the resulting jealousy presumably would not have existed if the employee had been male.

Tenge v. Phillips Modern Ag Co., like the present case, centered on a personal relationship between the owner of a small business and a valued employee of the business that was seen by the owner's wife as a threat to their marriage. 446 F.3d 903, 905–06 (8th Cir. 2006). In that case, unlike here, the plaintiff had pinched the owner's rear. *Id.* at 906. She admitted that the owner's wife "could have suspected the two had an intimate relationship." *Id.* Further, the plaintiff acknowledged she wrote "notes of a sexual or intimate nature" to the owner and put them in a location where others could see them. *Id.* In the end, the owner fired the plaintiff, stating that his wife was "'making me choose between my best employee or her and the kids.'" *Id.*

Reviewing this series of events, the Eighth Circuit affirmed the summary judgment in favor of the defendants. *Id.* at 911. The Eighth Circuit first noted the considerable body of authority that "'sexual favoritism,' where one employee was treated more favorably than members of the opposite sex because of a consensual relationship with the boss," does not violate Title VII. *Id.* at 908–909. . . .

. . .

Yet the court acknowledged that cases where the employee was treated less favorably would be "more directly analogous." *Id.* The court then discussed a decision of the Eleventh Circuit where an employee had been terminated for being a perceived threat to the marriage of the owner's son. . . . It also cited three federal district court cases, each of which had "concluded that terminating an employee based on the employee's consensual sexual conduct does not violate Title VII absent allegations that the conduct stemmed from unwelcome sexual advances or a hostile work environment." *Id.* (citing *Kahn v. Objective Solutions, Int'l*, 86 F. Supp. 2d 377, 382 (S.D.N.Y. 2000); *Campbell v. Masten*, 955 F. Supp. 526, 529 (D. Md. 1997); *Freeman v. Cont'l Technical Serv.*, Inc., 710 F. Supp. 328, 331 (N.D. Ga. 1988)).

After reviewing these precedents, the Eighth Circuit found the owner had not violated Title VII in terminating the employee at his wife's behest. As the court explained, "The ultimate basis for Tenge's dismissal was not her sex, it was Scott's desire to allay his wife's concerns over Tenge's admitted sexual behavior with him." *Id.* at 910.

In our case, the district court quoted at length from *Tenge*, stating it found that decision "persuasive." However, [plaintiff] argues there is a significant factual difference between the two cases. As the Eighth Circuit put it, "Tenge was terminated due to the consequences of her own admitted conduct with her employer, not because of her status as a woman." *Id.* . . .

[Plaintiff] contrasts [the situation in *Tenge*] with her own, where she claims she "did not do anything to get herself fired except exist as a female."

So the question we must answer is the one left open in *Tenge*—whether an employee who has not engaged in flirtatious conduct may be lawfully terminated simply because the boss's spouse views the relationship between the boss and the employee as a threat to her marriage. Notwithstanding the Eighth Circuit's care to leave that question unanswered, it seems odd at first glance to have the question of whether the employer engaged in unlawful discrimination turn on the employee's conduct, assuming that such conduct (whatever it is) would not typically be a firing offense. Usually our legal focus is on the employer's motivation, not on whether the discharge in a broader sense is fair. Title VII and the Iowa Civil

Rights Act are not general fairness laws, and an employer does not violate them by treating an employee unfairly so long as the employer does not engage in discrimination based upon the employee's protected status.

. . .

[Plaintiff]'s arguments warrant serious consideration, but we ultimately think a distinction exists between (1) an isolated employment decision based on personal relations (assuming no coercion or quid pro quo), even if the relations would not have existed if the employee had been of the opposite gender, and (2) a decision based on gender itself. In the former case, the decision is driven entirely by individual feelings and emotions regarding a specific person. Such a decision is not gender-based, nor is it based on factors that might be a proxy for gender.

. . .

[Plaintiff]'s viewpoint would allow any termination decision related to a consensual relationship to be challenged as a discriminatory action because the employee could argue the relationship would not have existed but for her or his gender. This logic would contradict federal caselaw to the effect that adverse employment action stemming from a consensual workplace relationship (absent sexual harassment) is not actionable under Title VII. [citing cases]

. . .

[Plaintiff] raises a legitimate concern about a slippery slope. What if Jeanne Knight demanded that her spouse terminate the employment of several women? Of course, a pretext does not prevail in a discrimination case. . . . If an employer repeatedly took adverse employment actions against persons of a particular gender, that would make it easier to infer that gender and not a relationship was a motivating factor. Here, however, it is not disputed that Jeanne Knight objected to this particular relationship as it had developed after [plaintiff] had already been working at the office for over ten years.

. . .

[Plaintiff] also raises a serious point about sexual harassment. Given that sexual harassment is a violation of anti-discrimination law, [plaintiff] argues that a firing by a boss to avoid committing sexual harassment should be treated similarly. But sexual harassment violates our civil rights laws because of the "hostile work environment" or "abusive atmosphere" that it has created for persons of the victim's sex (*see, e.g., Faragher v. City of Boca Raton*, (524 U.S. 775, 786–90 (1998)). On the other hand, an isolated decision to terminate an employee before such an environment arises, even if the reasons for termination are unjust, by definition does not bring about that atmosphere.

. . .

IV. Conclusion

As we have indicated above, the issue before us is not whether a jury could find that [defendant] treated [plaintiff] badly. We are asked to decide only if a genuine fact issue exists as to whether [defendant] engaged in unlawful gender discrimination when he fired [plaintiff] at the request of his wife. For the reasons previously discussed, we believe this conduct did not amount to unlawful discrimination, and therefore we affirm the judgment of the district court.

Cady, Chief Justice (concurring specially)

I concur in the majority opinion. . . . Melissa Nelson set forth a claim for sex discrimination recognized by law, but the facts of the case did not establish the claim.

. . .

. . . [O]ur law and this court remains [*sic*] devoted to carrying out the important legislative goal of eradicating discrimination from society, but this case simply lacked the facts to establish discrimination. Without proof of sex discrimination, the employment-at-will doctrine followed

> in Iowa guides the outcome. Id. (footnotes, and some citations, omitted).

Upon reflection, perhaps the decision in *Edwards* makes more sense in our modern world? The plaintiff was treated differently particularly because of her gender. If the plaintiff had instead been a male, it is likely that defendant wife would not have been jealous of a potential relationship between defendant husband and a male massage therapist. Of course, to carry this line further, one must disregard the fact that sexuality and sexual attractions—for some in society—are more fluid. However, in the general analysis under present law, the plaintiffs in both cases were treated differently than employees of the opposite sex/gender would have been treated. Even in the *Nelson* case, had plaintiff been a male (notwithstanding defendant only hired females), it does not appear that defendant's wife would have perceived any threat to the marriage. The plaintiffs in both *Edwards* and *Nelson* were terminated by the respective defendants precisely because the defendants' wives saw plaintiffs as attractive *females*, as a potential threat to the marriage of defendant husband and wife (and, in fact, in *Nelson*, the defendant himself thought that if more time passed he would try to have an affair with plaintiff, seemingly not considering whether plaintiff would have had anything to say about that).

Plaintiff's firing in *Edwards* was an adverse employment action finding its roots in a gender-based cause. However, the facts and circumstances in *Nelson* seem to undercut that argument, given the reasoning spelled out by that court. Further, defendant's action in *Nelson* seems to be justified in the court's eyes because the termination eliminated an issue before it rose to the level of sexual harassment or a similar matter that would be in violation of law. Is that the line, then? If a plaintiff does nothing wrong and engages in no inappropriate communications or actions inside or outside of the workplace, and there is the possibility of plaintiff's co-workers being both male and female such that plaintiff can be compared directly to the others on a gender basis (we don't know defendant's specific hiring practices in *Edwards*), we follow *Edwards*; but in other scenarios where there are entirely or almost entirely female employees, and one stands out as a potential direct threat to the employer's marriage vows, we follow *Nelson*? Is this an unworkable outcome? Or, rather, is this a strained distinction really owing more to different interpretations by two dissimilar courts in divergent parts of the United States?

Well, first, of course, follow the statutes and caselaw in your jurisdiction. *Edwards* is a decision of the Appellate Division, First Department in New York, which is binding across all of New York State unless and until another Department or the Court of Appeals holds to the contrary.[67] *Nelson*, a decision of the Iowa Supreme Court, is binding across that state. Beyond that, employers should take care, explore the precedents—both binding and persuasive—with legal counsel, and be certain that actions taken cannot be interpreted as having a gender-based rationale, or serving as the proxy for a gender-based factor (particularly as a pretext for sexual harassment), which would violate the laws against unequal treatment of persons based on gender or gender stereotypes.

[1.3] IV. SPECIFIC PROVISIONS OF SECTION 1981, SECTION 1983, FEDERAL TITLE VI, AND FEDERAL TITLE VII

Persons within the United States enjoy specific protections against discrimination, and have access to remedies, damages and attorneys' fees provisions, under the Civil Rights Laws[68]—and particularly actions against state actors[69]—commonly referred to as Title VI, Title VII, Section 1981, Section 1983 and/or Section 1988 claims, among others.

Section 1983 provides:

> Every person who, under color of any statute, ordinance, regulation, custom, or usage, of any State or Territory or the District of Columbia, subjects, or causes to be subjected, any citizen of the United States or other person within the jurisdiction thereof to the deprivation of any rights, privileges, or immunities secured by the Constitution and laws, shall be liable to the party injured in an action at law, suit in equity, or other proper proceeding for redress, except that in any action brought against a

67 It is generally accepted (with one potential disagreement out of the First Department) that the separate Appellate Divisions in the State of New York exist for administrative convenience, and the holding of one Division is binding across the State absent a contrary decision by another Division or the Court of Appeals. *See People v. Turner*, 5 N.Y.3d 476, 482 (2005) (Smith, J.); *Mountain View Coach Lines, Inc. v. Storms*, 102 A.D.2d 663, 664, 476 N.Y.S.2d 918 (2d Dep't 1984) (citing, *inter alia*, *Waldo v. Schmidt*, 200 N.Y. 199, 202 (1910), and collecting other cases); *see also* Michael Gordon, *Which Appellate Division Rulings Bind Which Trial Courts?*, N.Y.L.J., Sept. 8, 2009, https://www.law.com/newyorklawjournal/almID/1202433574138/?id=1202433574138 (citing cases, and discussing status of the statewide binding nature of Appellate Division decisions).

68 *See, inter alia*, 42 U.S.C. §§ 1981, *et seq.*; 42 U.S.C. §§ 2000d, *et seq.*; 42 U.S.C. §§ 2000e, *et seq.*

69 42 U.S.C. § 1983.

> judicial officer for an act or omission taken in such officer's judicial capacity, injunctive relief shall not be granted unless a declaratory decree was violated or declaratory relief was unavailable. For the purposes of this section, any Act of Congress applicable exclusively to the District of Columbia shall be considered to be a statute of the District of Columbia.[70]

For reference, Section 1981 (also existing under the Civil Rights Laws, and providing protection in "all phases and incidents of the contractual relationship"[71]) provides in its entirety as follows:

> **(a) Statement of equal rights**
>
> All persons within the jurisdiction of the United States shall have the same right in every State and Territory to make and enforce contracts, to sue, be parties, give evidence, and to the full and equal benefit of all laws and proceedings for the security of persons and property as is enjoyed by white citizens, and shall be subject to like punishment, pains, penalties, taxes, licenses, and exactions of every kind, and to no other.
>
> **(b) "Make and enforce contracts" defined**
>
> For purposes of this section, the term "make and enforce contracts" includes the making, performance, modification, and termination of contracts, and the enjoyment of all benefits, privileges, terms, and conditions of the contractual relationship.

---

70 *Id. But see Monell v. Dep't of Soc. Servs. of City of N.Y.*, 436 U.S. 658, 694, 98 S.Ct. 2018, 2037-2038 (1978) (Brennan, J.) ("We conclude, therefore, that a local government may not be sued under § 1983 for an injury inflicted solely by its employees or agents. Instead, it is when execution of a government's policy or custom, whether made by its lawmakers or by those whose edicts or acts may fairly be said to represent official policy, inflicts the injury that the government as an entity is responsible under § 1983"); *Knights v. City Univ. of N.Y.*, 2020 WL 1676484 at *2 (E.D.N.Y. Apr. 6, 2020) (Block, Senior D.J.) ("The Second Circuit has held that a single act by a municipality may amount to policy 'if ordered by a person "whose edicts or acts may fairly be said to represent official policy."'. . . 'Where an official has final authority over significant matters involving the exercise of discretion, the choices he makes represent government policy'") (citing *Rookard v. Health & Hosps. Corp.*, 710 F.2d 41, 45 (2d Cir. 1983) (quoting *Monell*, 436 U.S. at 694)).

71 *Comcast Corp. v. Nat'l Assoc. of African Am.-Owned Media*, 140 S.Ct. 1009, 1020 (2020) (Ginsburg, J., concurring).

(c) Protection against impairment

> The rights protected by this section are protected against impairment by nongovernmental discrimination and impairment under color of State law.[72]

In order for a plaintiff to allege a claim under Section 1983, not only must there be a deprivation of a right secured by the Constitution or laws of the United States, but the deprivation must be by one acting under color of state law, "which means the person exercised power 'possessed by virtue of state law and made possible only because the wrongdoer is clothed with the authority of state law.'"[73] Failure to adequately allege same will result in dismissal of plaintiff's claim.[74] Additionally, a but-for causation standard is applied in Section 1983 actions, such that "a plaintiff pursuing a claim for employment discrimination under § 1983 rather than Title VII must establish that the defendant's discriminatory intent was a 'but-for' cause of the adverse employment action or the hostile environment. It is insufficient to establish simply that invidious discrimination was 'a motivating factor' of the offending conduct. Accordingly, a court considering a § 1983 claim at summary judgment must determine whether, construing the evidence in a light most favorable to the plaintiff, a reasonable jury could find that the adverse employment action would not have occurred 'but-for' sex discrimination."[75]

---

72 42 U.S.C. § 1981. Section 1988 concerns the applicability of law, as well as the awarding of attorneys' and experts' fees to prevailing parties.

73 *Brown v. Patterson*, 2016 WL 3080825 at *2 (E.D. Wis. May 30, 2016) (Adelman, D.J.) (citing *Rodriguez v. Plymouth Ambulance Serv.*, 577 F.3d 816, 822 (7th Cir. 2009); *West v. Atkins*, 487 U.S. 42, 49 (1988)). Note further that regardless of whether plaintiff's claims fall under the auspices of Title VI, Title VII, Section 1981 or Section 1983, if filed against a state or arm of a state, the doctrine of sovereign immunity under the Eleventh Amendment to the U.S. Constitution may apply to shield the state defendant from liability—unless, under Title VII, the plaintiff properly pleads an *Ex parte Young* exception for "reinstatement to previous employment." *See Blamah v. N.Y.*, 2020 WL 1812690 at *4-7 (S.D.N.Y. Apr. 8, 2020) (Halpern, D.J.) ("*Ex parte Young* is an exception to Eleventh Amendment immunity which permits a plaintiff to sue a state official acting in his official capacity for prospective, injunctive relief from violations of federal law.... The *Ex parte Young* Doctrine is only applicable in cases in which the Plaintiff alleges 'a violation of federal law by a state official [that] is ongoing as opposed to cases in which federal law has been violated at one time or over a period of time in the past.'. . . If the injunctive relief sought by a plaintiff would not 'directly end[ ] the violation of federal law,' but rather 'is intended indirectly to encourage compliance with federal law through deterrence,' *Ex parte Young* does not apply") (citing *State Emps. Bargaining Agent Coal. v. Rowland*, 494 F.3d 71, 95 (2d Cir. 2007); *Papasan v. Allain*, 478 U.S. 265, 277–78 (1986)).

74 *Id.*

75 *Naumovski v. Norris*, 934 F.3d 200, 213 (2d Cir. 2019) (Cabranes, J.) (citations and footnotes omitted) (noting different, "lessened causation" standard, a "motivating factor" standard, applied under Title VII versus Section 1983's "but-for causation" standard).

Under *Section 1981*, a plaintiff is not restricted to suits against only state actors or actions under color of state law. Section 1981 claims may be brought against non-governmental (i.e. private) defendants. Further, just as with Section 1983, a Section 1981 plaintiff must prove their case pursuant to a "but-for causation standard." As the Supreme Court of the United States made clear:

> It is "textbook tort law" that a plaintiff seeking redress for a defendant's legal wrong typically must prove but-for causation. . . . Under this standard, a plaintiff must demonstrate that, but for the defendant's unlawful conduct, its alleged injury would not have occurred. This ancient and simple "but for" common law causation test, we have held, supplies the "default" or "background" rule against which Congress is normally presumed to have legislated when creating its own new causes of action. . . . We don't doubt that most rules bear their exceptions. But, taken collectively, clues from the statute's text, its history, and our precedent persuade us that § 1981 follows the general rule. Here, a plaintiff bears the burden of showing that race was a but-for cause of its injury. And, while the materials the plaintiff can rely on to show causation may change as a lawsuit progresses

> from filing to judgment, the burden itself remains constant.[76]

Title VI of the Civil Rights Acts of 1964[77] provides: "No person in the United States shall, on the ground of race, color, or national origin, be excluded from participation in, be denied the benefits of, or be subjected to discrimination under any program or activity receiving Federal financial assistance."[78] Title VI permits a private right of action by an aggrieved plaintiff,[79] and "[t]he Supreme Court [of the United States] has ruled that there must be a showing of intentional discrimination to succeed on a title VI claim. . . . [That case] involved a challenge to the hiring

76 *Comcast Corp.*, 140 S.Ct. at 1014-1015 (Gorsuch, J.). The Supreme Court's decision in *Price Waterhouse v. Hopkins*, 490 U.S. 228, 109 S.Ct. 1775 (1989), was deemed superseded by statute, because Congress codified a motivating factor test when it passed the Civil Rights Act of 1991 and amended Title VII; but Congress also amended Section 1981 at the same time, and did not add a motivating factor standard there. *See Comcast Corp.*, 140 S.Ct. at 1017-1018. *See also Fukelman v. Delta Air Lines, Inc.*, 2020 WL 2781662 at *2 & n.3 (E.D.N.Y. May 29, 2020) (Chen, D.J.) ("In order to prevail on a Section 1981 claim, a plaintiff must 'initially plead and ultimately prove that, but for race, it would not have suffered the loss of a legally protected right.'... The Court agrees with the R&R's conclusion that, as Plaintiffs do not allege facts sufficient to give rise to an inference of discrimination under Title VII, Plaintiffs have not plausibly alleged that 'their ethnicity was a but-for cause of the actions against them.'") (citing, *inter alia*, *Comcast Corp.*). *But see* Erwin Chemerinsky, *Chemerinsky: SCOTUS Comcast Case Is A Serious Loss for Civil Rights*, ABA Journal, Apr. 2, 2020, https://www.abajournal.com/news/article/chemerinsky-a-serious-loss-for-civil-rights (with the author explaining, as counsel for the unsuccessful party, the reasons why the *Comcast* decision may cause more dismissals at the pleading stage because of the heightened standard). Plaintiff, whether under Title VII or Section 1981, though, must allege facts sufficient for a court to find or infer intent to discriminate on the part of the defendant – and the *McDonnell Douglas* burden shift test (*see* § 1.6 *infra*) only shifts the burden of production, but never the burden of persuasion, which is always on the plaintiff. *Calvelos v. City of N.Y.*, 2020 WL 3414886 at *9-10 (S.D.N.Y. June 22, 2020) (McMahon, C.J.) (citing, *inter alia*, *Comcast Corp.*); *Comcast Corp.*, 140 S.Ct. at 1019; *Farooqi v. N.Y. Dep't of Educ.*, 2020 WL 1809290 at *2 (S.D.N.Y. Apr. 9, 2020) (Cote, D.J.) (arbitrator sustained charges of misconduct following N.Y. Educ. Law § 3020-a hearing, thus "but-for" showing of discriminatory intent by plaintiff not possible, § 1981 and § 1983 claims dismissed; "[a]s recently clarified by the Supreme Court in the context of § 1981, and the Second Circuit in the context of § 1983, the 'motivating factor' standard from Title VII does not apply") (citing *Comcast Corp.*; *Naumovksi*, 934 F.3d at 212-14). *See also Paige v. Metro. Sec. Servs.*, 2020 WL 3714737 (S.D. Miss. July 6, 2020) (Aycock, D.J.) ("'To prevail [on a section 1981 claim], a plaintiff must initially plead and ultimately prove that, but for race, [he] would not have suffered the loss of a legally protected right.'") (citing and quoting *Comcast Corp.*).

77 42 U.S.C. § 2000d, *et seq.*.

78 *Id. See also* Executive Order No. 13160, 65 F.R. 39775 (June 23, 2000) (Clinton) ("Nondiscrimination on the Basis of Race, Sex, Color, National Origin, Disability, Religion, Age, Sexual Orientation, and Status as a Parent in Federally Conducted Education and Training Programs"); Executive Order No. 13899, 84 F.R. 68779 (Dec. 11, 2019) (Trump) ("Combating Anti-Semitism") (recognizing that while religion is not protected under Title VI, if anti-Semitism results from race, color or national origin discrimination, then it would be addressed by Title VI).

79 *Cannon v. Univ. of Chicago*, 441 U.S. 677, 99 S.Ct. 1946 (1979) (Stevens, J.).

and firing practices of New York City's police department. The principal issue was whether compensation could be awarded for a violation of title VI in the absence of proof of discriminatory intent. Although the Court was divided and no majority opinion issued, seven Justices concluded that proof of discriminatory intent is required in order to make out a violation of title VI."[80] With regard to the elements of a successful claim, courts have held:

> "To establish a claim under Title VI, a plaintiff must show . . . : (1) that the entity involved engaged in racial or national origin discrimination; (2) the entity involved is receiving federal financial aid; and (3) plaintiff was an entitled beneficiary of the program or activity receiving the aid."
>
> Courts apply the three-part burden-shifting framework announced in *McDonnell Douglas Corp. v. Green*, 411 U.S. 792, 93 S.Ct. 1817... (1973), to Title VI claims,. . . .
>
> In order to satisfy the first element of a Title VI claim, Plaintiffs must demonstrate "that the defendant discriminated against [plaintiff] on the basis of race, that the discrimination was intentional, and that the discrimination was a substantial or motivating factor for the defendant's actions.". . . Plaintiffs may assert a prima facie case through direct evidence of discrimination, or when there is no direct evidence of discriminatory conduct, they may show that: (1) [plaintiff] is a member of a protected class; (2) [plaintiff] suffered an adverse action in pursuit of [their] education by defendant [this was a federally funded education case]; (3) [plaintiff] was treated differently from similarly situated students who were not members of the protected class; and (4) [plaintiff] was qualified to continue in [their] educational pursuit [the pursuit/activity at issue in this case]."[81]

80 *Campaign for Fiscal Equity, Inc. v. State*, 86 N.Y.2d 307, 321-322, 655 N.E.2d 661, 669 (1995) (Ciparick, J.) (citing *Guardians Ass'n v. Civil Serv. Comm'n*, 463 U.S. 582, 103 S.Ct. 3221 (1983)).

81 *JF v. Carmel Cent. Sch. Dist.*,168 F.Supp.3d 609, 623 (S.D.N.Y. 2016) (Román, D.J.) (citing, *inter alia, Babiker v. Ross Univ. Sch. of Med.*, 2000 WL 666342 at *4 (S.D.N.Y. May 19, 2000), *aff'd sub nom. Babiker v. Ross Univ. Sch. of Med.*, 86 Fed.Appx. 457 (2d Cir. 2004)).

Title VII of the Civil Rights Act of 1964,[82] provides protection against discrimination in employment based on race, color, religion, sex or national origin, and as discussed above, allows application of the lessened "motivating factor" causation standard.

The inclusion of only a handful of protected classes under Title VI and Title VII is not to say federal law fails to protect any other classes of persons. Rather, while New York placed virtually all protections under the Human Rights Law, the federal legislature created different statutory protections for different protected classes and circumstances. For instance, there is the federal Genetic Information Non-Discrimination Act (GINA),[83] the federal Fair Housing Act (FHA),[84] the Americans with Disabilities Act (ADA; *see* Chapter 6, *infra*),[85] the Individuals with Disabilities in Education Act (IDEA),[86] and the Age Discrimination in Employment Act (ADEA; *see* § 1.5, *infra*).[87]

As discussed further in § 1.7, *infra*, Title VII of the Civil Rights Act of 1964 also contains an anti-retaliation provision, which prohibits an employer from taking adverse actions against an employee who makes a complaint or charge, or who supports another in the making of a complaint or charge, under the Act.

> **(a) Discrimination for making charges, testifying, assisting, or participating in enforcement proceedings**
>
> It shall be an unlawful employment practice for an employer to discriminate against any of his employees or applicants for employment, for an employment agency, or joint labor-management committee controlling apprenticeship or other training or retraining, including on-the-job training programs, to discriminate against any individual, or for a labor organization to discriminate against any member thereof or applicant for membership, because he has opposed any practice made an unlawful

82 Pub. L. 88-352 (Title VII), *as amended*, codified at 42 U.S.C. §§ 2000e, *et seq.*

83 42 U.S.C. §§ 2000ff-1, *et seq.*

84 42 U.S.C. §§ 3601, *et seq.*

85 42 U.S.C. §§ 12101, *et seq.*

86 20 U.S.C. §§ 1400, *et seq. See also* Rehabilitation Act, 29 U.S.C. §§ 791, *et seq.* (particularly Section 504 of the Rehabilitation Act, 29 U.S.C. § 794).

87 29 U.S.C. §§ 621, *et seq.*

> employment practice by this subchapter, or because he has made a charge, testified, assisted, or participated in any manner in an investigation, proceeding, or hearing under this subchapter.[88]

Title VII, by its terms, does not apply to "employment of aliens outside of any State," or to "a religious corporation, association, educational institution, or society with respect to the employment of individuals of a particular religion to perform work connected with the carrying on by such corporation, association, educational institution, or society of its activities."[89] However, the Act does have extraterritoriality provisions, such that

> **(b) Compliance with statute as violative of foreign law**
>
> It shall not be unlawful under section 2000e-2 or 2000e-3 of this title for an employer (or a corporation controlled by an employer), labor organization, employment agency, or joint labor-management committee controlling apprenticeship or other training or retraining (including on-the-job training programs) to take any action otherwise prohibited by such section, with respect to an employee in a workplace in a foreign country if compliance with such section would cause such employer (or such corporation), such organization, such agency, or such committee to violate the law of the foreign country in which such workplace is located.
>
> **(c) Control of corporation incorporated in foreign country**
>
> (1) If an employer controls a corporation whose place of incorporation is a foreign country, any practice prohibited by section 2000e-2 or 2000e-3 of this title engaged in by such corporation shall be presumed to be engaged in by such employer.
>
> (2) Sections 2000e-2 and 2000e-3 of this title shall not apply with respect to the foreign operations of an

88 42 U.S.C. § 2000e-3. Also see the discussion about "Retaliation" in § 1.7 *infra*.

89 42 U.S.C. § 2000e-1(a).

employer that is a foreign person not controlled by an American employer.[90]

Given the importance of Title VII's anti-discrimination provisions in employment, a large portion of the statute section is provided below, verbatim, for analysis:

(a) Employer practices

It shall be an unlawful employment practice for an employer—

(1) to fail or refuse to hire or to discharge any individual, or otherwise to discriminate against any individual with respect to his compensation, terms, conditions, or privileges of employment, because of such individual's race, color, religion, sex, or national origin; or

(2) to limit, segregate, or classify his employees or applicants for employment in any way which would deprive or tend to deprive any individual of employment opportunities or otherwise adversely affect his status as an employee, because of such individual's race, color, religion, sex, or national origin.

(b) Employment agency practices

It shall be an unlawful employment practice for an employment agency to fail or refuse to refer for employment, or otherwise to discriminate against, any individual because of his race, color, religion, sex, or national origin, or to classify or refer for employment any individual on the basis of his race, color, religion, sex, or national origin.

(c) Labor organization practices

It shall be an unlawful employment practice for a labor organization—

90 42 U.S.C. § 2000e-1(b), (c)(1), (2).

(1) to exclude or to expel from its membership, or otherwise to discriminate against, any individual because of his race, color, religion, sex, or national origin;

(2) to limit, segregate, or classify its membership or applicants for membership, or to classify or fail or refuse to refer for employment any individual, in any way which would deprive or tend to deprive any individual of employment opportunities, or would limit such employment opportunities or otherwise adversely affect his status as an employee or as an applicant for employment, because of such individual's race, color, religion, sex, or national origin; or

(3) to cause or attempt to cause an employer to discriminate against an individual in violation of this section.

(d) Training programs

It shall be an unlawful employment practice for any employer, labor organization, or joint labor-management committee controlling apprenticeship or other training or retraining, including on-the-job training programs to discriminate against any individual because of his race, color, religion, sex, or national origin in admission to, or employment in, any program established to provide apprenticeship or other training.

(e) Businesses or enterprises with personnel qualified on basis of religion, sex, or national origin; educational institutions with personnel of particular religion

Notwithstanding any other provision of this subchapter, **(1) it shall not be an unlawful employment practice** for an employer to hire and employ employees, for an employment agency to classify, or refer for employment any individual, for a labor organization to classify its membership or to classify or refer for employment any individual, **or for an employer, labor organization, or joint labor-management committee controlling apprenticeship or other training or retraining programs to admit or employ any individual in any such**

program, on the basis of his religion, sex, or national origin in those certain instances where religion, sex, or national origin is a bona fide occupational qualification reasonably necessary to the normal operation of that particular business or enterprise, and (2) it shall not be an unlawful employment practice for a school, college, university, or other educational institution or institution of learning to hire and employ employees of a particular religion if such school, college, university, or other educational institution or institution of learning is, in whole or in substantial part, owned, supported, controlled, or managed by a particular religion or by a particular religious corporation, association, or society, or if the curriculum of such school, college, university, or other educational institution or institution of learning is directed toward the propagation of a particular religion.

(f) Members of Communist Party or Communist-action or Communist-front organizations

As used in this subchapter, the phrase "unlawful employment practice" shall not be deemed to include any action or measure taken by an employer, labor organization, joint labor-management committee, or employment agency with respect to an individual who is a member of the Communist Party of the United States or of any other organization required to register as a Communist-action or Communist-front organization by final order of the Subversive Activities Control Board pursuant to the Subversive Activities Control Act of 1950.

(g) National security

Notwithstanding any other provision of this subchapter, it shall not be an unlawful employment practice for an employer to fail or refuse to hire and employ any individual for any position, for an employer to discharge any individual from any position, or for an employment agency to fail or refuse to refer any individual for employment in any position, or for a labor organization to fail or refuse to refer any individual for employment in any position, if—

(1) the occupancy of such position, or access to the premises in or upon which any part of the duties of such position is performed or is to be performed, is subject to any requirement imposed in the interest of the national security of the United States under any security program in effect pursuant to or administered under any statute of the United States or any Executive order of the President; and

(2) such individual has not fulfilled or has ceased to fulfill that requirement.

(h) Seniority or merit system; quantity or quality of production; ability tests; compensation based on sex and authorized by minimum wage provisions

Notwithstanding any other provision of this subchapter, it shall not be an unlawful employment practice for an employer to apply different standards of compensation, or different terms, conditions, or privileges of employment pursuant to a bona fide seniority or merit system, or a system which measures earnings by quantity or quality of production or to employees who work in different locations, provided that such differences are not the result of an intention to discriminate because of race, color, religion, sex, or national origin, nor shall it be an unlawful employment practice for an employer to give and to act upon the results of any professionally developed ability test provided that such test, its administration or action upon the results is not designed, intended or used to discriminate because of race, color, religion, sex or national origin. It shall not be an unlawful employment practice under this subchapter for any employer to differentiate upon the basis of sex in determining the amount of the wages or compensation paid or to be paid to employees of such employer if such differentiation is authorized by the provisions of section 206(d) of Title 29.

. . .

(k) Burden of proof in disparate impact cases

(1)(A) An unlawful employment practice based on disparate impact is established under this subchapter only if—

(i) a complaining party demonstrates that a respondent uses a particular employment practice that causes a disparate impact on the basis of race, color, religion, sex, or national origin and the respondent fails to demonstrate that the challenged practice is job related for the position in question and consistent with business necessity; or

(ii) the complaining party makes the demonstration described in subparagraph (C) with respect to an alternative employment practice and the respondent refuses to adopt such alternative employment practice.

(B)(i) With respect to demonstrating that a particular employment practice causes a disparate impact as described in subparagraph (A)(i), the complaining party shall demonstrate that each particular challenged employment practice causes a disparate impact, except that if the complaining party can demonstrate to the court that the elements of a respondent's decisionmaking process are not capable of separation for analysis, the decisionmaking process may be analyzed as one employment practice.

(ii) If the respondent demonstrates that a specific employment practice does not cause the disparate impact, the respondent shall not be required to demonstrate that such practice is required by business necessity.

(C) The demonstration referred to by subparagraph (A)(ii) shall be in accordance with the law as it existed on June 4, 1989, with respect to the concept of "alternative employment practice."

(2) A demonstration that an employment practice is required by business necessity may not be used as a defense against a claim of intentional discrimination under this subchapter.

(3) Notwithstanding any other provision of this subchapter, a rule barring the employment of an individual who

> currently and knowingly uses or possesses a controlled substance, as defined in schedules I and II of section 102(6) of the Controlled Substances Act (21 U.S.C. 802(6)), other than the use or possession of a drug taken under the supervision of a licensed health care professional, or any other use or possession authorized by the Controlled Substances Act or any other provision of Federal law, shall be considered an unlawful employment practice under this subchapter only if such rule is adopted or applied with an intent to discriminate because of race, color, religion, sex, or national origin....[91]

Just as under the former New York law, not every entity that employs a person is considered an employer under Title VII. It is, therefore, important for one to understand the following:

> **(b)** The term "employer" means a person engaged in an industry affecting commerce who has fifteen or more employees for each working day in each of twenty or more calendar weeks in the current or preceding calendar year, and any agent of such a person, but such term does not include (1) the United States, a corporation wholly owned by the Government of the United States, an Indian tribe, or any department or agency of the District of Columbia subject by statute to procedures of the competitive service (as defined in section 2102 of Title 5), or (2) a bona fide private membership club (other than a labor organization) which is exempt from taxation under section 501(c) of Title 26, except that during the first year after March 24, 1972, persons having fewer than twenty-five employees (and their agents) shall not be considered employers.[92]

91 42 U.S.C. § 2000e-2(a)-(k) (emphasis added).

92 42 U.S.C. § 2000e(b).

Thus, as a shorthand, covered employers under these federal laws have 15 or more employees.[93]

When it comes to discrimination on the basis of pregnancy, the Pregnancy Discrimination Act was created as an amendment to Title VII.[94] According to the U.S. Equal Employment Opportunity Commission:

> Pregnancy discrimination involves treating a woman (an applicant or employee) unfavorably because of pregnancy, childbirth, or a medical condition related to pregnancy or childbirth. . . . The Pregnancy Discrimination Act (PDA) forbids discrimination based on pregnancy when it comes to any aspect of employment, including hiring, firing, pay, job assignments, promotions, layoff, training, fringe benefits, such as leave and health insurance, and any other term or condition of employment. . . . Pregnant employees may have additional rights under the Family and Medical Leave Act (FMLA), which is enforced by the U.S. Department of Labor. Nursing mothers may also have the right to express milk in the workplace under a provision of the Fair Labor Standards

93 Note an exception, however. "Normally, Title VII applies to employers with 15 or more employees. But, 'an individual qualifies as an employer under Title VII solely for purposes of imputing liability to the true employer if he or she serves in a supervisory position and exercises significant control over the plaintiff's hiring.'" *Paige*, 2020 WL 3714737 (citing *Vance v. Union Planters Corp.*, 279 F.3d 295, 299 (5th Cir. 2002) (quoting *Haynes v. Williams*, 88 F.3d 898, 899 (10th Cir. 1996))).

94 42 U.S.C. § 2000e(k). Separately, but related, an amendment to Section 7 of the federal Fair Labor Standards Act, which was part of President Obama's signature Patient Protection and Affordable Care Act, requires covered employers to allow nursing mothers a reasonable break time to express milk, and a place other than a bathroom in which to do so—shielded and free from intrusion by others. Although, employers with less than 50 employees are not required to subscribe to the Act's provisions on this matter, if doing so would create an undue hardship. *See* 29 U.S.C. § 207(r)(1)-(4), *held unconstitutional by Texas v. U.S.*, 340 F.Supp.3d 579 (N.D. Tex. 2018) (O'Connor, D.J.), *stay pending appeal*, 352 F. Supp. 3d 665 (N.D. Tex. 2018) (O'Connor, D.J.), *aff'd in part, vacated in part, remanded*, 945 F.3d 355 (5th Cir. 2019), *rehearing en banc denied*, 949 F.3d 182 (5th Cir. 2020), *cert. granted*, 140 S.Ct. 1262 (2020). *See also* Avi Lew, *New Lactation Room Laws in NYC: What Employers Need to Know*, N.Y.L.J. at p. 4, Apr. 30, 2019 (New York law contains similar provisions protecting and providing for nursing mothers); *see* Labor Law § 206-c ("Right of nursing mothers to express breast milk"); Exec Law § 292(21-f).

Act enforced by the U.S. Department of Labor's Wage and Hour Division.[95]

Among the claims a plaintiff employee may allege is a hostile work environment. "In order to establish a hostile work environment claim under Title VII, a plaintiff must produce enough evidence to show that "the workplace is permeated with discriminatory intimidation, ridicule, and insult, that is sufficiently severe or pervasive to alter the conditions of the victim's employment and create an abusive working environment."[96]

For a claim of discrimination to be made under Title VII, unless it is a disparate impact or disparate treatment claim—where the single incident is the discrimination suffered—a claim must be more than episodic.[97] In what is a split with New York law,[98] under the federal law incidents forming the basis of a claim must be more than occasional slights; they must be either severe (i.e., a sexual touching[99]) or pervasive, and if pervasive they must take place frequently enough that the workplace is considered to be pervaded or permeated by the abuse.[100] Generally, unless an incident of harassment is sufficiently severe, "incidents must be more than episodic; they must be sufficiently continuous and concerted in order to be

95 *Pregnancy Discrimination*, U.S. EEOC, https://www.eeoc.gov/laws/types/pregnancy.cfm. However, it should be noted that there is some dispute concerning whether a mother who has already given birth, and who experiences "lactation discrimination" in the workplace for needing to pump breast milk, is covered under the Pregnancy Discrimination Act and Title VII because of "pregnancy, childbirth, or related medical conditions"—i.e., courts have split concerning whether lactation is related to pregnancy, childbirth or medical conditions associated therewith sufficiently to provide a category for claims of discrimination under Title VII and the PDA. *See* Jayme Jonat, *The Precarious Position of the Working and Breastfeeding Mother*, N.Y.L.J., July 24, 2020, at https://www.law.com/newyorklawjournal/2020/07/24/the-precarious-position-of-the-working-and-breastfeeding-mother/ (citing, *inter alia, Fejes v. Gilpin Ventures, Inc.*, 960 F.Supp. 1487 (D. Colo. 1997); *Ames v. Nationwide Mut. Ins. Co.*, 2012 WL 12861597 (S.D. Iowa Oct. 16, 2012); *Hicks v. City of Tuscaloosa, Ala.*, 870 F.3d 1253 (11th Cir. 2013); *E.E.O.C. v. Houston Funding II, Ltd.*, 717 F.3d 425 (5th Cir. 2013)).

96 *Demoret v. Zegarelli*, 451 F.3d 140, 149 (2d Cir.2006) (Cardamone, J.) (internal quotation marks omitted) (overruled on other grounds).

97 *See Moore v. City of New York*, 2018 WL 3491286 (S.D.N.Y. July 20, 2018) (Cott, M.J.).

98 *Cf.* Exec. Law § 296(1)(h); N.Y.C. Admin. Code § 8-107.

99 *See Kyser v. D.J.F. Services, Inc.*, 2017 WL 5690889 at *3 (E.D. Okla. Nov. 27, 2017) (West, M.J.).

100 *See* 42 U.S.C. § 2000e-2; *Kotcher v. Rosa & Sullivan Appliance Ctr., Inc.*, 957 F.2d 59 (2d Cir. 1992) (Pratt, J.); *Galimore v. City Univ. of N.Y. Bronx Comm. Coll.*, 641 F.Supp.2d 269 (S.D.N.Y. 2009) (Sullivan, D.J.).

deemed pervasive."[101] A plaintiff claiming hostile work environment must show not only that she subjectively perceived the environment to be abusive, but also that the environment was objectively hostile and abusive,[102] thus requiring what are known as both subjective and objective hostile elements. Absent both, a claim will not survive.[103] Despite best efforts to create a legal landscape that is inclusive, tolerant and unbiased, the law does not require that a workplace be cordial, friendly or civil.[104]

An employee must, additionally, suffer an adverse employment action for their hostile work environment claim(s) to survive. Absent that, they also will not succeed. As has been defined by federal courts in New York:

> '"An adverse employment action is one which is more disruptive than a mere inconvenience or an alteration of job responsibilities."' . . . The Second Circuit has found examples of adverse employment actions to include 'termination of employment, a demotion evidenced by a decrease in wage or salary, a less distinguished title, a material loss of benefits, significantly diminished material responsibilities, or other indices unique to a particular situation.'[105]

In order to succeed on a claim under Title VII, a plaintiff employee must first

> carry the initial burden under the statute of establishing a prima facie case of racial discrimination. This may be done by showing (i) that he belongs to a racial minority [a protected class]; (ii) that he applied and was qualified for a job for which the employer was seeking applicants; (iii) that, despite his qualifications, he was rejected; and (iv) that, after his rejection, the position remained open

---

101 *Alfano v. Costello*, 294 F.3d 365, 374 (2d Cir. 2002) (Jacobs, J.); *Gorzynski v. JetBlue Airways Corp.*, 596 F.3d 93, 102 (2d Cir. 2010) (Calabresi, J.).

102 *Hayut v. State Univ. of N.Y.*, 352 F.3d 733, 745 (2d Cir. 2003) (Calabresi, J.). *See also Jamiel v. Viveros*, 2020 WL 1847566 at *3 (S.D.N.Y. Apr. 13, 2020).

103 *Jeanty v. Precision Pipeline Solutions, LLC*, 2019 WL 3532157 at *4-5 (S.D.N.Y. Aug. 2, 2019) (Briccetti, D.J.). *See also Barton v. Cty. of Warren*, 2020 WL 4569465 (N.D.N.Y. Aug. 7, 2020) (Suddaby, C.J.).

104 *Id.*

105 *See Gibson v. N.Y.S. Office of Mental Health*, 372 F.Supp.3d 23, 31 (N.D.N.Y. 2019) (Suddaby, C.J.).

> and the employer continued to seek applicants from persons of complainant's qualifications.[106]

A plaintiff need not, however, establish every element of a *prima facie* case to survive a motion to dismiss, although courts will "determin[e] whether a Title VII plaintiff has pleaded an actionable claim."[107] However, a plaintiff does carry the burden to at least identify the protected class of which they claim to be a member, their qualification for the position sought, or the circumstances giving rise to the inference of discriminatory animus, or the claim will fail.[108] While a low bar, plaintiffs have been unsuccessful.[109]

When a claim is made alleging intentional discrimination under Title VII, courts have commented concerning when an inference of intent is found. Specifically, in 2017, U.S. Magistrate Judge Lisa Margaret Smith of the Southern District of New York stated:

> "[a]n inference of discriminatory intent 'may be derived from a variety of circumstances, including, but not limited to: "the employer's continuing, after discharging the plaintiff, to seek applicants from persons of the plaintiff's qualifications to fill that position; or the employer's criticism of the plaintiff's performance in ethnically degrading terms; or its invidious comments about others in the employee's protected group; or the more favorable treatment of employees not in the protected group; or the sequence of events leading to the plaintiff's dis-

106 *McDonnell Douglas Corp. v. Green*, 411 U.S. 792, 802 (1973); *Miller v. Zinke for Dep't of Interior*, 324 F.Supp.3d 1032, 1041-42 (D. Alaska 2018) (Sedwick, Senior D.J.). The remainder of the *McDonnell Douglas* test is discussed in subsection 1.6, *infra*. For disparate impact claims, "[t]o make a *prima facie* case, the plaintiff must produce sufficient evidence 'demonstrating a causal connection' between the policy and the disparate impact." *Figueroa v. Pompeo*, 923 F.3d 1078, 1086 (D.C. Cir. 2019) (Wilkins, J.) (citing *Tex. Dep't of Hous. & Cmty. Affairs v. Inclusive Cmtys. Proj., Inc.*, 135 S. Ct. 2507, 2523 (2015); *accord* 42 U.S.C. § 2000e-2(k)(1)(A)(i)).

107 *Towns v. Memphis/Shelby Cty. Health Dep't*, 2019 WL 639050 at *4 (W.D. Tenn.Jan. 25, 2019) (Pham, M.J.).

108 *McCarrick v. Corning, Inc.*, 2019 WL 2106506 at *3 (W.D.N.Y. May 14, 2019) (Geraci, C.J.).

109 *Jamiel v. Viveros*, 2020 WL 1847566 at *3-4 (S.D.N.Y. Apr. 13, 2020) (defendants' motion to dismiss granted in part, with several claims under Title VII dismissed, but plaintiff's hostile work environment claim under Title VII survived, as did claims under the New York State and City Human Rights Laws); *Johnson v. Jack Parker Corp.*, 2019 WL 3428825 at *3-*4 (E.D.N.Y. July 30, 2019) (Donnelly, D.J.) (Title VII and 1981 claims dismissed, plaintiff failed to make *prima facie* showing, did not establish circumstances give rise to an inference of discrimination).

> charge.'"... In order to raise an inference of discriminatory intent by asserting that an employer treated a plaintiff less favorably than a similarly situated employee outside the plaintiff's protected group, the plaintiff must show he or she was similarly situated in 'all material respects' to the comparator employee."[110]

The court continued to explain, in its Report & Recommendation on a motion for summary judgment, that there is no requirement of but-for causation on these claims.[111] While a non-discriminatory reason may be proffered when the burden shifts to the defendant following plaintiff's *prima facie* showing—and although the "employer's explanation of its

110 *Kalola v. Int'l Bus. Mach. Corp.*, 2017 WL 3394115 at *7-*8 (S.D.N.Y. Feb. 28, 2017) (L. Smith, M.J.), *adopted* 2017 WL 3381896 (S.D.N.Y. Aug. 4, 2017) (Briccetti, D.J.), *appeal dismissed* 2018 WL 894064 (2d Cir. Jan. 24, 2018) (citing *Leibowitz v. Cornell Univ.*, 584 F.3d 487, 502 (2d Cir. 2009) (quoting *Chambers v. TRM Copy Ctrs. Corp.*, 43 F.3d 29, 37 (2d Cir. 1994)), *superseded by statute on other grounds*; *Graham v. Long Island R.R.*, 230 F.3d 34, 39 (2d Cir. 2000)). While placement of an employee on a performance improvement plan, absent more, is generally not sufficient for a finding of an adverse employment action, some courts have found that if the PIP is used to undermine an employee, or as a de facto step toward planned termination, a claim might survive, depending upon how a plaintiff pleads the remainder of the claim under the *McDonnell Douglas* analysis. *See Heap v. CenturyLink, Inc.*, 2020 WL 1489801 at *8 (S.D.N.Y. Mar. 27, 2020) (Preska, Senior D.J.) (citing, while distinguishing, *Kalola*, 2017 WL 3394115 at *9).

111 Claims such as those under Title VII can be "mixed motives," meaning that if one of the motivating factors behind an employer's adverse actions was based on discriminatory motive, the plaintiff can succeed on a claim. However, courts have held that mixed motives do not apply under the ADEA (*see* § 1.5 *infra*), which statutory framework instead requires a "because of" or "but-for" causation standard to apply, meaning a showing that the adverse action was taken because of age. This is a significant distinction between claims and must be understood. *Gross v. FBL Fin. Servs., Inc.*, 557 U.S. 167 (2009) (Thomas, J.). Additionally, the U.S. Supreme Court further clarified the application of the ADEA in a 2020 decision, finding that when a federal employer is involved, "[t]he plain meaning of the critical statutory language ('made free from any discrimination based on age') demands that personnel actions be untainted by any consideration of age. This does not mean that a plaintiff may obtain all forms of relief that are generally available for a violation of § 633a(a), including hiring, reinstatement, backpay, and compensatory damages, without showing that a personnel action would have been different if age had not been taken into account. To obtain such relief, a plaintiff must show that age was a but-for cause of the challenged employment decision. But if age discrimination played a lesser part in the decision, other remedies may be appropriate." *Babb v. Wilkie*, 140 S.Ct. 1168, 1171 (2020) (Alito, J.). Thus, the but-for causation standard is generally applicable for most relief to be awarded, although a mixed-motives standard, where age is only one potential consideration for an action that is taken, can be applied in certain cases for some lesser relief under the Act. The Court's decision in *Gross* still applies to private-sector employers, while *Babb* clarifies for public-sector employers. *Babb*, 140 S.Ct. at 1175-1176. Finally, "the Supreme Court's decision in *Gross* set forth an evidentiary standard of proof, rather than a pleading standard." *Zoulas v. N.Y.C. Dep't of Educ.*, 400 F.Supp.3d 25, 52 (S.D.N.Y. 2019) (Woods, D.J.). *See also* Marcia Coyle, *How Justice Alito Signaled Defeat for the Justice Department in Key Age-Bias Case*, N.Y.L.J. at p. 2, Apr. 8, 2020.

legitimate nondiscriminatory reasons must be 'clear and specific'"—any stated reason will be enough, and the defendant does not bear any burden to convince the court that the stated reason is or was the real reason for the action taken against plaintiff.[112] Indeed, according to the court, "[a] defendant's 'burden is satisfied if the proffered evidence taken as true, would permit the conclusion that there was a nondiscriminatory reason for the adverse action.'"[113]

Under the analysis, if the defendant meets its burden, there is a shift once more, to place the final burden on the plaintiff.

> "Upon the defendant's articulation of such a non-discriminatory reason for the employment action, the presumption of discrimination arising with the establishment of the prima facie case drops from the picture." . . . The burden then shifts "back to the plaintiff to demonstrate by competent evidence that the legitimate reasons offered by the defendant were not its true reasons, but were a pretext for discrimination." . . . The plaintiff must "produce not simply 'some' evidence, but 'sufficient evidence to support a rational finding that the legitimate, non-discriminatory reasons proffered by the [defendant] were false, and that more likely than not [discrimination] was the real reason for the [employment action].'" . . . "[T]he ultimate burden of persuading the trier of fact that the defendant intentionally discriminated against the plaintiff remains at all times with the plaintiff."[114]

The burden is not an easy one to bear, and not all plaintiffs survive the burden shifting analysis under *McDonnell Douglas*. Indeed, the plaintiff in *Kalola* was found by that court not to have established a *prima facie* case of discrimination.[115] See more on the *McDonnell Douglas* analysis below in § 1.6.

---

112 *Kalola*, 2017 WL 3394115 at *8 (citing *Mandell v. Cty. of Suffolk*, 316 F.3d 368, 381 (2d Cir. 2003); *Tarshis v. Riese Org.*, 211 F.3d 30, 36 (2d Cir. 2000), *abrogated on other grounds by Swierkiewicz v. Sorema N.A.*, 534 U.S. 506 (2002)).

113 *Kalola*, 2017 WL 3394115 at *8 (citing *Ricci v. DeStefano*, 530 F.3d 88, 110 (2d Cir. 2008)).

114 *Kalola*, 2017 WL 3394115 at *8 (citing *Weinstock v. Columbia Univ.*, 224 F.3d 33, 42 (2d Cir. 2000); *Leibowitz v. Cornell Univ.*, 584 F.3d 487, 499 (2d Cir. 2009); *Texas Dep't of Commun. Affairs v. Burdine*, 450 U.S. 248, 253 (1981)).

115 *Kalola*, 2017 WL 3394115 at *9.

It is important to recognize that in addition to the other statutory frameworks discussed in this section, the conversation would not be complete without mentioning the interplay of Title IX of the Education Amendments Act of 1972.[116] As discussed by courts, Title IX[117]

> provides in pertinent part that "[n]o person in the United States shall, on the basis of sex, be excluded from participation in, be denied the benefits of, or be subjected to discrimination under any education program or activity receiving Federal financial assistance."… The definition of a "program or activity" under Title IX is broad, and encompasses the operations of, inter alia: a "department, agency, special purpose district, or other instrumentality of a State or of a local government"; a local educational agency; an "entire corporation, partnership, or other private organization, or an entire sole proprietorship"; and any other entity that is established by two or more of the foregoing entities…. Thus, for an entity to be liable under Title IX, it must be both a "program or activity" as defined under § 1687, and a recipient of "Federal financial assistance."[118]

The analysis, and standard, when a plaintiff brings a Title IX claim against an educational institution resembles—although does not mirror—that applied under Title VII.

> The Supreme Court [has] rejected vicarious liability and constructive notice as bases for Title IX liability. For a plaintiff to proceed on a claim against an educational institution under Title IX, a plaintiff must establish a prima facie case showing that: 1) [sic] she was subjected to *quid pro quo* sexual harassment or a sexually hostile environment; b) she provided actual notice of the situa-

116 20 U.S.C. §§ 1681, *et seq.*

117 *Compare with* New York's Education Law Article 129-B (the "Enough is Enough Law"). *See Doe v. Syracuse Univ.*, 2019 WL 2021026 at *8 (N.D.N.Y. May 8, 2019) (Hurd, D.J.) ("In 2015, New York enacted article 129–B of the Education Law, known as the Enough is Enough Law (see L 2015, ch 76). The purpose of this law was to require all colleges and universities in the State of New York to implement uniform prevention and response policies and procedures relating to sexual assault, domestic violence, dating violence and stalking") (citing and quoting *Jacobson v. Blaise*, 157 A.D.3d 1072, 1074 (Sup. Ct. App. Div. 3d Dep't 2018)).

118 *A.B. by C.B. v. Hawaii State Dep't of Educ.*, 386 F.Supp.3d 1352, 1355 (D. Haw. 2019) (Kobayashi, D.J.).

> tion to an "appropriate person," who was, at a minimum, an official of the educational entity with authority to take corrective action and to end discrimination; and c) the institution's response to the harassment amounted to "deliberate indifference."[119]

Colleges and universities must be cautious when investigating or adjudicating claims of discrimination or sexual misconduct by a student or employee. Understand that Title IX applies to cases of gender discrimination in education programs and activities. *Gender* discrimination—not specifically discrimination against women. That means that students and employees of any gender may assert a claim under the statute when circumstances warrant.[120] Furthermore, in the case of *Menaker v. Hofstra Univ.,*[121] the Second Circuit U.S. Court of Appeals held that

> where a university (1) takes an adverse action against a student or employee, (2) in response to allegations of sex-

119 *Klemencic v. Ohio State Univ.*, 263 F.3d 504, 510 (6th Cir. 2001) (Siler, J.) (citing *Morse v. Regents of the Univ. of Colorado*, 154 F.3d 1124, 1127–28 (10th Cir. 1998) (citing *Gebser v. Lago Vista Indep. Sch. Dist.*, 524 U.S. 274, 280, 289-91 (1998))). As of 2020, a Circuit split exists as to the standard applied in Title IX cases at the pleading stage with the Second Circuit applying the *McDonnell Douglas* analysis (a lower standard); while the Sixth Circuit applies *Bell Atl. Corp. v. Twombly* and *Ashcroft v. Iqbal*; the Ninth Circuit rejects the Second Circuit's application; and the Tenth Circuit applies *McDonnell Douglas* at the summary judgment stage. *See Lee v. Univ. of N.M.*, 2020 WL 1515381 at *44-46 (D.N.M. Mar. 30, 2020) (Browning, D.J.) (citing, and discussing, *inter alia, Bell Atl. Corp. v. Twombly*, 550 U.S. 544, 127 S.Ct. 1955 (2007); *Ashcroft v. Iqbal*, 556 U.S. 662, 129 S.Ct. 1937 (2009); *Doe v. Columbia Univ.*, 831 F.3d 46 (2d Cir. 2016); *Doe v. Miami Univ.*, 882 F.3d 579 (6th Cir. 2018); *Austin v. Univ. of Or.*, 925 F.3d 1133, 1137 (9th Cir. 2019); *Hiatt v. Colo. Seminary*, 858 F.3d 1307, 1315 n.8 (10th Cir. 2017)).

120 *See, e.g., Doe v. Columbia Univ.*, 831 F.3d 46 (2d Cir. 2016) (Leval, J.); *Feibleman v. Trustees of Columbia Univ.*, 2020 WL 882429 (S.D.N.Y. Feb. 24, 2020) (Carponi, D.J.) (plaintiff male student, accused of sexual misconduct, alleged bias/discrimination on the basis of gender in defendant university's proceedings in violation of Title IX; Court denied motion to dismiss as to certain claims). The U.S. Supreme Court's decision in *Bostock v. Clayton County*, 140 S. Ct. 1731 (June 15, 2020) (Gorsuch, J.), may also serve to expand protections for gender identity, and prohibit discrimination based thereon under Title IX and other statutes, given the Court's interpretation of Title VII's "because of…sex" statutory language, and its extension to include sexual orientation and gender identity in that decision. *See* Erwin Chemerinsky, *Chemerinsky: Gorsuch Wrote His 'Most Important Opinion' in SCOTUS Ruling Protecting LGBTQ Workers*, ABA Journal, July 1, 2020, https://www.abajournal.com/news/article/chemerinsky-justice-gorsuch-just-wrote-his-most-important-opinion. Separately, the Trump Administration issued new regulations under Title IX in the spring of 2020, which included increased procedural due process rights for students accused of sexual misconduct on a college campus. *See* Debra Cassens Weiss, *New Title IX Regulations Give More Rights to College Students Accused of Sexual Misconduct*, ABA Journal, May 7, 2020, https://www.abajournal.com/news/article/new-title-ix-regs-give-more-rights-to-students-accused-of-sexual-misconduct.

121 935 F.3d 20 (2d Cir. 2019) (Cabranes, J.).

> ual misconduct, (3) following a clearly irregular investigative or adjudicative process, (4) amid criticism for reacting inadequately to allegations of sexual misconduct by members of one sex, these circumstances provide the requisite support for a *prima facie* case of sex discrimination.[122]

In May 2020, the U.S. Department of Education released new Final Regulations on Title IX, which, among other things, defined "sexual harassment," strengthened protections for survivors of sexual assault on campuses, and also increased due process for those accused of sexual misconduct.[123]

Additionally, bear in mind, that law schools are required to demonstrate a commitment to diversity and inclusion, for students, faculty and staff, as part of the American Bar Association's Section of Legal Education & Admissions to the Bar's Standards of Approval.[124] The *Standards and Rules of Procedure for Approval of Law Schools*, as implemented by the Section's Council, provide at Standard 206 as follows:

> **Standard 206. DIVERSITY AND INCLUSION**
>
> (a) Consistent with sound legal education policy and the Standards, a law school shall demonstrate by concrete action a commitment to diversity and inclusion by pro-

122 *Id.* at 33–34 (citing *Doe v. Columbia Univ.*). *But see Vengalattore v. Cornell Univ.*, 2020 WL 2104706 at *7-8 (N.D.N.Y. May 1, 2020) (Sharpe, Senior D.J.) (discussing whether "[d]iscriminatory intent of subordinates may . . . be imputed to ultimate decisionmakers," and finding *Menaker* distinguishable because there "the 'officials specifically referenced [the student's] accusations in the course of terminating [the plaintiff], thereby acknowledging that she had "played a meaningful role in the decision"'").

123 *See Secretary DeVos Takes Historic Action to Strengthen Title IX Protections for All Students*, Press Office, U.S. Dep't of Educ., May 6, 2020, https://www.ed.gov/news/press-releases/secretary-devos-takes-historic-action-strengthen-title-ix-protections-all-students; Kimberly C. Lau, *et al.*, *Due Process for Campus Sexual Misconduct Cases*, N.Y.L.J. at p. 4, June 25, 2020. *See also* 85 Fed. Reg. 30026 (May 19, 2020).

124 When it comes to accreditation of law schools, the American Bar Association Section of Legal Education & Admissions to the Bar states this on its website concerning its Council: "The Section's Council is recognized by the U.S. Department of Education (DOE) as the national accrediting agency for programs leading to the J.D. In this function, the Council and the Section are independent of the ABA, as required by DOE regulations. All state supreme courts recognize ABA-approved law schools as meeting the legal education requirements to qualify for the bar examination; forty-six states limit eligibility for bar admission to graduates of ABA-approved schools." *Law School Accreditation*, ABA Section of Legal Education & Admissions to the Bar, https://www.americanbar.org/groups/legal_education.

> viding full opportunities for the study of law and entry into the profession by members of underrepresented groups, particularly racial and ethnic minorities, and a commitment to having a student body that is diverse with respect to gender, race, and ethnicity.
>
> (b) Consistent with sound educational policy and the Standards, a law school shall demonstrate by concrete action a commitment to diversity and inclusion by having a faculty and staff that are diverse with respect to gender, race, and ethnicity.[125]

Federal law sets out a framework of protections based on race, color, religion, sex, or national origin, with other specific classes covered by other statutes, as discussed in the ensuing portions of this book. While New York laws are more expansive in the number and types of protected classes created and protected, nevertheless federal law exists as the "floor" for protections, below which no U.S. jurisdiction may fall.[126] The applications of federal law extend far and wide, and, as noted above, have found their way into the standards for accreditation of American law schools—the training ground for future attorneys, the guardians of the Constitution and the Republic in the years to come.

---

125 Standard 206, *2019-2020 Standards and Rules of Procedure for Approval of Law Schools*, ABA Section of Legal Education & Admissions to the Bar, https://www.americanbar.org/groups/legal_education/resources/standards/ (note that pursuant to Standard 207, law schools must assure reasonable accommodations for those students, faculty and staff with qualifying disabilities).

126 *Supremacy Clause*, U.S. Const. Art. VI ("This Constitution, and the Laws of the United States which shall be made in Pursuance thereof; and all Treaties made, or which shall be made, under the Authority of the United States, shall be the supreme Law of the Land; and the Judges in every State shall be bound thereby, any Thing in the Constitution or Laws of any State to the Contrary notwithstanding.").

[1.4] V. RELIGIOUS ACCOMMODATION

When it comes to protections based on religious beliefs & accommodations, this area hinges on the actions of both employers and employees.[127] To begin, however, a baseline exists whereby religious organizations that are also employers have protections stemming from the First Amendment, such that a "ministerial exception" will apply to certain employment actions. In summer 2020, the U.S. Supreme Court solidified this protec-

127 Note that with regard to a juxtaposition of Title VII and protection for religion, a broad exception also exists under the Religious Freedom Restoration Act, 42 U.S.C. § 2000bb. "RFRA provides 'very broad protection for religious liberty' by exempting religious believers from laws that substantially burden the exercise of their religious beliefs.... The Government must provide such an exemption unless the application of the law to the believer is the 'least restrictive means' of furthering a 'compelling government interest.'... A RFRA claim may be brought as an affirmative defense to criminal charges.... The Act was passed after the Supreme Court held—reversing prior case law—that the Free Exercise Clause of the First Amendment 'does not relieve an individual of the obligation to comply with a valid and neutral law of general applicability.'... Congress enacted RFRA in response, seeking to 'restore' religious exemptions from nondiscriminatory 'rule[s] of general applicability.'... RFRA therefore reflected Congress' judgment that 'laws [that are] "neutral" toward religion may burden religious exercise as surely as laws intended to interfere with religious exercise.'... To succeed on a RFRA defense, a claimant must first make two showings: (1) governmental action burdens a sincere 'exercise of religion' and (2) the burden is 'substantial.'... A RFRA claim that does not establish these two elements fails.... If a claimant does demonstrate a substantial burden on her sincere exercise of religious belief, a court must find a RFRA violation unless the Government demonstrates that 'application of the burden to the person' both (1) 'furthers a compelling governmental interest' and (2) 'is the least restrictive means of furthering that compelling government interest.'" *U.S. v. Hoffman*, 436 F.Supp.3d 1272, 1279-1280 (D. Ariz. 2020) (Márquez, D.J.) (citing, *inter alia*, *Burwell v. Hobby Lobby Stores, Inc.*, 573 U.S. 682, 693, 134 S.Ct. 2751 (2014); *Employment Div. v. Smith*, 494 U.S. 872, 879, 110 S.Ct. 1595 (1990); 42 U.S.C. § 2000bb). In a civil action, "'A person who brings a challenge under RFRA bears the initial burden of proving that (1) the Government's policy or action implicates her religious exercise, (2) the relevant religious exercise is grounded in a sincerely held religious belief, and (3) the policy or action substantially burdens that exercise.'... If the person establishes a *prima facie* RFRA violation, then the burden shifts to the government to demonstrate that the government interest is compelling, and its action is the least restrictive means." *Sabra v. Pompeo*, 2020 WL 1643676 at *24 (D.D.C. Apr. 2, 2020) (Sullivan, D.J.) (The protections instituted by Congress in the RFRA exceed those in the First Amendment to the U.S. Constitution). Following the U.S. Supreme Court's decision in *Bostock v. Clayton County*, 140 S.Ct. 1731, some question what the impact will be if an individual discriminates against another because of sexual orientation or gender identity, and concomitantly seeks the shelter of the RFRA and First Amendment. *See* E. Chemerinsky, *Chemerinsky: Gorsuch Wrote His 'Most Important Opinion', supra.* For further reference, the Supreme Court, in a decision at the end of the October 2019 Term (issued in summer 2020), evaluating arguments under the RFRA, ruled with regard to the contraceptive mandate that developed under the Patient Protection and Affordable Care Act ("Obamacare") "that the [federal] Departments had the authority to provide exemptions from the regulatory contraceptive requirements for employers with religious and conscientious objections." *See Little Sisters of the Poor Sts. Peter & Paul Home v. Pa.*, 140 S. Ct. 2367 (2020) (Thomas, J.).

tion with its holding in *Our Lady of Guadalupe School v. Morrissey-Berru*,[128] in which the Court stated:

> These cases require us to decide whether the First Amendment permits courts to intervene in employment disputes involving teachers at religious schools who are entrusted with the responsibility of instructing their students in the faith. The First Amendment protects the right of religious institutions "to decide for themselves, free from state interference, matters of church government as well as those of faith and doctrine." *Kedroff v. Saint Nicholas Cathedral of Russian Orthodox Church in North America*, 344 U. S. 94, 116 (1952). Applying this principle, we held in *Hosanna-Tabor Evangelical Lutheran Church and School v. EEOC*, 565 U. S. 171 (2012), that the First Amendment barred a court from entertaining an employment discrimination claim brought by an elementary school teacher, Cheryl Perich, against the religious school where she taught. Our decision built on a line of lower court cases adopting what was dubbed the "ministerial exception" to laws governing the employment relationship between a religious institution and certain key employees. We did not announce "a rigid formula" for determining whether an employee falls within this exception, but we identified circumstances that we found relevant in that case, including Perich's title as a "Minister of Religion, Commissioned," her educational training, and her responsibility to teach religion and participate with students in religious activities. *Id.* at 190–191.
>
> In the cases now before us, we consider employment discrimination claims brought by two elementary school teachers at Catholic schools whose teaching responsibilities are similar to Perich's. Although these teachers were not given the title of "minister" and have less religious training than Perich, we hold that their cases fall within the same rule that dictated our decision in *Hosanna-Tabor*. The religious education and formation of students is the very reason for the existence of most private religious schools, and therefore the selection and supervision of the teachers upon whom the schools rely to do this

128 140 S. Ct. 2049 (2020) (Alito, J.).

> work lie at the core of their mission. Judicial review of the way in which religious schools discharge those responsibilities would undermine the independence of religious institutions in a way that the First Amendment does not tolerate.
>
> . . .
>
> Respondents argue that the *Hosanna-Tabor* exception is not workable unless it is given a rigid structure, but we declined to adopt a "rigid formula" in *Hosanna-Tabor*, and the lower courts have been applying the exception for many years without such a formula. Here, as in *Hosanna-Tabor*, it is sufficient to decide the cases before us. When a school with a religious mission entrusts a teacher with the responsibility of educating and forming students in the faith, judicial intervention into disputes between the school and the teacher threatens the school's independence in a way that the First Amendment does not allow.[129]

The holding in *Morrissey-Berru* notwithstanding, there are other instances when employers and employees have interactions that do fall under the employment laws—such as when religious obligations or practices interfere or conflict with job responsibilities. In such cases, if religious discrimination is claimed by the employee, the plaintiff must have a genuine religious practice, which conflicts with a requirement of the job (this usually concerns work schedules and observance of Sabbath days).

> In order to establish a prima facie case of religious discrimination based on a failure to accommodate, the plaintiff must show that "(1) a bona fide religious practice

129 *Id.* (determining that allegations of discrimination by the employees against the employers in this case under the ADA and ADEA could not survive). In the dissent, however, Justice Sotomayor contrasted the judge-made "ministerial exception" with statutory carve-out provisions: "Some antidiscrimination laws, like the Americans with Disabilities Act, permit a religious institution to consider religion when making employment decisions. 42 U. S. C. §12113(d)(1). Under that Act, a religious organization may also 'require that all applicants and employees conform' to the entity's 'religious tenets.'... Title VII further permits a school to prefer 'hir[ing] and employ[ing]' people 'of a particular religion' if its curriculum 'propagat[es]' that religion.... These statutory exceptions protect a religious entity's ability to make employment decisions—hiring or firing—for religious reasons. The 'ministerial exception,' by contrast, is a judge-made doctrine. This Court first recognized it eight years ago in *Hosanna-Tabor*, concluding that the First Amendment categorically bars certain antidiscrimination suits by religious leaders against their religious employers...." *Id.* (Sotomayor, J., dissenting) (citations omitted).

> conflicts with an employment requirement, (2) he or she brought the practice to the [Union's] attention, and (3) the religious practice was the basis for the adverse employment decision." . . . Once the plaintiff has established this prima facie case, the burden shifts to the union to show that it made a reasonable accommodation of the religious practice or show that any accommodation would result in undue hardship.[130]

It is essential that the employee demonstrates a "bona fide religious belief" for the religious accommodation claim to succeed.[131] An employer or labor organization is not required to accommodate "purely personal preference" under Title VII.[132] The plaintiff must show that the religious practice or belief that is creating the conflict that is sincerely held.[133]

Thereafter, an employer, when on notice, must offer a reasonable accommodation (which will be discussed more during discussion of the Americans with Disabilities Act, in Chapter 6, *infra*). If the employer offers a full accommodation, such accommodation does not have to be what the employee requests. It must simply resolve the conflict completely.[134] However, if the employer fails to reasonably accommodate, or the accommodation offered does not fully resolve the conflict, then the employer may face liability (of course subject to the employer having the defense that any accommodation would cause an undue hardship).[135]

On the reverse side, though, if the employee fails to act in good faith, and rejects a reasonable accommodation for an unacceptable reason (such as preference versus religious practices), then the employer generally will

---

130 *EEOC v. Union Independiente de la Autoridad de Acueductos y Alcantarillados de Puerto Rico*, 279 F.3d 49, 55 (1st Cir. 2002) (Torruella, J.) (citing *EEOC v. United Parcel Serv.*, 94 F.3d 314, 317 (7th Cir. 1996); *Seaworth v. Pearson*, 203 F.3d 1056, 1057 (8th Cir.) (per curiam), *cert. denied*, 531 U.S. 895 (2000); *Tiano v. Dillard Dep't Stores, Inc.*, 139 F.3d 679, 682 (9th Cir. 1998)); *Mereigh v. N.Y. & Presbyterian Hosp.*, 16-cv-5583, 2017 WL 5195236 at *5 (S.D.N.Y. Nov. 9, 2017) (Forrest, D.J.).

131 *Union Independiente*, 279 F.3d at 55-56.

132 *Id.* (citing *Vetter v. Farmland Indus., Inc.*, 120 F.3d 749, 751 (8th Cir. 1997)).

133 *Id.* (citing *Redmond v. GAF Corp.*, 574 F.2d 897, 901 n. 12 (7th Cir. 1978); *Hager v. Sec. of Air Force*, 938 F.2d 1449, 1454 (1st Cir. 1991)).

134 *See Mereigh*, 2017 WL 5195236 at *5, *8.

135 *Id.* at *5; *Jamil v. Sessions*, 2017 WL 913601 (E.D.N.Y. Mar. 6, 2017) (Chen, D.J.); Exec. Law § 296(10).

not face liability for religious discrimination or failure to accommodate.[136]

Recognize the importance of acting in good faith—both as an employer and employee—when addressing *bona fide* religious beliefs and practices and attempting to provide for an inclusive and accommodating work environment.

[1.5] VI. A NOTE ON AGE—ADEA

The Age Discrimination in Employment Act (ADEA)[137] is a federal statute, which provides, in relevant part:

> **(a) Employer practices**
>
> It shall be unlawful for an employer—
>
> **(1)** to fail or refuse to hire or to discharge any individual or otherwise discriminate against any individual with respect to his compensation, terms, conditions, or privileges of employment, because of such individual's age;
>
> **(2)** to limit, segregate, or classify his employees in any way which would deprive or tend to deprive any individual of employment opportunities or otherwise adversely affect his status as an employee, because of such individual's age; or
>
> **(3)** to reduce the wage rate of any employee in order to comply with this chapter.[138]

The ADEA also applies to employment agencies, labor organizations, and foreign corporations controlled by American employers.[139] The ADEA likewise contains its own anti-retaliation provision:

> **(d) Opposition to unlawful practices; participation in investigations, proceedings, or litigation**

136 *See Mereigh*, 2017 WL 5195236 at *5, *8; *Moore v. City of N.Y.*, 2018 WL 3491286 (S.D.N.Y. July 20, 2018) (Cott, M.J.).

137 29 U.S.C. §§ 621, *et seq.*

138 29 U.S.C. § 623(a).

139 29 U.S.C. § 623(b), (c), (h).

> It shall be unlawful for an employer to discriminate against any of his employees or applicants for employment, for an employment agency to discriminate against any individual, or for a labor organization to discriminate against any member thereof or applicant for membership, because such individual, member or applicant for membership has opposed any practice made unlawful by this section, or because such individual, member or applicant for membership has made a charge, testified, assisted, or participated in any manner in an investigation, proceeding, or litigation under this chapter.[140]

To establish a claim under the ADEA, a plaintiff must meet the following burden (which is comparable to that under Title VII, and should be familiar to the reader by this point):

> To establish a prima facie case of age discrimination under the ADEA, a plaintiff must show that: (1) he 'was within the protected age group'; (2) he 'was qualified for the position'; (3) he 'experienced [an] adverse employment action'; and (4) 'such action occurred under circumstances giving rise to an inference of discrimination.'[141]

In addition, as compared to cases of mixed-motives under Title VII, "[a] plaintiff in an ADEA case must also 'allege that [his] age was the "but-for" cause of the adverse action.'"[142] Stray remarks, alone, will not carry the day to establish employment discrimination,[143] although employers and supervisors should be very careful because a stray remark can quickly become more pervasive in the workplace, if it appears management is tolerant of such behavior toward and treatment of others.

The ADEA is mentioned herein for attention to specific court holdings, wherein it appears that the protections of the ADEA concerning disparate impact claims are only applicable to employees, not to job applicants. The

---

140 29 U.S.C. § 623(d).

141 *Tsismentzoglou v. Milos Estiatorio Inc.*, 2019 WL 2287902 at *3 (S.D.N.Y. May 29, 2019) (Abrams, D.J.) (citing *Gorzynski v. JetBlue Airways Corp.*, 596 F.3d 93, 107 (2d Cir. 2010)).

142 *Tsismentzoglou*, 2019 WL 2287902 at *3 (citing *Marcus v. Leviton Mfg. Co., Inc.*, 661 Fed. App'x 29, 32 (2d Cir. 2016) (citing *Vega v. Hempstead Union Free Sch. Dist.*, 801 F.3d 72, 87 (2d Cir. 2015))).

143 *Tsismentzoglou*, 2019 WL 2287902 at *4.

case referred to is *Kleber v. CareFusion Corp.*,[144] an *en banc* decision of the Seventh Circuit that referred to *Villarreal v. R.J. Reynolds Tobacco Co.*,[145] an *en banc* decision of the Eleventh Circuit.

Kleber was filed seeking relief under ADEA provisions prohibiting both disparate treatment (§4 (a)(1)) and disparate impact (§ 4(a)(2)) based on age. In *Kleber*, the attorney applicant, aged 58 with many years of experience, was passed over for a 29-year-old applicant who had many fewer years of experience. "The job description required applicants to have '3 to 7 years (no more than 7 years) of relevant legal experience.'"[146] The 29-year old applicant met but did not exceed the range specified for years of experience. The district court dismissed Kleber's § 4(a)(2) disparate impact claim, citing earlier Seventh Circuit precedent. In addition, Kleber voluntarily dismissed his § 4(a)(1) disparate treatment claim.[147]

A panel of the Seventh Circuit reversed the district court's holding on the 4(a)(2) claim, but the Seventh Circuit granted re-hearing *en banc*.[148] The full court affirmed the district court and reversed the panel decision. According to the *en banc* decision, the plain language of § 4(a)(2) makes clear that Congress, while protecting employees from disparate impact age discrimination, did not extend the same protection to outside job applicants. The *en banc* majority believed its holding was reinforced by the ADEA's structure and history.

> By its terms, § 4(a)(2) proscribes certain conduct by employers and limits its protection to employees. The prohibited conduct entails an employer acting in any way to limit, segregate, or classify its employees based on age. The language of § 4(a)(2) then goes on to make clear that its proscriptions apply only if an employer's actions have a particular impact—"depriv[ing] or tend[ing] to deprive any individual of employment opportunities or otherwise adversely affect[ing] his status as an employee." This language plainly demonstrates that the requisite impact must befall an individual with "status as an employee." Put most simply, the reach of § 4(a)(2)

144 914 F.3d 480 (7th Cir. 2019) (en banc).

145 839 F.3d 958, 964 (11th Cir. 2016) (en banc).

146 *Kleber*, 914 F.3d at 481-82.

147 *Id.*

148 *Id.*

> does not extend to applicants for employment, as common dictionary definitions confirm that an applicant has no "status as an employee."
>
> . . .
>
> Subjecting the language of §4(a)(2) to even closer scrutiny reinforces our conclusion. Congress did not prohibit just conduct that "would deprive or tend to deprive any individual of employment opportunities." It went further. Section 4(a)(2) employs a catchall formulation—"or otherwise adversely affect his status as an employee"—to extend the proscribed conduct. Congress's word choice is significant and has a unifying effect: the use of "or otherwise" serves to stitch the prohibitions and scope of § 4(a)(2) into a whole, first by making clear that the proscribed acts cover all conduct "otherwise affect[ing] his status as an employee," and, second, by limiting the reach of the statutory protection to an individual with "status as an employee.""'[149]

The dissenting judges of the *en banc* court, after examining the language of 29 U.S.C. § 623(a), stated:

> The disparate-treatment provision, paragraph (a)(1), does not refer to job applicants, but it clearly applies to them by making it unlawful for the employer "to fail or refuse to hire . . . any individual . . . because of such individual's age." The disparate-impact provision, paragraph (a)(2), also does not refer specifically to applicants or hiring decisions, but its broad language easily reaches employment practices that hurt older job applicants as well as current older employees.[150]

It will eventually be left to the Supreme Court of the United States to resolve this issue of statutory interpretation and application on this issue.

149 *Id.* at 482-83 (citing *Villarreal*, 839 F.3d at 964).

150 *Id.* at 491 (Hamilton, J., dissenting, joined by Wood, C.J., & Rovner, J.).

[1.6] VII. THE *MCDONNELL DOUGLAS* BURDEN SHIFTING TEST

When it comes to cases concerning discrimination, harassment or retaliation, and the evidence is indirect or circumstantial[151] in nature (as it is in many cases), courts apply what has become known as the *McDonnell Douglas* burden shifting test or analysis.[152] Often, because an employer that has engaged in discrimination is unlikely to leave a "smoking gun," a plaintiff usually must rely on "the cumulative weight of circumstantial evidence" when proving bias.[153] The test comes from the seminal 1973 United States Supreme Court case *McDonnell Douglas Corp. v. Green.*[154] The *McDonnell Douglas* burden shift places the initial burden on the plaintiff, but once that burden is met the burden next falls on the defendant. While placing the burden on defendants is not usual in the American legal system, in essence the shift to the defendant resembles (but certainly is not the same as) a defendant proving an affirmative defense (which is a burden regularly placed on defendants[155]), although as mentioned earlier, it is really a burden of production, a showing, and not a burden of persuasion.[156] As stated by then-New York State Chief Judge Lawrence H. Cooke, for a unanimous Court in *N.Y.C. Bd. of Ed., Community School*

---

151 "Circumstantial evidence is 'evidence that points to discriminatory animus through a longer chain of inferences,'... and sets out a 'convincing mosaic of discrimination.'... Such evidence generally falls into one of three categories: (1) suspicious timing, ambiguous oral or written statements, or behavior toward or comments direct at other employees in the protected group; (2) evidence, whether or not rigorously statistical, that similarly situated employees outside the protected class received systematically better treatment; and (3) evidence that the employer offered a pretextual reason for the adverse employment action." *Larbi v. Advocate Christ Med. Ctr.*, 2012 WL 6019107 at *3 (N.D. Ill. Dec. 3, 2012) (Kennelly, D.J.).

152 Worth noting, after the Civil Rights Act of 1991, and the Supreme Court's ruling in *Desert Palace, Inc. v. Costa*, 539 U.S. 90 (2003), it is no longer necessary for a Title VII plaintiff to offer direct evidence of discriminatory motive to proceed under a mixed-motive analysis. *See Dare v. Wal-Mart Stores, Inc.*, 267 F.Supp.2d 987 (D. Minn. 2003) (Magnuson, D.J.).

153 *Luciano v. Olsten Corp.*, 110 F.3d 210, 215 (2d Cir. 1997) (Altimari, J.).

154 411 U.S. 792 (1973) (Powell, J.). Following the U.S. Supreme Court's decision in *Comcast Corp.*, the *McDonnell Douglas* analysis is still applied to both Title VII and Section 1981 claims. *See Mann v. XPO Logistics Freight, Inc.*, 2020 WL 3397737 at *6 & n.15 (10th Cir. June 19, 2020).

155 *Hardaway v. Hartford Public Works Dep't*, 879 F.3d 486, 491 (2d Cir. 2018) (Pooler, J.); *Waters v. ShopRite Supermarkets, Inc.*, 2011 WL 6029248 at *3 (D.N.J. Dec. 5, 2011) (Martini, D.J.); *Averbuck v. Becher*, 134 N.Y.S. 1112, 1113 (App. Term 1912) (Gerard, J.).

156 *See Comcast Corp.*, 140 S.Ct. at 1019.

Dist. No. 1 v. Batista,[157] "to overcome a prima facie showing of discrimination in a firing an employer must make 'a showing that the employee was terminated for some independently legitimate reason which was neither a pretext for discrimination nor was substantially influenced by impermissible discrimination.'"[158] If defendant meets its burden, the final shift does place the ultimate burden back on the plaintiff, where it belongs, to prove the case and liability.

As made clear by the U.S. District Court for the Eastern District of Pennsylvania in *McCarty v. Marple Tp. Ambulance Corps*, when discussing the burden shifting analysis:

> A plaintiff asserting an ADA claim or a Title VII claim may proceed using a three-step burden-shifting framework set forth by the Supreme Court in *McDonnell Douglas*. . . .
>
> First, the *McDonnell Douglas* approach requires a plaintiff to establish a prima facie case of discrimination.... Under this approach, a plaintiff must show that:
>
> (1) [h]e is a member of a protected class;
>
> (2) [h]e was qualified for the position he sought to attain or retain;
>
> (3) [h]e suffered an adverse employment action; and
>
> (4) the action occurred under circumstances that could give rise to an inference of intentional discrimination.
>
> . . . Courts vary the precise components required for a prima facie case because "the elements... depend on the facts of a particular case.". . . The burden to establish a prima facie case is not an onerous one, but a prima facie case can allow a court "to eliminate the most obvious, lawful reasons for the defendant's action.". . .
>
> If a plaintiff successfully establishes a prima facie case, the burden shifts to the defendant to articulate some legit-

157 54 N.Y.2d 379, 384 & n.* (1981) (Cooke, C.J.).

158 *Id.* at 384 & n.* (citing *Pace Coll. v. Comm'n on Human Rights of City of N.Y.*, 38 N.Y.2d 28, 40 (1975) (Breitel, C.J.)).

> imate, non-discriminatory reason for its decision. . . . If the defendant succeeds, the burden returns to the plaintiff to show that the employer's stated reason for termination was merely a pretext for intentional discrimination. . . . To survive a motion for summary judgment, a nonmoving plaintiff must point to evidence that: "1) casts sufficient doubt upon each of the legitimate reasons proffered by the defendant so that a factfinder could reasonably conclude that each reason was a fabrication;" or 2) permits the factfinder to reasonably conclude "that discrimination was more likely than not a motivating or determinative cause of the adverse employment action.". . .[159]

While the initial burden is not usually a high one, there are cases where plaintiffs have failed to make out a *prima facie* showing sufficient to survive motion practice.[160] For instance, in the case of *Whigham-Williams v. Am. Broadcasting Co., Inc.*,[161]

> [p]laintiff [did] not sufficiently allege a specific position she applied for and was rejected from. Plaintiff does not allege anywhere in the complaint that there was an opening for a coanchor position on Good Morning America, Plaintiff concedes that her talent agency contacted executives at ABC regarding "potential openings" for a co-host position on Good Morning America. . . . Additionally, Plaintiff does not sufficiently allege that she was "qualified for [the] job.". . . Plaintiff alleges that she has an Associate's degree, is studying law and theology, and is a member of two professional organizations. . . . However, she fails to explain how those credentials qualify her to be a co-anchor on Good Morning America.[162]

---

159 *McCarty v. Marple Tp. Ambulance Corps*, 869 F.Supp.2d 638, 645-46 (E.D. Pa. 2012) (Brody, D.J.) (citations omitted). The burden shift also applies to other claims, such as ADEA cases (*Granica v. Town of Hamburg*, 237 F.Supp.3d 60 (W.D.N.Y. 2017) (Skretny, D.J.)), and FMLA cases (*Hurlbert v. St. Mary's Health Care Sys., Inc.*, 439 F.3d 1286 (11th Cir. 2006) (Wilson, J.)).

160 *See Cardoza v. Healthfirst, Inc.*, 210 F.Supp.2d 224 (S.D.N.Y. 1999) (Berman, D.J.).

161 2018 WL 4042110 (S.D.N.Y. Aug. 22, 2018) (Nathan, D.J.).

162 *Id.* at *3. *But cf. Collins v. Res. Ctr. for Indep. Living*, 2018 WL 5983377 (N.D.N.Y. Nov. 14, 2018) (Kahn, D.J.) (plaintiff did make *prima facie* case for first step, Title VII claim survived motion for judgment on the pleadings).

Michael Strahan was hired as the new co-anchor. Plaintiff's case was dismissed. Plaintiffs will not survive summary judgment when unable to rebut the employer defendant's legitimate, non-discriminatory reason, as part of the shift back to plaintiff under *McDonnell Douglas*.[163]

In addition to applying to disparate treatment claims under Title VII, the *McDonnell Douglas* test also applies to retaliation claims under Title VII.[164] Its reach is universally applied in this field.[165]

Generally, the same standard is applied for claims under the federal statutes, as well as under the New York State statutes. Although the *McDonnell Douglas* test applies in New York City,[166] courts have also held that claims under the New York City Administrative Code must be analyzed separately, independently and construed more broadly in favor of plaintiffs, as compared with the federal and state laws.[167] In more recent years, New York City's law is no longer coterminous with federal and state law in this field. It was noted by the Eastern District of New York federal court that:

> NYCHRL claims "have typically been treated as coextensive with state and federal counterparts.". . . "However, the New York City Council has rejected such equivalence.". . . Pursuant to the Local Civil Rights Restoration Act of 2005, N.Y.C. Local Law No. 85 ("Restoration Act"), interpretations of New York state or federal statutes with similar wording may only be used "'to aid

163 *Concha v. Purchase Coll. State Univ. of N.Y.*, 2019 WL 3219386 (S.D.N.Y. July 17, 2019) (McCarthy, M.J.) (Title VII, §1983, and N.Y.S. Human Rights Law claims dismissed).

164 *See Rafael v. Conn. Dep't of Children & Families*, 2017 WL 27393 (D. Conn. Jan. 3, 2017) (Bryant, D.J.).

165 *See Quaintance v. City of Columbia*, 2018 WL 264177 (W.D. Mo. Jan. 2, 2018) (Laughrey, D.J.) (Plaintiff failed to make *prima facie* showing under *McDonnell Douglas* of discrimination under the ADA, or discrimination or retaliation under Title VII, and therefore summary judgment granted to defendant); *see also Murray v. Cerebal Palsy Assoc. of N.Y., Inc.*, 2018 WL 264112 (S.D.N.Y. Jan. 2, 2018) (Ramos, D.J.).

166 *James v. City of N.Y.*, 144 A.D.3d 466, 41 N.Y.S.3d 221 (Sup. Ct. App. Div. 1st Dep't 2016).

167 "Claims asserted under Title VII and the NYSHRL are analyzed pursuant to the same standard; therefore, analysis of identical claims brought by an individual under both of these laws can be performed in tandem," however "the Court of Appeals notes that district courts 'must analyze NYCHRL claims separately and independently from any federal and state law claims' and 'constru[e] the NYCHRL's provisions broadly in favor of discrimination plaintiffs, to the extent that such a construction is reasonably possible.'" *E.E.O.C. v. Bloomberg L.P.*, 967 F. Supp. 2d 816, 831, 835 (S.D.N.Y. 2013) (Preska, C.J.) (citing *Pucino v. Verizon Wireless Commc'ns, Inc.*, 618 F.3d 112, 117 n. 2 (2d Cir. 2010)).

> in interpretation of New York City Human Rights Law, viewing similarly worded provisions of federal and state civil rights laws as a floor below which the City's Human Rights law cannot fall.'". . . [However] because a motion for summary judgment inquires only as to whether a "rational factfinder could find in favor of the non-moving party," as opposed to what the "ceiling" of a claim may be, the court [in this cited case did apply] an identical analysis to plaintiff's ADA, NYSHRL, and NYCHRL claims."[168]

Finally, make a note that following the Amendments Act in New York, signed by the Governor on August 12, 2019, there has been an elimination of the "severe or pervasive" standard for claims of hostile work environment under the New York State law, aligning it with the New York City law.[169] Under the law, effective October 11, 2019, it is unlawful to subject an individual to "inferior terms, conditions or privileges of employment because of the individual's membership" in any protected class under the Human Rights Law, but there is no need to show repetitive violations exist.[170] However, an affirmative defense will remain for defendant employers: where "harassing conduct does not rise above the level of what a reasonable victim of discrimination with the same protected characteristic would consider petty slights or trivial inconveniences."[171] The statutory change, though, only applies to actions filed after the effective date of October 11, 2019, thus for some time trial court decisions and appellate dispositions may still apply the old law requiring severe or pervasive conduct.[172]

Additionally, for cases filed on or after the 60th day from Governor Cuomo's signing of the Amendments Act, plaintiffs no longer need to compare themselves to others similarly situated but not belonging to the same protected class for employment discrimination claims (i.e., employee not in a protected class violates a policy, and is punished less

---

168 *Morse v. JetBlue Airways Corp.*, 941 F.Supp.2d 274, 292 (E.D.N.Y. 2013) (Matsumoto, D.J.) (citing *Loeffler v. Staten Isl. Univ. Hosp.*, 582 F.3d 268, 278 (2d Cir. 2009); *Graves v. Finch Pruyn & Co., Inc.*, 353 Fed.Appx. 558, 560 (2d Cir. 2009)).

169 *See* Exec. Law § 296(1)(h) (*eff.* Oct. 11, 2019); N.Y.C. Admin. Code § 8-107 and Case Note 136.

170 Exec. Law § 296(1)(h) (*eff.* Oct. 11, 2019).

171 *Id.*

172 *Golston-Green v. City of N.Y.*, 123 N.Y.S.3d 656, 669 & n.3 (Sup. Ct. App. Div. 2d Dep't 2020) (Brathwaite Nelson, J).

harshly than others who are in protected classes). Instead, the statute provides "[n]othing . . . shall imply that an employee must demonstrate the existence of an individual to whom the employee's treatment must be compared."[173]

One final note for this subchapter. The initial discussion concerned the *McDonnell Douglas* analysis and cumulative circumstantial evidence. Some cases, however, do have direct evidence that plaintiffs may utilize to prevail on their claims.[174] "Direct evidence is something close to an explicit admission by the employer that a particular decision was motivated by discrimination; this type of evidence is rare, but it 'uniquely reveals' the employer's intent to discriminate. . . . More common is circumstantial evidence, which 'suggests discrimination albeit through a longer chain of inferences.'"[175]

In the end, it is vital to understand the proof in a particular case, and ensure that the actions taken by a business or employer are legitimate, and non-discriminatory, thus not only providing a defense in litigation, but also helping to eliminate bias and discrimination in the first place.

---

173 *Id.*

174 *Larbi v. Advocate Christ Med. Ctr.*, 2012 WL 6019107 at *3 (N.D. Ill. Dec. 3, 2012) (Kennelly, D.J.) ("Under the direct method of proof, a plaintiff may avoid summary judgment by presenting evidence, either direct or circumstantial, from which a reasonable jury could find that the employer's discrimination motivated the adverse employment action of which she complains.... Direct evidence is 'an outright admission that an action was taken for discriminatory reasons.'") (citing *Lewis v. Sch. Dist. # 70*, 523 F.3d 730, 741 (7th Cir. 2008); *Everett v. Cook Cnty.*, 655 F.3d 723, 729 (7th Cir. 2011)).

175 *Diaz v. Kraft Foods Global, Inc.*, 653 F.3d 582, 586-87 (7th Cir. 2011) (Wood, J.).

[1.7] VIII. RETALIATION[176]

In the context of this book, retaliation means getting or exacting revenge.[177] Particularly, when an employer takes adverse action against an employee because they have asserted their rights, filed a claim or raised an objection under the anti-discrimination or anti-harassment laws. It could be that the employee filed an internal complaint with human resources, an external charge with a human rights agency or court, or supported a fellow employee in same.[178] Courts have been clear in their pronouncements on retaliation, its reaches, and what engagement in protected activity means:

> An employee has engaged in protected activity if he has (1) opposed any practice made an unlawful employment practice by the statute, or (2) made a charge, testified, assisted, or participated in any manner in a Title VII investigation, proceeding, or hearing. . . . The opposition

176 As addressed in other chapters of this book, since the emergence of the COVID-19 pandemic in the winter of 2020, the field of employment law and anti-discrimination law has experienced an eruption of potential claims, with attorneys and commentators alike warning that it may be only a matter of time before there is an increase in discrimination, harassment and retaliation claims against employers related to COVID-19 health, safety and security concerns. The concern is that workers might also raise allegations of retaliation in response to layoffs, shift changes or downsizing of workforces, if those same workers raised health concerns within the workplace. This is yet another matter with which businesses and attorneys should be familiar. *See* Lisa Helm, *As Some States Are Beginning to Reopen, What Should Employers Know? A Seyfarth Shaw Partner Weighs In*, N.Y.L.J. at p.4, May 1, 2020; Milton L. Williams & Derek Borchardt, *After the COVID-19 Layoffs, Brace Yourselves for Retaliation Claims*, N.Y.L.J. at p. 4, Apr. 13, 2020; Gary D. Friedman, *et al.*, *WARN Act During COVID-19: When Predicting Business Health is Murky*, N.Y.L.J. at p. 4, Apr. 15, 2020. Although not covered in this text, for the reader's information, the WARN (Worker Adjustment and Retraining Notification) Act (29 U.S.C. § 2101, *et seq.*; 20 C.F.R. Part 639) is a federal law that covers private or quasi-public employers of 100 or more workers (full-time, employed more than 6 months), and requires in certain cases of plant closings or mass layoffs, that 60 days' advance notice be given to the workers, with concomitant information about, *inter alia*, when the closing or layoff will start, if it will be temporary or permanent, and contact information for questions. *See Employer's Guide to Advance Notice of Closings and Layoffs*, U.S. Dep't of Labor, https://www.dol.gov/sites/dolgov/files/ETA/Layoff/pdfs/_EmployerWARN2003.pdf; *see also In re MF Global Holdings Ltd.*, 481 B.R. 268, 277-278 (Bankr. S.D.N.Y. 2012) (Glenn, B.J.) (discussing/describing WARN Act).

177 *Worbetz v. Ward N. Am., Inc.*, 54 Fed.Appx. 526, 536-37 (3d Cir. 2002) (Fuentes, J.) ("The definition of 'retaliation,' read to the jury [in a New Jersey Conscientious Employee Protection Act] was: 'to repay, as an injury, in kind. To return like for like, especially, to get revenge.'").

178 While not addressed in this text, one should also be aware that retaliation might arise in another context when an employer takes adverse action against an employee who reports the company or a supervisor for other illegal activities besides alleged violations of the human rights laws called "whistleblowing." *See, generally, Collette v. St. Luke's Roosevelt Hosp.*, 132 F.Supp.2d 256 (S.D.N.Y. 2001) (Lynch, D.J.). *See also* Labor Law § 215.

> clause requires the employee to show that he had at least a reasonable belief that the practices he opposed were unlawful. . . . However, proof of an actual unlawful employment practice is not required to state a claim for unlawful retaliation. . . . Title VII's retaliation provision is not limited to actions and harms that relate to employment or occur at the workplace. It covers employer actions materially adverse to a reasonable employee, that is, actions that well might have dissuaded a reasonable worker from making or supporting a charge of discrimination.[179]

The reason one might engage in retaliation? To deter employees from engaging in activities otherwise protected under the law.[180]

Under both New York law[181] and federal law,[182] it is a *separate* violation if an employee suffers an adverse employment action, termination or otherwise, in retaliation for their having opposed discrimination suffered by another, participated in an investigation, supported the claim of another, or filed a claim alleging discrimination on their own behalf.[183] Although, in New York, if both claims (discrimination and retaliation) arise from the same facts and occurrences, plaintiff's choice of remedies (i.e., choosing to proceed in court or New York State's Division of Human

---

179 *LeBlanc v. Greater Baton Rouge Port Comm'n*, 676 F.Supp.2d 460, 472 (M.D. La. 2009) (Tyson, C.J.; Riedlinger, M.J.) (citing *Grimes v. Texas Dep't of Mental Health & Mental Retardation*, 102 F.3d 137, 140 (5th Cir. 1996); *Long v. Eastfield Coll.*, 88 F.3d 300, 304 (5th Cir. 1996)).

180 *See Guerrero v. Hawaii*, 662 F. Supp. 2d 1242, 1256 (D. Haw. 2009) (Ezra, D.J).

181 Exec. Law § 296(7); N.Y.C. Admin. Code § 8-107(7).

182 *See* 29 U.S.C. § 623 (ADEA) ("Opposition to unlawful practices; participation in investigations, proceedings, or litigation. It shall be unlawful for an employer to discriminate against any of his employees or applicants for employment, for an employment agency to discriminate against any individual, or for a labor organization to discriminate against any member thereof or applicant for membership, because such individual, member or applicant for membership has opposed any practice made unlawful by this section, or because such individual, member or applicant for membership has made a charge, testified, assisted, or participated in any manner in an investigation, proceeding, or litigation under this chapter"); 42 U.S.C. § 2000e-3 (Title VII) (similar).

183 *See Sherman v. Standard Rate Data Serv., Inc.*, 709 F.Supp. 1433, 1441-42 (N.D. Ill. 1989) (Rovner, D.J.) ("[Plaintiff] does not contest [defendant's] assertion that the retaliation claim is a separate and distinguishable claim from the sexual discrimination claim alleged in her EEOC charge. Indeed, [plaintiff] would be hardpressed to argue this point. [Plaintiff's] retaliatory discharge claim in Count III 'injects an entirely new theory of liability into the case alleging unlawful activity of a much different nature" than the sexual discrimination alleged in her original EEOC charge') (citing *Steffen v. Meridian Life Ins. Co.*, 859 F.2d 534, 545 (7th Cir. 1988)).

Rights, see Chapter 5, *infra*) will be binding for both claims; retaliation cannot be raised in court while the discrimination claim proceeds in the DHR, or vice versa.[184]

Importantly, even if the employee's underlying claim of discrimination fails, the employee may still maintain a separate and substantiated claim of retaliation.[185] This also includes wrongful actions taken against an employee after an internal complaint.[186]

For instance, under both New York City and New York State law, and federal law in the Rehabilitation Act and Americans with Disabilities Act (*see* Chapter 6, *infra*), a plaintiff can bring a claim for retaliatory action based on the same standard:

> In order to make out a claim for unlawful retaliation under state or federal law, a plaintiff must show that "(1) she has engaged in protected activity, (2) her employer was aware that she participated in such activity, (3) she suffered an adverse employment action based upon her

184 *See Bonfiglio v. N.Y. Presbyterian Hosp. Weill Cornell Med. Ctr.*, 2011 WL 2436706 at *3 (S.D.N.Y. June 16, 2011) (Scheindlin, D.J.).

185 *See Nurriddin v. Bolden*, 674 F. Supp. 2d 64, 80 (D.D.C. 2009) (Bates, D.J.) ("[S]ome allegations are stronger than others; indeed, the present record indicates that, of all of plaintiff's legal theories, his claim of retaliation is far better supported (and more plausible) than any other claim. However, at this early stage of litigation, the Court is limited to assessing whether plaintiff's complaint states a claim upon which relief can be granted, and whether the record is sufficient to warrant the entry of summary judgment on any claims. As discussed below, plaintiff's claims of retaliation under Title VII are supported by detailed factual allegations indicating retaliatory animus and will be allowed to proceed to discovery. The factual allegations in support of discrimination based on race, gender and religion are far less substantial, but suffice to survive defendants' motion to dismiss or for summary judgment under the law of this circuit. In contrast, his claims of conspiracy, disability discrimination, and hostile work environment fail as a matter of law.").

186 *See Cook v. EmblemHealth Servs. Co., LLC*, 167 A.D.3d 459 (1st Dep't 2018) ("The temporal proximity between plaintiff's complaints to his employer that he was subjected to racial stereotyping and discrimination and the termination of his employment in close succession to his last complaint is sufficient to raise an inference of a causal connection between plaintiff's protected activity and the disadvantaging employment action taken against him").

> activity, and (4) there is a causal connection between the protected activity and the adverse action."[187]

The standard under Title VII is similar, as stated by the U.S. District Court for the Middle District of Louisiana: "A plaintiff establishes a prima facie case for unlawful retaliation under 42 U.S.C. § 2000e–3(a) and § 1981 by proving: (1) that he engaged in activity protected by Title VII or § 1981, (2) that an adverse employment action occurred, and (3) that a causal connection exists between the protected activity and the adverse employment action."[188]

The U.S. District Court in *Rajcoomar* further expounded: "[a]fter plaintiff presents a prima facie case of retaliation, 'defendant then has the burden of pointing to evidence that there was a legitimate, non-retaliatory reason for the complained of action, and . . . if the defendant meets its burden, plaintiff must demonstrate that there is sufficient potential proof for a reasonable jury to find the proffered legitimate reason merely a pretext for impermissible retaliation,'. . . and that the employment decision was a result of unlawful discrimination."[189]

Therefore, the reader is now aware that not only does respect for diversity and inclusion in the workplace mean not taking adverse actions against an individual because of their protected class traits or characteristics, but it also involves not taking adverse action against them or a supportive co-worker as revenge if they assert rights or claims under the protective statutes.

---

187 *Calhoun v. Cty. of Herkimer*, 114 A.D.3d 1304, 1306, 980 N.Y.S.2d 664, 666 (4th Dep't 2014) (mem) (citing *Forrest v. Jewish Guild for the Blind*, 3 N.Y.3d 295, 313 (2004); *Adeniran v. State of New York*, 106 A.D.3d 844, 844–845, 965 N.Y.S.2d 163 (2d Dep't 2013); *Treglia v. Town of Manlius*, 313 F.3d 713, 719 (2d Cir. 2002)); *see also Collins v. Indart–Etienne*, 59 Misc.3d 1026, 1041-42, 72 N.Y.S.3d 332, 347-48 (Sup. Ct. Kings Cty. 2018) (K. Levine, J.); *Rajcoomar v. Wal-Mart Stores East, L.P.*, 2008 WL 11417101 at *4 (S.D.N.Y. Apr. 15, 2008) (Brieant, D.J.) (citing *Kessler v. Westch. Cty. Dep't of Soc. Servs.*, 461 F.3d 199, 205-06 (2d Cir. 2006)).

188 *LeBlanc*, 676 F.Supp.2d at 472 (citing, *inter alia*, *LeMaire v. State of Louisiana*, 480 F.3d 383 (5th Cir. 2007)). The *LeBlanc* court also noted that "Section 1981 protects against retaliation for opposition to race discrimination in the workplace." *LeBlanc*, 676 F.Supp.2d at 472 & n.39 (citing *Foley v. Univ. of Houston Sys.*, 355 F.3d 333, 339 (5th Cir. 2003); *Swanson v. City of Bruce, Miss.*, 105 Fed.Appx. 540, 543 (5th Cir. 2004)).

189 *Rajcoomar*, 2008 WL 11417101 at *4.

[1.8] IX. EMPLOYER DEFENSES BASED ON EXISTING POLICIES

Specific defenses exist for employers in particular circumstances – although the defenses are narrowing under New York law. In cases alleging a hostile work environment, employers have a potential defense available pursuant to the line of cases stemming from *Faragher v. City of Boca Raton*[190] and *Burlington Indus., Inc. v. Ellerth,*[191] i.e., the *Faragher-Ellerth* defense. Courts have explained the defense as follows:

> The *Faragher/Ellerth* defense, named for two cases the Supreme Court decided the same day, . . . provides that "an employer is strictly liable for supervisory harassment that 'culminates in a tangible employment action, such as discharge, demotion, or undesirable reassignment.'" . . . *See also Ellerth*, 524 U.S. at 761 (identifying as tangible employment actions "hiring, firing, failing to promote, reassignment with significantly different responsibilities, or a decision causing a significant change in benefits"). The *Faragher/Ellerth* defense also shields an employer from liability where the employer maintains an anti-harassment policy with which an employee has failed to demonstrate compliance.
>
> The *Faragher/Ellerth* defense consists of two elements providing that even if a supervisor's behavior resulted in a tangible employment action against the plaintiff, the employer will not be liable if (1) "the employer exercised reasonable care to prevent and correct promptly any [discriminatory] harassing behavior," and (2) "the plaintiff employee unreasonably failed to take advantage of any preventative or corrective opportunities provided by the employer or to avoid harm otherwise.". . . With regard to the first element, the maintenance of a written anti-harassment policy providing a procedure for an employee who is the victim of harassment to report the harassment to the Defendant for investigation satisfies the first element. . . . "With regard to the second element, 'proof that an employee has unreasonably failed to use the

190 524 U.S. 775 (1998) (Souter, J.).

191 524 U.S. 742 (1998) (Kennedy, J.).

> employer's complaint procedure normally suffices to satisfy the employer's burden.'"[192]

New York City, however, eliminated the *Faragher-Ellerth* defense under the New York City Human Rights Law: "The NYCHRL imposes strict liability on employers for discriminatory acts of managerial employees."[193]

While the defense did exist in New York State at one time, not so any longer following the Amendments Act signed by the Governor on August 12, 2019.[194] Thus, even in situations where the plaintiff employee does not make use of an employer's policies and procedures, and does not complain to the employer or put the employer on notice pursuant to a stated policy, the defendant employer has no *Faragher-Ellerth* defense under New York law.

That being said, the defense remains under federal law. Therefore, when a company or a supervisor receives a complaint, there are several best practices that should be followed. First, always remember the *Faragher-Ellerth* defense in the case of sexual harassment claims, and that it only provides a defense if the employer also follows its established policy and takes the complaint seriously.[195] Do not discount an employee's complaint. Take action. Additionally, become familiar with the Supreme

192 *Green v. Avis Budget Group, Inc.*, 2017 WL 35452 at *21 (W.D.N.Y. Jan. 4, 2017) (Foschio, M.J.) (citing, *inter alia*, *Faragher* and *Ellerth*; *Pennsylvania State Police v. Suders*, 542 U.S. 129, 137 (2004); *Ferraro v. Kellwood Co.*, 440 F.3d 96, 102 (2d Cir. 2006)). *See also Poolt v. Brooks*, 38 Misc.3d 1216(A), 967 N.Y.S.2d 869 (Table) (Sup. Ct. N.Y. Cty. 2013) (Singh, J.) (providing that a first element is that no adverse action was taken).

193 *Roberts v. United Parcel Service, Inc.*, 115 F.Supp.3d 344, 368 (E.D.N.Y. 2015) (Weinstein, Senior D.J.) (citing *Garrigan v. Ruby Tuesday, Inc.*, 2014 WL 2134613 at *6 (S.D.N.Y. May 22, 2014); N.Y.C. Admin. Code § 8–107(13)(b)(1)). *See also Belton v. Lal Chicken, Inc.*, 138 A.D.3d 609 (1st Dep't 2016); *Zakrzewska v. The New Sch.*, 598 F.Supp.2d 426, 435 (S.D.N.Y. 2009) (Kaplan, D.J.) ("the plain language of Section 8–107, subd. 13 (b), is inconsistent with the defense crafted by the Supreme Court in *Faragher* and *Ellerth*. It creates vicarious liability for the acts of managerial and supervisory employees even where the employer has exercised reasonable care to prevent and correct any discriminatory actions and even where the aggrieved employee unreasonably has failed to take advantage of employer-offered corrective opportunities. Likewise, it provides for employer liability for the discriminatory acts of co-workers in like circumstances provided only that a managerial or supervisory employee knew of and acquiesced in such conduct or should have known of what was going on and failed to take reasonable preventive measures.").

194 *See* Exec. Law § 296(1)(h) (*eff.* Oct. 11, 2019).

195 *See Faragher*, 524 U.S. 775; *Ellerth*, 524 U.S. 742.

Court's holding in *Vance v. Ball State University*.[196] The *Vance* majority expanded on the *Faragher-Ellerth* holdings, and in the opening paragraphs of the opinion, Justice Alito made clear:

> In this case, we decide a question left open in [*Ellerth*] and [*Faragher*], namely, who qualifies as a "supervisor" in a case in which an employee asserts a Title VII claim for workplace harassment?
>
> Under Title VII, an employer's liability for such harassment may depend on the status of the harasser. If the harassing employee is the victim's co-worker, the employer is liable only if it was negligent in controlling working conditions. In cases in which the harasser is a "supervisor," however, different rules apply. If the supervisor's harassment culminates in a tangible employment action, the employer is strictly liable. But if no tangible employment action is taken, the employer may escape liability by establishing, as an affirmative defense, that (1) the employer exercised reasonable care to prevent and correct any harassing behavior and (2) that the plaintiff unreasonably failed to take advantage of the preventive or corrective opportunities that the employer provided. . . .
>
> Under this framework, therefore, it matters whether a harasser is a "supervisor" or simply a co-worker.
>
> We hold that an employee is a "supervisor" for purposes of vicarious liability under Title VII if he or she is empowered by the employer to take tangible employment actions against the victim, and we therefore affirm the judgment of the Seventh Circuit.[197]

The Court, furthermore, established what is meant by "tangible employment actions." As currently outlined in the caselaw:

> We hold that an employer may be vicariously liable for an employee's unlawful harassment only when the employer has empowered that employee to take tangible employment actions against the victim, *i.e.*, to effect a

196 570 U.S. 421 (2013) (Alito, J.).

197 *Id.* at 423-24 (citing *Faragher* and *Ellerth*).

> "significant change in employment status, such as hiring, firing, failing to promote, reassignment with significantly different responsibilities, or a decision causing a significant change in benefits.". . . We reject the nebulous definition of a "supervisor" advocated in the EEOC Guidance4 and substantially adopted by several courts of appeals. Petitioner's reliance on colloquial uses of the term "supervisor" is misplaced, and her contention that our cases require the EEOC's abstract definition is simply wrong.[198]

After *Vance*, for these purposes, no longer is an employee having only the title of "supervisor" or "manager," but none of the authority or responsibility to enact tangible employment actions, able to vicariously bind the company or cause vicarious liability. But if a true "*Vance* supervisor" fails to investigate complaints, "turns a blind eye," takes part in the discrimination through silence or constructive approval, or otherwise fails to protect an employee's rights, the employer defendant may face liability.

If an employee makes a complaint or report under an existing company policy, make sure that the person or team appointed to make the investigation is not in any way named or involved in the complaint itself. Interviews should be handled discreetly, but thoroughly. Speak to all witnesses, and document, document, document. The company investigators should keep records/notes of all interviews, investigation avenues, and findings. Investigators or Human Resources should meet with the complaining employee and keep them apprised of the final decision of the company, but should never meet one-on-one, and always have at least two managers/company representatives present.

If the complaint is determined to be unfounded, the company and its established policy should explain whether the employee has any internal appeal routes. Of course, if the workplace is unionized, the union representatives should be kept apprised, and the collective bargaining agreement should be followed concerning any grievance procedures and appeals.

As mentioned in § 1.7, *supra*, companies, executives and *Vance* supervisors must always remember that retaliation can be the basis for a separate lawsuit, even if the discrimination complaint is unfounded or baseless. Therefore, inform all supervisors and managers that they are to

198 *Id.* at 431–32 (citing *Ellerth*, 524 U.S. at 761).

treat all employees and all investigations with respect, regardless of their feelings concerning the subject of the complaint or about the person making the complaint, with the instruction that Human Resources, the corporation's attorneys and official company investigators will handle any complaints or reports from employees.

[1.9] X. BRIEFLY ON DAMAGES AND FEE SHIFTING

At one time, there was a distinct difference in the kinds of damages available to prevailing New York employment plaintiffs in discrimination, harassment and retaliation actions, and the difference was based on whether the claims were asserted under federal laws or state laws.[199] Particularly, under federal law, successful employee plaintiffs may recover compensatory and punitive damages, and attorneys' fees, although punitive damages are only available against private entities and individuals, not governments or municipalities (with punitives also not available under the ADEA),[200] and with federal courts limiting an award of punitive damages to those cases where plaintiff demonstrates intentional discrimination and malice or reckless indifference, or where discrimination happens "in the face of a perceived risk that [defendant's] actions w[ould] violate federal law."[201]

> Title VII authorizes punitive damages only when a plaintiff makes two showings. First, the plaintiff must show that the employer "engaged in unlawful intentional dis-

199 *Heinemann v. Howe & Rusling*, 260 F.Supp.2d 592, 599 (W.D.N.Y. 2003) (Larimer, D.J.); Exec. Law §297(10).

200 *See Titus v. Moon Area Sch. Dist.*, 2006 WL 752961 (W.D. Pa. Mar. 17, 2006) (Ambrose, C.J.) ("[P]unitive damages are unavailable as against the School District under Title I of the ADA); *Doe v. Cty. of Centre*, 242 F.3d 437, 457 (3d Cir. 2001) (stating that the Civil Rights Act of 1991 'expressly amended Title I of the ADA . . . to allow awards of punitive damages against individuals and private entities, but not against municipalities and government entities.'); *Raie v. City of Phila.*, 2001 WL 884707 at *9 (E.D. Pa. July 31, 2001) (Hutton, D.J.) (stating that '[t]he law is clear that a municipality is not liable for punitive damages under Title VII or the ADA'). Finally, while liquidated damages are available under the ADEA, punitive damages (in the sense of an uncapped award) are not. *See Potence v. Hazelton Area School District*, 357 F.3d 366 (3d Cir. 2004) (Sloviter, J.) (recognizing that liquidated damages are available against a municipality under the ADEA); *Cross v. N.Y. Trans. Auth.*, 417 F.3d 241 (2d Cir. 2005) (Raggi, J.); *Castillo v. Homan*, 2005 WL 2000675 at *5 (S.D. Tex. Aug.16, 2005) (Hittner, D.J.) (stating that, '[w]hile the ADEA does not permit punitive damages, it does allow liquidated damages, which are seen as punitive in nature, and limits the amount awarded to an equivalent of back pay')"); *see also U.S. E.E.O.C. v. AIC Sec. Investigations, Ltd.*, 55 F.3d 1276 (7th Cir. 1995) (Kanne, J.).

201 *Brady v. Wal-Mart Stores, Inc.*, 531 F.3d 127, 137 (2d Cir. 2008) (Calabresi, J.).

> crimination (not an employment practice that is unlawful because of its disparate impact). . . ." Second, the plaintiff must show that the employer engaged in the discriminatory practice "with malice or with reckless indifference to the federally protected rights of an aggrieved individual.". . . That is, "an employer must at least discriminate in the face of a perceived risk that its actions will violate federal law[.]"
>
> When a plaintiff relies on vicarious liability to hold an employer liable for punitive damages under Title VII, as [plaintiff] did, he must do so under traditional principles of agency law. Agency law provides only four ways an employer can be held vicariously liable for punitive damages based on the act of an employee: (1) when the employer authorizes the employee's tortious act; (2) when an employee is unfit and the employer acts recklessly in employing the employee; (3) when the employee served in a managerial capacity and was acting within the scope of employment; or (4) when the employer or managerial agent of the employer ratified or approved the act.[202]

In addition, pursuant to federal law, damages awards for successful plaintiffs are capped (including under Title VII and Section 1981). According to EEOC guidance:

> **Limits On Compensatory & Punitive Damages**
>
> There are limits on the amount of compensatory and punitive damages a person can recover. These limits vary depending on the size of the employer:

202 *Ward v. AutoZoners, LLC*, 958 F.3d 254 (4th Cir. 2020) (Floyd, J.) (citing *Kolstad v. Am. Dental Ass'n*, 527 U.S. 526, 536, 542-43, 119 S.Ct. 2118 (1999); 42 U.S.C. § 1981); *Wiercinski v. Mangia 57, Inc.*, 787 F.3d 106 (2d Cir. 2015) (B. Parker, J.); *E.E.O.C. v. Boh Bros. Const. Co., L.L.C.*, 731 F.3d 444 (5th Cir. 2013) (Elrod, J.); *McInnis v. Fairfield Communities, Inc.*, 458 F.3d 1129 (10th Cir. 2006) (Ebel, J.); *Zisumbo v. Ogden Reg. Med. Ctr.*, 801 F.3d 1185, 1202–03 (10th Cir. 2015) (Moritz, J.) (distinguing *McInnis*, but noting "[i]ndeed, in *McInnis* we noted that if a retaliating supervisor's knowledge of retaliation was automatically imputed to the employer, it could spell the end of the *Kolstad* defense"); *Ash v. Tyson Foods, Inc.*, 664 F.3d 883(11th Cir. 2011) (Carnes, J.) (citing and following *Kolstad*); *Brady*, 531 F.3d 127. *See also* Michael W. Mitchell & Edward Roche, *Fourth Circuit Ruling Limits Punitive Damages*, N.Y.L.J. at p.2, June 9, 2020.

> For employers with 15-100 employees, the limit is $50,000.
>
> For employers with 101-200 employees, the limit is $100,000.
>
> For employers with 201-500 employees, the limit is $200,000.
>
> For employers with more than 500 employees, the limit is $300,000.[203]

The same is also set forth pursuant to federal statutory language, specifically stated in the text of 42 U.S.C. § 1981a:

> **Limitations**
>
> The sum of the amount of compensatory damages awarded under this section for future pecuniary losses, emotional pain, suffering, inconvenience, mental anguish, loss of enjoyment of life, and other nonpecuniary losses, and the amount of punitive damages awarded under this section, shall not exceed, for each complaining party—
>
> (A) in the case of a respondent who has more than 14 and fewer than 101 employees in each of 20 or more calendar weeks in the current or preceding calendar year, $50,000;
>
> (B) in the case of a respondent who has more than 100 and fewer than 201 employees in each of 20 or more calendar weeks in the current or preceding calendar year, $100,000; and
>
> (C) in the case of a respondent who has more than 200 and fewer than 501 employees in each of 20 or more calendar weeks in the current or preceding calendar year, $200,000; and

203 *Remedies For Employment Discrimination*, U.S. EEOC, https://www.eeoc.gov/remedies-employment-discrimination.

(D) in the case of a respondent who has more than 500 employees in each of 20 or more calendar weeks in the current or preceding calendar year, $300,000.[204]

If damages awarded by a jury exceed the cap, courts will reduce the award to at least the cap (although courts might not grant remittitur beyond any reduction to the level of the cap, such as when extreme mental anguish is proven, or where the award is not grossly disproportionate to the evidence of damages in the case).[205]

Under the former New York State law, by contrast, successful employee plaintiffs could recover compensatory damages, but not punitive damages, and attorneys' fees in only select actions at the discretion of the tribunal (for instance, in employment, as of January 2016, for discrimination based on sex).[206]

---

204 42 U.S.C. § 1981a(b)(3). *See also Lampley v. Onyx Acceptance Corp.*, 340 F.3d 478 (7th Cir. 2003) (Williams, J.), *rehearing and rehearing en banc denied, cert. denied* 124 S.Ct. 1421, 540 U.S. 1182 (2004); *E.E.O.C. v. AutoZone, Inc.*, 707 F.3d 824 (7th Cir. 2013) (Manion, J.); *Bennett v. Fairfax County, Va.*, 432 F.Supp.2d 596 (E.D. Va. 2006) (Lee, D.J.); *Orr v. Mukasey*, 631 F.Supp.2d 138, 153-154 (D.P.R. 2009) (Besosa, D.J.).

205 *Orr,* 631 F.Supp.2d 138 (court reduced $1.35 million award to $300,000 cap, but would not grant remittitur beyond that number because it was "not so high as to be grossly disproportionate to the evidence of damages in this case"); *Hudson v. Chertoff*, 473 F.Supp.2d 1286, 1291-1292 (S.D. Fla. 2007) (the cap applies per party or action, not per claim in a case; $1.5 million award reduced to $300,000 cap but no further, given "the deferential standard that applies to an award of compensatory damages by the jury, and that sufficient evidence exists, this Court finds that the plaintiff is entitled to an award of $300,000 for compensatory damages for the emotional pain and mental anguish that he suffered as a result of the defendant's violations of Title VII and the Rehabilitation Act") (citing, *inter alia*, for issue of per action and not per claim cap: *Smith v. Chicago Sch. Reform Bd. of Trustees*, 165 F.3d 1142 (7th Cir. 1999); *Baty v. Willamette Indus., Inc.*, 172 F.3d 1232 (10th Cir. 1999); *Hudson v. Reno*, 130 F.3d 1193 (6th Cir. 1997), *cert. denied*, 525 U.S. 822, 119 S.Ct. 64 (1998), *abrogated on other grounds, Pollard v. E.I. du Pont de Nemours & Co.*, 532 U.S. 843, 845, 121 S.Ct. 1946 (2001) (reversing *Hudson*'s inclusion of front pay as compensatory damages subject to the statutory cap); *Alexander v. Fulton Cty.*, 207 F.3d 1303, 1322 n. 13 (11th Cir. 2000); *Rau v. Apple–Rio Mgmt., Co.*, 85 F.Supp.2d 1344 (N.D.Ga. 1999), *aff'd*, 251 F.3d 161 (11th Cir. 2001)).

206 *Heinemann*, 260 F.Supp.2d at 599; Exec. Law § 297(10). Note that the New York City Human Rights Law has permitted punitive damages in some circumstances. *See Chauca v. Abraham*, 30 N.Y.3d 325, 328-29 (2017) (Garcia, J.) ("The New York City Human Rights Law makes clear that punitive damages are available for violations of the statute, but does not specify a standard for when such damages should be awarded. The Second Circuit has, by certified question, asked us to determine the applicable standard. We conclude that, consistent with the New York City Council's directive to construe the New York City Human Rights Law liberally, the common-law standard… applies. Accordingly, a plaintiff is entitled to punitive damages where the wrongdoer's actions amount to willful or wanton negligence, or recklessness, or where there is 'a conscious disregard of the rights of others or conduct so reckless as to amount to such disregard'") (citations omitted); N.Y.C. Admin. Code § 8-502.

With the enactment of the Amendments Act in New York, however (as signed by the Governor on August 12, 2019 and effective October 12, 2019), prevailing employee plaintiffs on discrimination, harassment or retaliation claims will be able to recover punitive damages and "shall" be awarded reasonable attorneys' fees.[207] The prevailing party's attorneys' fees and costs are to be paid *by the party that does not prevail.*[208] Defendant/respondent employers, though, if they prevail, may usually only seek fees and costs if plaintiff's suit is determined on motion to be frivolous.[209]

This text does not delve much more deeply into the issue of damages, costs and fee shifting. However, one big issue we will address briefly is who qualifies as a "prevailing party" and how much success must they achieve in the lawsuit to be a "prevailing party." A case out of the U.S. District Court for the Southern District of New York addressed this matter with regard to a party that did not obtain any of the specific relief sought in the complaint under the Americans with Disabilities Act (*see* Chapter 6, *infra*).[210] In *Lazarus v. County of Sullivan*, a consent decree was reached providing plaintiff with relief. Under the Americans with Disabilities Act, consent decrees can be the basis for an award of attorneys' fees under the law's fee-shifting provisions. Defendants objected to plaintiff's application for attorneys' fees. The question: whether obtaining a consent decree that did not contain the specific relief sought in the complaint "created" the "material alteration" necessary for "prevailing party" status and fee-shifting.

In other cases, looked to for guidance, plaintiffs obtained a consent decree or judgment and at least some of the relief sought in the complaint. In *Lazarus*, plaintiff reached a consent decree, but none of the specific relief sought in her complaint. U.S. Magistrate Judge Mark D. Fox, of the Southern District of New York, determined that consent decrees require judicial oversight that private settlement agreements do not, therefore there is a judicial imprimatur of the change in relationship of the parties. As held by Judge Fox:

---

207 Exec. Law § 297(8), (9), (10) (*eff.* Oct. 12, 2019) (2019 Sess. Law News of N.Y. Ch. 160 (A. 8421)).

208 *See, inter alia*, 42 U.S.C. § 12205 (A.D.A); 42 U.S.C. § 1988 (Title VII, et al.); 42 U.S.C. § 2000e-5(k) (Equal Employment); N.Y.C Admin. Code § 8-502(g); Exec. Law § 297(10) (*eff.* Oct. 11, 2019 attorneys' fees "shall" be awarded to prevailing party); *Diggs v. Oscar De La Renta, LLC*, 169 A.D.3d 1003, 94 N.Y.S.3d 574 (2d Dep't 2019) (standard under § 8-502 is, and prior standard under § 297 was, discretionary for award of attorneys' fees to prevailing party).

209 *See, e.g.*, Exec. Law § 297(10).

210 *Lazarus v. County of Sullivan*, 269 F.Supp.2d 419 (S.D.N.Y. 2003) (M. Fox, M.J.).

> A party prevails when actual relief on the merits of his [or her] claim materially alters the legal relationship between the parties by modifying the defendant's behavior in a way that directly benefits the plaintiff. . . . Although consent decrees do not always contain an admission of liability, they nonetheless effectuate a change in the legal relationship of the parties . . . [and therefore] create the material alteration of the legal relationship of the parties necessary to permit an award of attorney's fees.[211]

Additionally, plaintiff achieved some relief *similar* to that sought in the complaint. Therefore, an award of attorneys' fees to plaintiff's counsel was approved by the court in *Lazarus*.[212] An analogous holding was true for a plaintiff who accepted a Federal Rule of Civil Procedure 68 offer of judgment.[213]

Damages and fees are also available to prevailing plaintiffs under the statutes in realms beyond employment, such as education, housing or public accommodations. Therefore, as always, be aware that failing to foster a diverse and inclusive environment could have judicially imposed and costly results, measured in dollars and cents, not just potential bad press or loss of goodwill.

[1.10] XI. CONCLUSION

Diversity and inclusion, and elimination of bias, in order to permeate all facets of life in our society, will require the adherence to and enforcement of the state and federal statutory frameworks discussed in this chapter. Employers and business owners (operators of places of public accommodation), as members of society, must integrate their daily practices and treatment of employees and customers with the standards created and implemented by the representative legislatures and departments/agencies around the country. And, we have not addressed what is perhaps

211 *Id.* at 421 (citing *Farrar v. Hobby*, 506 U.S. 103, 111-12 (1992); *Buckhannon Bd. & Care Home, Inc. v. W. Va. Dep't. of Health & Human Res.*, 532 U.S. 598, 604 (2001)); *see also Indep. Project, Inc. v. Ventresca Bros. Constr. Co., Inc.*, 397 F.Supp.3d 482 (S.D.N.Y. 2019) (Karas, D.J.) (citing, *inter alia*, *Lazarus*); *Swartz v. HCIN Water Street Assoc., LLC*, 2018 WL 5629903, at *1 (S.D.N.Y. Oct. 31, 2018) (Ramos, D.J.) (same); 13 N.Y. Prac., Employment Litigation in New York § 9:4 (2018) (citing, *inter alia*, *Lazarus*); Am. Jur. 2d Job Discrimination § 2634 (2019) (same); 27 Mental & Phys. Disab. L. Rep. 679 (Sept./Oct. 2003) (same).

212 269 F.Supp.2d at 423–24.

213 *See Glenn v. Fuji Grill Niagara Falls, LLC*, 2016 WL 1557751 (W.D.N.Y. Apr. 18, 2016) (Skretny, D.J.).

just as insidious as explicit discriminatory bias—that is unfavorable, negative or discriminatory "implicit bias."[214] Implicit bias, however, will likely require more time, effort and focus to combat and eradicate, given the fact that it has largely permeated the subconscious of large swaths of people—of all races and creeds—throughout our Nation. Ultimately, efforts in all of these areas are not only a matter of political correctness or of compassion—they are very much a matter of societal imperative and of law.

214 Implicit Bias "refers to the attitudes or stereotypes that affect our understanding, actions, and decisions in an unconscious manner. These biases, which encompass both favorable and unfavorable assessments, are activated involuntarily and without an individual's awareness or intentional control." *Understanding Implicit Bias*, Kirwan Institute for the Study of Race & Ethnicity, The Ohio State Univ., http://kirwaninstitute.osu.edu/research/understanding-implicit-bias.

CHAPTER TWO

SHIFTING GROUND ON PROTECTION FOR SEXUAL ORIENTATION, LGBT STATUS

[2.0] INTRODUCTION

The class of individuals characterized by sexual orientation, gender dysphoria, transgender status, and gender identity has been, until recently, an "unsettled class" in society, as we will call it. It was "unsettled" because while in some jurisdictions these individuals enjoyed the full protection of law as extended to other classes such as race, national origin, gender, age and religion, in many jurisdictions within the United States members of this unsettled class were not subject to protection under the umbrella of anti-discrimination laws—that is, until a landmark U.S. Supreme Court case, decided in June 2020. Studies have found that LGBT (lesbian, gay, bisexual, and transgender) individuals comprise an estimated 4.5% (11.3 million) of the overall adult population in the United States, with transgender individuals comprising approximately 0.6% (1.4 million) of that population.[1] Prior to the U.S. Supreme Court's decision in *Bostock v. Clayton County*, discussed later in this chapter, the 11.3 million people in this "unsettled" class could be fired, demoted, passed over for promotion, denied housing, excluded from some services of public accommodations, or suffer other adverse actions with no recourse in a number of U.S. jurisdictions, including under federal law.[2] Now, since the *Bostock* decision, members of the sexual orientation and gender identity classes are only unprotected if state laws do not provide protection, and employers have less than the requisite 15 employees to be covered by Title VII.

Prior to *Bostock*, protection only existed in the Seventh and Second Circuits within federal jurisdiction, or in certain state and local jurisdictions, such as in New York under state and New York City laws. Therefore, this chapter explores the provisions of New York law, and federal law, to assist in understanding where diversity and inclusion has been extended for members of this once "unsettled class."

---

1 *See* Daniel Trotta, *Some 4.5 Percent of U.S. Adults Identify as LGBT: Study*, Reuters, Mar. 5, 2019, https://www.reuters.com/article/us-usa-lgbt/some-4-5-percent-of-u-s-adults-identify-as-lgbt-study-idUSKCN1QM2L6 (discussing data developed by The Williams Institute at UCLA School of Law, examining and performing a deeper dive on Gallup Daily Tracker survey; includes findings related to LGBT population density, identifying a high of 9.8% of the population in Washington, D.C., and a low of 2.7% in North Dakota).

2 Of course, so long as the adverse action they suffer is not based on another protected class characteristic, i.e., an Asian homosexual *cannot* be excluded from the services of a public accommodation (business) because they are Asian, a race and national origin protected class.

[2.1] II. PROTECTIONS IN NEW YORK

Prior to *Bostock*, New York's jurisdictions provided much more expansive protections than federal law, and even surpass protections in many states that have provided for LGBT individuals. For example, New York State and New York City laws have created the protected classes of sexual orientation, gender identity and gender expression.[3] Discrimination and retaliation claims based on membership in the protected class of sexual orientation now have a basis in law across New York State and New York City,[4] although still subject to the *McDonnell* burden shift, and defendant's legitimate, non-discriminatory, non-pretextual reason (if any) for the action taken,[5] as discussed in Chapter 1, *supra*. Until fairly recently, though, gender identity was not protected across New York State.[6] In October 2015, several months after the *Roberts* decision was issued, New York's Governor Andrew Cuomo was the first to issue a directive for statewide regulations specifically and extensively prohibiting harassment and discrimination on the basis of transgender status, gender identity or gender dysphoria—regulations issued through the State Division of Human Rights.[7] More recently, the Dignity for All Students Act provided

3 *See* N.Y. Executive Law § 296 (sexual orientation, gender identity and gender expression); N.Y.C. Admin. Code § 8-107 (sexual orientation). *Cf. Nacinovich v. Tullet & Tokyo Forex, Inc.*, 257 A.D.2d 523, 685 N.Y.S.2d 17 (1st Dep't 1999) (N.Y.C. law provided for sexual orientation protected class, N.Y.S. law did not at that time).

4 *See Harrington v. City of New York*, 157 A.D.3d 582, 70 N.Y.S.3d 177 (1st Dep't 2018).

5 *See Andaya v. Atlas Air, Inc.*, 146 A.D.3d 740, 44 N.Y.S.3d 553 (2d Dep't 2017) (citing *Forrest v. Jewish Guild for the Blind*, 3 N.Y.3d 295 (2004), which in turn cited *McDonnell Douglas Corp. v. Green*, 411 U.S. 792 (1973)).

6 *See Roberts v. United Parcel Serv., Inc.*, 115 F. Supp. 3d 344, 367 (E.D.N.Y. 2015) (Weinstein, Senior D.J.) (as of the time of the decision, 18 states had statewide protection for sexual orientation and gender identity, another 3 had protection for only sexual orientation – New York was once among the latter; citing *American Civil Liberties Union, Non–Discrimination Laws: State by State Information—Map*).

7 *See Governor Cuomo Introduces Regulations to Protect Transgender New Yorkers from Unlawful Discrimination*, Office of the Governor of the State of New York, Oct. 22, 2015, https://www.governor.ny.gov/news/governor-cuomo-introduces-regulations-protect-transgender-new-yorkers-unlawful-discrimination.

protections for transgender and gender-nonconforming students against bullying.[8]

It is also worth noting that in New York, particularly in New York City, individuals are entitled to utilize gender pronouns with which they most identify and expect that most others do the same in reference to them. For instance, the New York City Human Rights Commission provided guidance on the issue in 2019:

> The New York City Human Rights Law (NYCHRL) prohibits discrimination in employment, public accommodations, and housing. It also prohibits discriminatory harassment and bias-based profiling by law enforcement.
>
> The NYCHRL requires employers and covered entities to use the name, pronouns, and title (e.g., Ms./Mrs./Mx.) with which a person self-identifies, regardless of the person's sex assigned at birth, anatomy, gender, medical history, appearance, or the sex indicated on the person's identification. Most people and many transgender people use female or male pronouns and titles. Some transgender, non-binary, and gender non-conforming people use pronouns other than he/him/his or she/her/hers, such as they/them/theirs or ze/hir. They/them/theirs can be used to identify or refer to a single person (e.g., "Joan is going to the store, and they want to know when to leave"). Many transgender, non-binary, and gender non-conforming people use a different name than the one they were assigned at birth.
>
> All people, including employees, tenants, customers, and participants in programs, have the right to use and have others use their name and pronouns regardless of whether they have identification in that name or have obtained a court-ordered name change, except in very limited circumstances where certain federal, state, or local laws

---

8 *See Dignity for All Students Act*, N.Y. Educ. Law § 10, *et seq*. However, also note that a deeply divided N.Y. Court of Appeals determined that the Executive Law, (i.e., Human Rights Law) does not apply to public schools within New York State, as they are not an "education corporation or association" under the law. *North Syracuse Cent. Sch. Dist. v. N.Y.S. Div. of Human Rts.*, 19 N.Y.3d 481, 950 N.Y.S.2d 67 (2012). *See also Weiss v. City Univ. of N.Y.*, 2019 WL 1244508 at *11 (S.D.N.Y. Mar. 18, 2019) (Broderick, D.J.) (citing, *inter alia*, *North Syracuse*; N.Y. Exec. Law § 296(4); and N.Y.C. Admin. Code § 8-107(4)(f)).

> require otherwise (e.g., for purposes of employment eligibility verification with the federal government). Asking someone in good-faith for their name and gender pronouns is not a violation of the NYCHRL.
>
> Covered entities may avoid violations of the NYCHRL by creating a policy of asking everyone what their gender pronouns are so that no person is singled out for such questions and by updating their systems, intake forms, or other questionaires [*sic*] to allow all people to self-identify their name and gender. Covered entities should not limit the options for identification to male and female only.[9]

Thus, agencies, employers, and others who are "covered entities" must take care to observe and respect the gender pronouns that individuals request be utilized in reference to themselves. Repeated refusal, ultimately subjecting individuals to demeaning treatment for no legal reason, and only because of discriminatory animus, may well result in legal liability. Such was the case in *Doe v. City of New York*, in which the court held:

> Under the present HASA policy, a transgender person, such as plaintiff, cannot obtain a change to his/her birth certificate will not be able to obtain a benefits card to indicate a change in his/her gender despite legal name change and documentation from a doctor stating that the medical convertive surgery was complete. While plaintiff is still eligible for HASA benefits, the unchanged benefits card denies or hampers access to those benefits. As plaintiff had experienced, she was subjected to accusations of fraud, and denial of tangible benefits because she did not present as a man, contrary to the benefits card indication. Therefore, while plaintiff is eligible for HASA benefits, she risks loss of such benefits due to her hampered access to them. Thus, while HASA's policy appears to be equal across the board, its practical impact for the transgender community is not.

9 *Legal Enforcement Guidance on Discrimination on the Basis of Gender Identity or Expression*, N.Y.C. Commission on Human Rights, Feb. 15, 2019, https://www1.nyc.gov/assets/cchr/downloads/pdf/publications/2019.2.15%20Gender%20Guidance-February%202019%20FINAL.pdf.

> As for the treatment to which plaintiff was subjected, accepting the allegations as true for the purposes of this motion to dismiss, the purposeful use of masculine pronouns in addressing plaintiff, who presented as female, and the insistence that she sign a document with her birth name despite the court-issued name change order, is not a light matter, but one which is laden with discriminatory intent. HASA employees knew of her convertive surgery, and yet did not treat her accordingly or appropriately. Their acts are against the tenets of HASA which is to assist its clients with housing, medical and financial needs. It cannot be said that plaintiff felt demeaned for any reason other than abject discriminatory reasons... discussion of transgender people obtaining gender change marker in birth certificates). Thus, based on the foregoing, plaintiff has sufficiently stated a cause of action.[10]

The defendants' motion to dismiss in *Doe* was thus denied, and the case continued, allowing plaintiff's grievances to be heard, including those disparate impact claims related to disregard of plaintiff's gender pronouns.[11]

[2.2] III. THE STATUS UNDER FEDERAL LAW

In spite of the upward trajectory for expanding protections in some states, such as New York, federal law and federal court decisions across the United States did not protect sexual orientation as a class[12] until very recently. The basis for rejection of the claims in federal court, under Title VII, had historically been that:

> by considering the ordinary meaning of the word "sex" in Title VII, as enacted by Congress, and by determining that "[t]he phrase in Title VII prohibiting discrimination based on sex, in its plain meaning, implies that it is unlawful to discriminate against women because they are

10 42 Misc.3d 502, 506-07, 976 N.Y.S.2d 360 (Sup. Ct., N.Y. Co. 2013) (citations omitted).

11 *Id.*

12 *See Hinton v. Virginia Union Univ.*, 185 F.Supp.3d 807 (E.D. Va. 2016). *Cf. Roberts v. United Parcel Service, Inc.*, 115 F.Supp.3d at 362-363 (court, following exhaustive review and looking at EEOC determination, held that there was sufficient evidence for the jury to consider the sexual orientation discrimination and retaliation claims, including under New York City law).

> women and against men because they are men." . . . "Congress had a narrow view of sex in mind when it passed the Civil Rights Act." . . . "[courts] were confident that Congress had nothing more than the traditional notion of 'sex' in mind when it voted to outlaw sex discrimination, and that discrimination on the basis of sexual orientation and transsexualism, for example, did not fall within the purview of Title VII."[13]

An argument persisted that because gender stereotyping (gender nonconformity) and same-sex discrimination (discrimination by a male or a female against one of the same sex/gender) may be maintained as claims under Title VII,[14] the statute could therefore be expanded to include sexual orientation as the next logical, included class. The argument met with no success, although some courts did begin to "chip away" and question prior holdings prior to *Bostock v. Clayton County*.[15] Courts tended to

---

13 *Hively v. Ivy Tech. Comm. College, South Bend*, 830 F.3d 698, 699-700 (7th Cir. 2016) (citing multiple cases), *subsequently rev'd* 853 F.3d 339 (7th Cir. 2017) (*en banc*). *Cf. Troutman v. Hydro Extrusion USA, LLC*, 388 F.Supp.3d 400, 404 (M.D. Pa. 2019) (Munley, D.J.) (citing *Bibby v. Phila. Coca Cola Bottling Co.*, 260 F.3d 257, 261, 265 (3d Cir. 2001), and declining to follow *Hively* because, prior to the *Bostock v. Clayton County* decision, the Third Circuit Court of Appeals did not recognize sexual orientation as a protected class under Title VII's "because of sex" language).

14 *Price Waterhouse v. Hopkins*, 490 U.S. 228, 250–52 (1989) (plurality opinion), superseded by statute with regard to the motivating factor standard for Title VII claims due to amendment by Congress in the Civil Rights Act of 1991, and as to § 1981 claims as recognized in *Comcast Corp. v. Nat'l Ass'n of African Am.-Owned Media*, 140 S.Ct. 1009, 1017-1018 (2020) (Gorsuch, J.); *see also Oncale v. Sundowner Offshore Servs., Inc.*, 523 U.S. 75, 79–80 (1998).

15 *See Evans v. Georgia Regional Hosp.*, 850 F.3d 1248, 1256-57 (11th Cir. 2017), *cert. denied* 138 S.Ct. 557 (2017) (citing, *inter alia*, *Higgins v. New Balance Athletic Shoe, Inc.*, 194 F.3d 252, 259 (1st Cir. 1999)) (disagreed with by *Zarda v. Altitude Express, Inc.*, 883 F.3d 100 (2d Cir. 2018)); *Simonton v. Runyon*, 232 F.3d 33, 36 (2d Cir. 2000); ("Simonton has alleged that he was discriminated against not because he was a man, but because of his sexual orientation. Such a claim remains non-cognizable under Title VII") (overruled by *Zarda*); *Bibby v. Phila. Coca Cola Bottling Co.*, 260 F.3d 257, 261 (3d Cir. 2001) (*but see Guess v. Phila. Housing Auth.*, 354 F.Supp.3d 596, 602-605 (E.D. Pa. 2019) (McHugh, D.J.) (pre-*Bostock*, evaluating *Bibby* and sex stereotyping versus sexual orientation discrimination, and believing it time to perhaps re-examine *Bibby*; "I am at a loss to conceive of a sexual orientation discrimination claim that could occur in so much of a vacuum as to be free of any gender stereotyping"); *Vickers v. Fairfield Med. Ctr.*, 453 F.3d 757, 762 (6th Cir. 2006) (*but see Johnson v. CC Metals & Alloys, LLC*, 413 F.Supp.3d 654 (W.D. Ky. 2019) (Russell, Senior D.J.) (pre-*Bostock*, evaluating *Vickers* and sex stereotyping versus sexual orientation discrimination); *Hamner v. St. Vincent Hosp. & Health Care Ctr., Inc.*, 224 F.3d 701, 704 (7th Cir. 2000) ("[H]arassment based solely upon a person's sexual preference or orientation (and not on one's sex) is not an unlawful employment practice under Title VII") (overruled by *Hively v. Ivy Tech Comm. Coll.*, 853 F.3d 339 (7th Cir. 2017) (*en banc*) (Wood, C.J.)); *Williamson v. A.G. Edwards & Sons, Inc.*, 876 F.2d 69, 70 (8th Cir. 1989); *Rene v. MGM Grand Hotel, Inc.*, 305 F.3d 1061, 1063-64 (9th Cir. 2002); *Medina v. Income Support Div.*, 413 F.3d 1131, 1135 (10th Cir. 2005).

reject attempts at what they viewed as impermissible efforts to expand the language of Title VII through the courts rather than the legislature.

In 2014–2015, the EEOC tried once more to bring a claim under Title VII based on sexual orientation. It was initially rebuffed by the U.S. District Court for the Northern District of Indiana[16] and the Seventh Circuit Court of Appeals.[17] However, the landscape changed when the Seventh Circuit voted to rehear the case *en banc*. A decision by the full Seventh Circuit broke ground when that court reversed and vacated the panel opinion and held, for the first time, that Title VII does protect against discrimination based on sexual orientation—a bellwether on this front.[18]

From there, the ground started to shift—not an earthquake at first, but certainly some large rumbles. First came the Second Circuit's 2017 decision in *Christiansen v. Omnicom Group, Inc.*[19] That court was not as wide-sweeping as the Seventh Circuit in *Hively*, but rather addressed claims as they would be analyzed pursuant to gender stereotyping, sending the case back to the district court for further proceedings. The concurrence in *Christiansen*, though, spoke strongly about expanding protections for sexual orientation.[20]

Then came U.S. District Judge Alvin K. Hellerstein's decision in *Philpott v. New York*, which set forth in a stern and unmistakable holding: "Simply put, the line between sex discrimination and sexual orientation discrimination is 'difficult to draw' because that line does not exist, save as a lingering and faulty judicial construct," and "[t]he law with respect to this legal question is clearly in a state of flux, and the Second Circuit, or perhaps the Supreme Court, may return to this question soon. In light of the evolving state of the law, dismissal of plaintiff's Title VII claim is improper."[21] Thereafter, an opinion of the U.S. District Court for the

16 *Hively v. Ivy Tech Cmty. Coll.*, 2015 WL 926015 (N.D. Ind. Mar. 3, 2015).

17 *See Hively*, 830 F.3d 698, *supra*.

18 *See Hively*, 853 F.3d 339 (7th Cir. 2017) (*en banc*). For more on the *Hively* case, see: *Hively v. Ivy Tech Community College: Seventh Circuit Holds Sexual Orientation Discrimination is a Form of Sex Discrimination*, 131 Harv. L. Rev. 1489 (2018).

19 852 F.3d 195 (2d Cir. 2017).

20 *Id.*

21 252 F. Supp. 3d 313 (S.D.N.Y. 2017) (Hellerstein, D.J.) (citing *Videckis v. Pepperdine Univ.*, 150 F.Supp.3d 1151, 1159 (C.D. Cal. 2015) (collecting cases)). After further proceedings, however, the district court granted defendant employer's motion for summary judgment, which was affirmed on appeal (but not on the grounds that sexual orientation was not a protected class). *See Philpott v. State Univ. of N.Y.*, 805 Fed.Appx. 32 (2d Cir. Mar. 17, 2020).

Southern District of Ohio seemed to cite *Philpott* with approval but was ultimately constrained by Sixth Circuit precedent.[22]

Thereafter, we turn back to the Second Circuit, for discussion of the case of *Zarda v. Altitude Express.*[23] The three-judge panel of the Second Circuit in *Zarda* held that a panel of the court could not overrule prior precedent (another panel's decision), as that was within the purview and prerogative of the full court *en banc*.[24] Thus, the panel, similar to the court in *Grimsley*, found itself constrained by a prior holding in the Second Circuit that Title VII did not provide protection for sexual orientation.[25] Thereafter, the Second Circuit agreed to rehear the case *en banc*, and followed the lead of the Seventh Circuit in holding for an expansion of Title VII.[26] When resolving the troubling "because of . . . sex" wording in order to bring sexual orientation under Title VII, the majority of the full court held:

> Because one cannot fully define a person's sexual orientation without identifying his or her sex, sexual orientation is a function of sex. Indeed sexual orientation is doubly delineated by sex because it is a function of both a person's sex and the sex of those to whom he or she is

---

22 *Grimsley v. Am. Showa, Inc.*, 2017 WL 3605440 (S.D. Ohio Aug. 21, 2017) ("Plaintiff maintains, however, that heterosexuality is the most central of gender norms, based on the presumption that he should be attracted to women, not men. According to Plaintiff, because sexual orientation is inherently a 'sex-based consideration,' an allegation of discrimination based on sexual orientation is an allegation of sex discrimination under Title VII. This view has been adopted by the EEOC and, recently, by the Seventh Circuit Court of Appeals.... None of this authority is binding in the Sixth Circuit, however. Earlier this year, the Sixth Circuit acknowledged that there may be a sea change underway in this area of the law.... The court also acknowledged that it is difficult to discern 'the line between discrimination based on gender-non-conforming characteristics that supports a sex-stereotyping claim and discrimination based on sexual orientation.'... Nevertheless, the court pointed out that one panel of the court cannot overrule the decision of another panel. *Vickers* remains controlling law until overruled by the Sixth Circuit sitting *en banc*, or until the United States Supreme Court issues a contrary ruling") (citing *Baldwin v. Foxx*, E.E.O.C. Doc. No. 0120133080, 2015 WL 4397641 (July 15, 2015); *Hively*; *Philpott*; *Tumminello v. Father Ryan High Sch., Inc.*, 678 Fed.Appx. 281, 285 n.1 (6th Cir. 2017)).

23 855 F.3d 76 (2d Cir. 2017), *rev'd* 883 F.3d 100 (*en banc*), *cert. granted* 139 S.Ct. 1599 (2019), *aff'd, Bostock v. Clayton County*, 140 S. Ct. 1731 (2020) (Gorsuch, J.).

24 855 F.3d at 82 (citing *Christiansen v. Omnicom Grp.*, 852 F.3d 195, 199 (2d Cir. 2017); *United States v. Wilkerson*, 361 F.3d 717, 732 (2d Cir. 2004)).

25 855 F.3d at 82 (citing *Simonton v. Runyon*, 232 F.3d 33 (2d Cir. 2000), *subsequently overruled by Zarda*, 883 F.3d 100 (2d Cir. 2018)).

26 883 F.3d 100, *aff'd, Bostock*, 140 S. Ct. 1731.

> attracted. Logically, because sexual orientation is a function of sex and sex is a protected characteristic under Title VII, it follows that sexual orientation is also protected.[27]

Certiorari was granted for the appeal of the *Zarda en banc* decision to the U.S. Supreme Court. Additionally, although the Supreme Court declined to hear an appeal of the Eleventh Circuit's holding in *Evans v. Georgia Regional Hosp.*, another decision of the Eleventh Circuit that likewise held Title VII did not protect sexual orientation, was granted certiorari by the Court: *Bostock v. Clayton County, Georgia.*[28] *Bostock* was consolidated on appeal with *Zarda*,[29] and with a third case, *Equal Employment Opportunity Commission v. R.G. &. G.R. Harris Funeral Homes, Inc.*,[30] out of the Sixth Circuit, such that the Court's 2019–2020 Term was set for resolution of the Circuit split.[31]

27 *Id.* at 113 (citing *Hively*, 853 F.3d at 358) ("[D]iscriminating against [an] employee because they are homosexual constitutes discriminating against an employee because of (A) the employee's *sex*, and (B) their sexual attraction to individuals of the *same sex*") (emphasis in original).

28 723 Fed.Appx. 964 (11th Cir. 2018), *rehearing en banc denied*, 894 F.3d 1335 (11th Cir. 2018), *cert. granted* 139 S.Ct. 1599 (2019), *reversed, Bostock*, 140 S. Ct. 1731.

29 *See* Marcia Coyle, *Justices Will Hear Major LGBT Workplace Cases, Testing Title VII's Scope*, N.Y.L.J. at p. 2, Apr. 23, 2019.

30 884 F.3d 560 (6th Cir. 2018), *aff'd* 140 S. Ct. 1731 (2020).

31 Resolution of the matter could provide clarity for another claim—reverse discrimination, where a plaintiff claims they are discriminated and retaliated against because of their heterosexual sexual orientation. *See O'Daniel v. Indus. Serv. Solutions*, 922 F.3d 299 (5th Cir. 2019): *see also Welch v. Pepsi Co. Beverages Inc.*, 2020 WL 1450550 (N.D. Miss. Mar. 25, 2020) (Aycock, D.J.) (citing, *inter alia*, *O'Daniel*; "the scope of the retaliation provision 'is dictated by the scope of Title VII's prohibitions, not by freestanding conceptions of "retaliation" or "opposition."'... 'Title VII protects an employee only from "retaliation for complaining about the types of discrimination it prohibits."... [Plaintiff's] claim for discrimination and retaliation based on sexual orientation is clearly not protected by Title VII as interpreted by the Fifth Circuit. For these reasons, [plaintiff's] claim for discrimination based on his sexual orientation is dismissed *with prejudice*") (emphasis by court).In *O'Daniel* plaintiff alleged that she was terminated and retaliated against because of her heterosexuality—she had undertaken an online rant against an LGBT individual on Facebook, and over the following two months was reprimanded, disciplined and then terminated by her employer (one of the bosses/co-owners was a member of the LGBT community). The district court dismissed the claims, and the Fifth Circuit affirmed holding that Title VII does not protect sexual orientation, and thus there could also be no retaliation claim because there was no "engage[ment] in protected activity by [plaintiff] 'oppos[ing] any practice made an unlawful employment practice by this subchapter. . . .' 42 U.S.C. § 2000e-3(a). . . The threshold criterion for relief under this provision is a showing that the plaintiff 'participated in an activity protected under the statute.'" 922 F.3d at 305-06. With regard to this decision and the decision in *U.S. v. Varner*, 948 F.3d 250 (5th Cir. 2020), it appears that the Supreme Court's holdings in *Bostock v. Clayton County* would supersede going forward.

R.G. &. G.R. Harris Funeral Homes, Inc. was a case on a related issue: whether adverse action against transgender individuals violates Title VII, as discrimination "because of . . . sex" or "based on . . . sex." In *R.G. &. G.R. Harris Funeral Homes, Inc.,*[32] a case out of Michigan, the employer was alleged to have terminated the plaintiff, a transgender individual, because of her transitioning and transgender status, and gender stereotyping, among other claims.[33] The District Court dismissed plaintiff's claims, but the Sixth Circuit affirmed in part, reversed in part and remanded. The Circuit held, *inter alia*, that gender stereotyping is a violation of Title VII, that a claim could be brought alleging violation of Title VII due to discrimination on the basis of transgender and transitioning status, and that there was no substantial burden to the employer's religious practice meaning that employer could not utilize a defense under the Religious Freedom Restoration Act, and the strict scrutiny/compelling government interest standard was not applicable (although the Sixth Circuit did find the standard met, in any event).[34]

Interestingly, at the time of briefing over the summer of 2019, the Department of Justice's position and the EEOC's position—as two agencies in the Administration of Donald Trump—diverged. EEOC brought the case on behalf of the employee, but the Justice Department argued against it. The disagreement was so extreme that EEOC's General Counsel—who usually signs all of the agency's briefs to the Supreme Court—refused to sign onto the Justice Department's briefing that argued discrimination against a transgender female only exists and violates Title VII if treatment differed from that of a transgender male, because Title VII addresses unequal treatment of women and men; and, further, that transgender status is not protected and therefore discrimination on that basis does not violate Title VII.[35] In a further cause for division, the Justice Department's briefing, and defendant funeral home's briefing, took care never to refer to plaintiff employee by any gender pronouns, while the

32 201 F.Supp.3d 837 (E.D. Mich. 2016) (Cox, D.J.), *rev'd* 884 F.3d 560 (6th Cir. 2018) (Moore, J.), *cert. granted R.G. & G.R. Harris Funeral Homes, Inc. v. E.E.O.C.*, 139 S. Ct. 1599 (2019) (Mem.) ("Petition for writ of certiorari to the United States Court of Appeals for the Sixth Circuit granted limited to the following question: Whether Title VII prohibits discrimination against transgender people based on (1) their status as transgender (2) sex stereotyping under [*Price Waterhouse v. Hopkins*, 490 U.S. 228, 109 S.Ct. 1775 (1989)]"), *aff'd, Bostock*, 140 S. Ct. 1731.

33 *Id.*

34 *Id.*

35 *See* Debra Cassens Weiss, *EEOC Doesn't Sign US Brief Telling Supreme Court That Transgender Discrimination is Legal*, ABA Journal, Aug. 19, 2019, http://www.abajournal.com/news/article/eeoc-doesnt-sign-us-brief-telling-supreme-court-that-transgender-discrimination-is-legal.

ABA's *amicus curiae* brief and the Sixth Circuit's decision both used female pronouns, as plaintiff employee preferred.[36]

Finally, in 2020, the Earth did quake following the Supreme Court's holding in *Bostock v. Clayton County*.[37] Via a 6-3 decision, issued by Justice Neil Gorsuch over the dissents of Justices Thomas, Alito and Kavanaugh, the Court held that Title VII's "because of . . sex" language was inclusive of both sexual orientation and gender identity—affirming the Second Circuit's *Zarda* decision and Sixth Circuit's *R.G. & G.R.* decision, and reversing the Eleventh Circuit's *Bostock* decision. Given the importance of the holding, a large portion is quoted hereafter for consideration:

> **Bostock v. Clayton County (Supreme Court of the United States)**
> **Gorsuch, Justice**
>
> Sometimes small gestures can have unexpected consequences. Major initiatives practically guarantee them. In our time, few pieces of federal legislation rank in significance with the Civil Rights Act of 1964. There, in Title VII, Congress outlawed discrimination in the workplace on the basis of race, color, religion, sex, or national origin. Today, we must decide whether an employer can fire someone simply for being homosexual or transgender. The answer is clear. An employer who fires an individual for being homosexual or transgender fires that person for traits or actions it would not have questioned in members of a different sex. Sex plays a necessary and undisguisable role in the decision, exactly what Title VII forbids.
>
> Those who adopted the Civil Rights Act might not have anticipated their work would lead to this particular result. Likely, they weren't thinking about many of the Act's consequences that have become apparent over the years, including its prohibition against discrimination on the basis of motherhood or its ban on the sexual harassment of male employees. But the limits of the drafters' imagination supply no reason to ignore the law's demands.

36 *See* Debra Cassens Weiss, *Justice Department Avoids Gender Pronouns in Brief in Transgender Case*, ABA Journal, Aug. 21, 2019, http://www.abajournal.com/news/article/justice-department-avoids-gender-pronouns-in-brief-in-transgender-case.

37 140 S. Ct. 1731 (2020).

When the express terms of a statute give us one answer and extratextual considerations suggest another, it's no contest. Only the written word is the law, and all persons are entitled to its benefit.

. . .

A

The only statutorily protected characteristic at issue in today's cases is "sex"—and that is also the primary term in Title VII whose meaning the parties dispute. Appealing to roughly contemporaneous dictionaries, the employers say that, as used here, the term "sex" in 1964 referred to "status as either male or female [as] determined by reproductive biology." The employees counter by submitting that, even in 1964, the term bore a broader scope, capturing more than anatomy and reaching at least some norms concerning gender identity and sexual orientation. But because nothing in our approach to these cases turns on the outcome of the parties' debate, and because the employees concede the point for argument's sake, we proceed on the assumption that "sex" signified what the employers suggest, referring only to biological distinctions between male and female.

Still, that's just a starting point. The question isn't just what "sex" meant, but what Title VII says about it. Most notably, the statute prohibits employers from taking certain actions "because of" sex. And, as this Court has previously explained, "the ordinary meaning of 'because of' is 'by reason of' or 'on account of.'" *University of Tex. Southwestern Medical Center v. Nassar*, 570 U.S. 338, 350, 133 S.Ct. 2517, 186 L.Ed.2d 503 (2013) (citing *Gross v. FBL Financial Services, Inc.*, 557 U.S. 167, 176, 129 S.Ct. 2343, 174 L.Ed.2d 119 (2009); quotation altered). In the language of law, this means that Title VII's "because of " test incorporates the "'simple'" and "traditional" standard of but-for causation. *Nassar*, 570 U.S. at 346, 360, 133 S.Ct. 2517. That form of causation is established whenever a particular outcome would not have happened "but for" the purported cause. See *Gross*, 557 U.S. at 176, 129 S.Ct. 2343. In other words, a but-for test directs us to change one thing at a time and see if the outcome changes. If it does, we have found a but-for cause.

This can be a sweeping standard. Often, events have multiple but-for causes. So, for example, if a car accident occurred both because the defendant ran a red light and because the plaintiff failed to signal his turn at the intersection, we might call each a but-for cause of the collision. Cf. *Burrage v. United States*, 571 U.S. 204, 211–212, 134 S.Ct. 881, 187 L.Ed.2d 715 (2014). When it comes to Title VII, the adoption of the traditional but-for causation standard means a defendant cannot avoid liability just by citing some other factor that contributed to its challenged employment decision. So long as the plaintiff's sex was one but-for cause of that decision, that is enough to trigger the law. See *ibid.*; *Nassar*, 570 U.S. at 350, 133 S.Ct. 2517.

. . .

B

From the ordinary public meaning of the statute's language at the time of the law's adoption, a straightforward rule emerges: An employer violates Title VII when it intentionally fires an individual employee based in part on sex. It doesn't matter if other factors besides the plaintiff's sex contributed to the decision. And it doesn't matter if the employer treated women as a group the same when compared to men as a group. If the employer intentionally relies in part on an individual employee's sex when deciding to discharge the employee—put differently, if changing the employee's sex would have yielded a different choice by the employer—a statutory violation has occurred. Title VII's message is "simple but momentous": An individual employee's sex is "not relevant to the selection, evaluation, or compensation of employees." *Price Waterhouse v. Hopkins*, 490 U.S. 228, 239, 109 S.Ct. 1775, 104 L.Ed.2d 268 (1989) (plurality opinion).

The statute's message for our cases is equally simple and momentous: An individual's homosexuality or transgender status is not relevant to employment decisions. That's because it is impossible to discriminate against a person for being homosexual or transgender without discriminating against that individual based on sex. Consider, for example, an employer with two employees, both of whom are attracted to men. The two individuals are, to the employer's mind, materially identical in all respects, except that one is a man and the other a woman. If the employer fires the male employee for no reason other than the fact he is attracted to men, the employer discriminates against him for traits or actions it tolerates in his female colleague. Put differently, the employer intentionally singles out an employee to fire based in part on the employee's sex, and the affected employee's sex is a but-for cause of his discharge. Or take an employer who fires a transgender person who was identified as a male at birth but who now identifies as a female. If the employer retains an otherwise identical employee who was identified as female at birth, the employer intentionally penalizes a person identified as male at birth for traits or actions that it tolerates in an employee identified as female at birth. Again, the individual employee's sex plays an unmistakable and impermissible role in the discharge decision.

That distinguishes these cases from countless others where Title VII has nothing to say. Take an employer who fires a female employee for tardiness or incompetence or simply supporting the wrong sports team. Assuming the employer would not have tolerated the same trait in a man, Title VII stands silent. But unlike any of these other traits or actions, homosexuality and transgender status are inextricably bound up with sex. Not because homosexuality or transgender status are related to sex in some vague sense or because discrimination on these bases has some disparate impact on one sex or another, but because to discriminate on these grounds requires an employer to intentionally treat individual employees differently because of their sex.

, , ,

At bottom, these cases involve no more than the straightforward application of legal terms with plain and settled meanings. For an employer to discriminate against employees for being homosexual or transgender, the employer must intentionally discriminate against individual men and women in part because of sex. That has always been prohibited by Title VII's plain terms—and that "should be the end of the analysis." 883 F.3d at 135 (Cabranes, J., concurring in judgment).

C

If more support for our conclusion were required, there's no need to look far. All that the statute's plain terms suggest, this Court's cases have already confirmed.

. . .

Some of those who supported adding language to Title VII to ban sex discrimination may have hoped it would derail the entire Civil Rights Act. Yet, contrary to those intentions, the bill became law. Since then, Title VII's effects have unfolded with far-reaching consequences, some likely beyond what many in Congress or elsewhere expected.

But none of this helps decide today's cases. Ours is a society of written laws. Judges are not free to overlook plain statutory commands on the strength of nothing more than suppositions about intentions or guesswork about expectations. In Title VII, Congress adopted broad language making it illegal for an employer to rely on an employee's sex when deciding to fire that employee. We do not hesitate to recognize today a necessary consequence of that legislative choice: An employer who fires an individual merely for being gay or transgender defies the law.

The judgments of the Second and Sixth Circuits in Nos. 17–1623 and 18–107 are affirmed. The judgment of the Eleventh Circuit in No. 17–1618 is reversed, and the case is remanded for further proceedings consistent with this opinion.

It is so ordered.[38]

The Supreme Court's decision settled the law on the federal level—unless Congress should take any further action in the future—and resolved the Circuit-split to clarify the national standard, expanding Title VII protections beyond their decades-old limits.

[2.3] IV. MARRIAGE AND PUBLIC ACCOMMODATIONS

With the U.S. Supreme Court's rulings in *Obergefell v. Hodges*[39] and *U.S. v. Windsor*,[40] marriage between two people of the same sex has been deemed a fundamental right and liberty under the United States Constitution. Since then, new areas of dispute have arisen between business owners and same sex couples requesting services, particularly for weddings.

For example, say you operate a business in the wedding industry, and a customer comes in requesting your services for their wedding. You say, "Very well, let's discuss your plans." You then determine that the wedding will be of two same-sex partners. You advise the customer that this is against your religious beliefs, and you will not accept their wedding business. However, if they wish to have some other business services, you will provide those separate from anything specifically involved with or supporting the same-sex wedding. The client/customer declines, and then brings suit against you for discrimination. You still provide wedding services for heterosexual couples. What result?

This is generally the scenario in *Masterpiece Cakeshop, Ltd. v. Colorado Civil Rights Commission*.[41] The decision did not address First Amendment rights broadly but focused instead on narrowly ruling for the Cakeshop on First Amendment free exercise grounds: protection of religious beliefs against open hostility. The Court's majority decision is a surgical exercise. The rights of gays and lesbians can be exercised on equal terms to others, and are accorded great respect, but so are the religious and philosophical objections to gay marriage. However, it was determined

38 *Id. See* Marcia Coyle, *'No Contest:' Gorsuch Leads SCOTUS Ruling That Protects LGBT Employees Against Firing*, N.Y.L.J. at p. 2, June 16, 2020.

39 135 S. Ct. 2584 (2015).

40 570 U.S. 744, 133 S.Ct. 2675 (2013).

41 138 S. Ct. 1719 (June 4, 2018) (Kennedy, J.).

that the Colorado Commission did not comply with requirements for religious neutrality in its assessment of the baker's objections.[42]

The Supreme Court's majority made clear the decision was for this case only, and future cases would have to be resolved with further elaboration, and "tolerance, without undue disrespect to sincere religious beliefs, and without subjecting gay persons to indignities when they seek goods and services in an open market."[43] Justices Breyer and Kagan concurred in the Court's judgment, while Justices Ginsburg & Sotomayor dissented.

The Supreme Court briefly addressed, but then pushed aside, the idea of wedding cakes as art and pure speech. Only the concurrence of Justices Thomas and Gorsuch accepted that path, possibly because the other Justices wished to avoid strict scrutiny protection for opponents of same-sex marriage and those who might discriminate.[44] Therefore, the case has limited application to future cases, but indicates that the Court will not be receptive to decisions of lower tribunals that appear to be clearly hostile to religious beliefs when those beliefs, "based on sincere religious . . . convictions," are proffered as the basis for denial of services (as the Court held was the case with the Colorado Commission). It remains to be seen

42 *Id.*

43 *Id.* at 1732.

44 *See* Tony Mauro, *In 'Masterpiece' Case, Why Did SCOTUS Snub Wedding Cakes as Art?*, N.Y.L.J. at p. 2, June 7, 2018.

what additional elucidation the Court will provide in this area should the case return to the High Court for further proceedings.[45]

[2.4] V. CONCLUSION

Following the *Zarda* decision, the EEOC advanced arguments in support of claims for expansive protection in the Eighth Circuit on appeal in

45 Of note, two similar cases highlight the same issue. In Minnesota, a husband and wife operating a wedding videography business brought a pre-enforcement challenge against the state attorney general and Minnesota Human Rights Department. The Minnesota Human Rights Act prohibits discrimination in public accommodations based on sexual orientation. The couple challenging the law claimed their rights under the First and Fourteenth Amendments to the U.S. Constitution were violated, and that they had free speech, free exercise, and due process rights to create videos that match their creative and religious beliefs. According to the court: "The Larsens 'gladly work with all people—regardless of their race, sexual orientation, sex, religious beliefs, or any other classification.' But because they 'are Christians who believe that God has called them to use their talents and their company to . . . honor God,' the Larsens decline any requests for their services that conflict with their religious beliefs. This includes any that, in their view, 'contradict biblical truth; promote sexual immorality; support the destruction of unborn children; promote racism or racial division; incite violence; degrade women; or promote any conception of marriage other than as a lifelong institution between one man and one woman.'" *Telescope Media Group v. Lucero*, 936 F.3d 740, 748 (8th Cir. 2019) (Stras, J.). The district court had dismissed the Larsens' action, but the Eighth Circuit affirmed in part and reversed in part and remanded the case to the district court for further proceedings. "On remand, the district court must consider in the first instance whether the Larsens are entitled to a preliminary injunction, keeping in mind the principle that, '[w]hen a plaintiff has shown a likely violation of his or her First Amendment rights, the other requirements for obtaining a preliminary injunction are generally deemed to have been satisfied.'" *See id.* at 762. The other case comes from Kentucky, where a printing business owner refused to provide t-shirts for the Gay and Lesbian Service Organization to use during the Lexington Pride Festival 2012. The Lexington Fayette Urban County Human Rights Commission found a violation of the county's public accommodation law (Local Ordinance 201–99, § 2–33), but the state circuit court reversed the determination, and a majority of the Kentucky Court of Appeals affirmed. "[I]n situations where conduct is cited as the basis for refusing service, applying public accommodation laws is less straightforward. 'Some activities may be such an irrational object of disfavor that, if they are targeted, and if they also happen to be engaged in exclusively or predominantly by a particular class of people, an intent to disfavor that class can readily be presumed.'. . . By contrast, however, it is not the aim of public accommodation laws, nor the First Amendment, to treat speech as this type of activity or conduct. This is so for two reasons. First, speech cannot be considered an activity or conduct that is engaged in exclusively or predominantly by a particular class of people. Speech is an activity anyone engages in—regardless of religion, sexual orientation, race, gender, age, or even corporate status. Second, the right of free speech does not guarantee to any person the right to use someone else's property, even property owned by the government and dedicated to other purposes, as a stage to express ideas.... As it held in its order, the Commission argues on appeal that 'Acceptance of [HOO's] argument [for why it did not print the GLSO's t-shirts] would allow a public accommodation to refuse *service* to an individual or group of individuals who *hold and/or express pride* in *their status*.'. . . We disagree." *See Lexington Fayette Urban Cty. Human Rights Comm'n v. Hands on Originals, Inc.*, 2017 WL 2211381 (Ky. Ct. Apps. May 12, 2017) (unpublished) (emphasis in opinion), *aff'd*, 592 S.W.3d 291 (Ky. 2019).

Horton v. Midwest Geriatric Mgmt., LLC.[46] *Horton*, still pending at the time of this writing, could be moot now, though, given the U.S. Supreme Court's resolution of the consolidated *Zarda*, *R.G.* and *Bostock* appeals. The resolution of the Circuit split created common ground across the Nation, providing benefit overall when it comes to understanding which individuals are entitled to protection under law, and how people will be expected to interact and treat each other in an ever more diverse society. However, the Supreme Court will need to resolve further issues in this field in years to come—for instance, the Court may address a dispute between Texas and California based on the latter's apparent "blacklisting" of states with laws that permit discrimination against LGBT individuals; and another case challenging Philadelphia's anti-discrimination rules in the context of foster care.[47] Additionally, in 2020 the U.S. Department of Health and Human Services, as part of the Administration of Donald Trump, at the time of this writing, planned to remove protections for sexual orientation and gender identity from federal health care regulations, arguing that the Administration of President Barack Obama misinterpreted Section 1557 of the Patient Protection and Affordable Care Act in previously allowing protections.[48] Of course, regardless of the holdings of the courts, Congress could choose to act at any time and amend Title VII and other federal laws to add protections for other specified protected classes.

46 2017 WL 6536576 (E.D. Mo. Dec. 21, 2017) (Hamilton, D.J.), *appeal pending* No. 18-1104 (8th Cir. Jan. 12, 2018).

47 *See* Marcia Coyle, *After Landmark LGBT Rights Ruling, Unresolved Questions Await Supreme Court*, N.Y.L.J. at p. 2, June 19, 2020 (including reference to *Fulton v. City of Phila.*, 140 S.Ct. 1104 (Mem) (Feb. 24, 2020) (granting cert.)).

48 *See* Allison Bell, *HHS To Let Agents Reject Gay Medicare And Exchange Plan Prospects*, N.Y.L.J. at p. 3, June 17, 2020.

CHAPTER THREE

SHIFTING GROUND ON EQUAL PAY

[3.0] I. STATUTORY PROVISIONS ON EQUAL PAY

In New York State, the Labor Law provides for equal pay between men and women, among other protected classes, statewide. In the summer of 2019, Governor Cuomo signed legislation amending § 194 of the Labor Law, such that it provides as of October 8, 2019:

> 1. No employee with status within one or more protected class or classes shall be paid a wage at a rate less than the rate at which an employee without status within the same protected class or classes in the same establishment is paid for: (a) equal work on a job the performance of which requires equal skill, effort and responsibility, and which is performed under similar working conditions, or (b) substantially similar work, when viewed as a composite of skill, effort, and responsibility, and performed under similar working conditions; except where payment is made pursuant to a differential based on:
>
> (i) a seniority system;
>
> (ii) a merit system;
>
> (iii) a system which measures earnings by quantity or quality of production; or
>
> (iv) a bona fide factor other than status within one or more protected class or classes, such as education, training, or experience. Such factor: (A) shall not be based upon or derived from a differential in compensation based on status within one or more protected class or classes and (B) shall be job-related with respect to the position in question and shall be consistent with business necessity. Such exception under this paragraph shall not apply when the employee demonstrates (1) that an employer uses a particular employment practice that causes a disparate impact on the basis of status within one or more protected class or classes, (2) that an alternative employment practice exists that would serve the same business purpose and not produce such differential, and (3) that the employer has refused to adopt such alternative practice.

> 2. For the purpose of subdivision one of this section: (a) "business necessity" shall be defined as a factor that bears a manifest relationship to the employment in question, and (b) "protected class" shall include age, race, creed, color, national origin, sexual orientation, gender identity or expression, military status, sex, disability, predisposing genetic characteristics, familial status, marital status, or domestic violence victim status, and any employee protected from discrimination pursuant to paragraphs (a), (b), and (c) of subdivision one of section two hundred ninety-six and any intern protected from discrimination pursuant to section two hundred ninety-six-c of the executive law.
>
> 3. For the purposes of subdivision one of this section, employees shall be deemed to work in the same establishment if the employees work for the same employer at workplaces located in the same geographical region, no larger than a county, taking into account population distribution, economic activity, and/or the presence of municipalities.....[1]

Furthermore, the New York State Department of Labor states the following:

> An employer may not pay different rates based on gender. Men and women must receive the same rate of pay if they work:

- In the same establishment
- On jobs that need equal effort, skill and responsibility
- Under similar conditions

> The law does permit different rates of pay based on factors other than gender, such as:

- Length of service
- Quality of work

1 N.Y. Labor Law § 194 (as amended by L.2019, c. 93, § 1, eff. Oct. 8, 2019) (Lab. Law).

- Quantity of work

> The Commissioner of Labor can enforce claims of workers based on violations of the Equal Pay Law similar to other wage payment laws.[2]

Consider another legislative act, a local law in New York City: Local Law 67 of 2017, codified at N.Y.C. Administrative Code § 8-107(25). The law generally prohibits employers from inquiring about prior salaries at any stage of interview or the process of setting the starting salary. If the interviewer already knows the prior history, that information cannot be relied upon in determining compensation of the employee. However, the employer may inquire as to salary and benefits expectations, and if the interviewee truly volunteers information on prior salary, the employer may verify the information, and is then permitted to consider the history.[3]

When considered, the prohibitions make sense. If one has their starting salary established based on her salary at her prior employment, and that prior salary was unequal with a comparable male's salary, then the new job and starting salary would have a significant probability of perpetuating the discrimination and unequal pay. These changes in the law included in this chapter seek to break the chain and create a level field.

With that in mind, there is yet another recent change in New York State law that occurred in the summer of 2019, when Governor Cuomo signed legislation that added a new section to the Labor Law, mirroring the 2017 provision of the New York City Administrative Code.[4] The full text of new Labor Law § 194-a (effective January 6, 2020) is provided here for review:

> No employer shall:

---

2 N.Y.S. Dep't of Labor, https://www.labor.ny.gov/workerprotection/laborstandards/workprot/equalpay.shtm.

3 N.Y.C. Admin. Code § 8-107(25).

4 New York is one of many states to take action in this area. In 2017, it was reported that 25 states and the District of Columbia were considering similar legislation barring inquiries into prior salaries, with Massachusetts and California having already passed laws; and California and Arkansas having previously passed legislation prohibiting employers from justifying pay differentials with salary history alone. *See* Yuki Noguchi, *Proposals Aim To Combat Discrimination Based On Salary History*, N.P.R., May 30, 2017, https://www.npr.org/2017/05/30/528794176/proposals-aim-to-combat-discrimination-based-on-salary-history.

a. rely on the wage or salary history of an applicant in determining whether to offer employment to such individual or in determining the wages or salary for such individual.

b. orally or in writing seek, request, or require the wage or salary history from an applicant or current employee as a condition to be interviewed, or as a condition of continuing to be considered for an offer of employment, or as a condition of employment or promotion.

c. orally or in writing seek, request, or require the wage or salary history of an applicant or current employee from a current or former employer, current or former employee, or agent of the applicant or current employee's current or former employer, except as provided in subdivision three of this section.

d. refuse to interview, hire, promote, otherwise employ, or otherwise retaliate against an applicant or current employee based upon prior wage or salary history.

e. refuse to interview, hire, promote, otherwise employ, or otherwise retaliate against an applicant or current employee because such applicant or current employee did not provide wage or salary history in accordance with this section.

f. refuse to interview, hire, promote, otherwise employ, or otherwise retaliate against an applicant or current or former employee because the applicant or current or former employee filed a complaint with the department alleging a violation of this section.

2. Nothing in this section shall prevent an applicant or current employee from voluntarily, and without prompting, disclosing or verifying wage or salary history, including but not limited to for the purposes of negotiating wages or salary.

3. An employer may confirm wage or salary history only if at the time an offer of employment with compensation is made, the applicant or current employee responds to

the offer by providing prior wage or salary information to support a wage or salary higher than offered by the employer.

4. For the purposes of this section, "employer" shall include but not be limited to any person, corporation, limited liability company, association, labor organization, or entity employing any individual in any occupation, industry, trade, business or service, or any agent thereof. For the purposes of this section, the term "employer" shall also include the state, any political subdivision thereof, any public authority or any other governmental entity or instrumentality thereof, and any person, corporation, limited liability company, association or entity acting as an employment agent, recruiter, or otherwise connecting applicants with employers.

5. An applicant or current or former employee aggrieved by a violation of this section may bring a civil action for compensation for any damages sustained as a result of such violation on behalf of such applicant, employee, or other persons similarly situated in any court of competent jurisdiction. The court may award injunctive relief as well as reasonable attorneys' fees to a plaintiff who prevails in a civil action brought under this paragraph.

6. Nothing in this section shall be deemed to diminish the rights, privileges, or remedies of any applicant or current or former employee under any other law or regulation or under any collective bargaining agreement or employment contract.

7. This section shall not supersede any federal, state or local law enacted prior to the effective date of this section that requires the disclosure or verification of salary history information to determine an employee's compensation.

8. The department shall conduct a public awareness outreach campaign, which shall include making information

> available on its website, and otherwise informing employers of the provisions of this section.[5]

On the federal level, since 1963, the Equal Pay Act (EPA)[6] has existed, in an effort to balance and provide for equal wages, with mixed success. The EPA's provisions are clear:

> **(d) Prohibition of sex discrimination**
>
> **(1)** No employer having employees subject to any provisions of this section shall discriminate, within any establishment in which such employees are employed, between employees on the basis of sex by paying wages to employees in such establishment at a rate less than the rate at which he pays wages to employees of the opposite sex in such establishment for equal work on jobs the performance of which requires equal skill, effort, and responsibility, and which are performed under similar working conditions, except where such payment is made pursuant to (i) a seniority system; (ii) a merit system; (iii) a system which measures earnings by quantity or quality of production; or (iv) a differential based on any other factor other than sex: Provided, That an employer who is paying a wage rate differential in violation of this subsection shall not, in order to comply with the provisions of this subsection, reduce the wage rate of any employee.
>
> **(2)** No labor organization, or its agents, representing employees of an employer having employees subject to any provisions of this section shall cause or attempt to

5 Lab. Law § 194-a (Added L.2019, c. 94, § 1, eff. Jan. 6, 2020). *See also* Keith Fall & Ross Weil, *What Not To Talk About In Lateral Partner Discussions*, N.Y.L.J. at p. 9, Apr. 20, 2020 (recommending that firms cease asking about past salary history, despite an argument that the prohibition should not apply to candidates seeking to join firms as partners/shareholders/owners; and further arguing that the salary "expectations" question should be less relevant today).

6 Pub. L. 88-38, 29 U.S.C. § 206(d). The Equal Pay Act is enforced by the U.S. Equal Employment Opportunity Commission and is incorporated into the federal Fair Labor Standards Act, 29 U.S.C. § 201, *et seq*. According to the EEOC, the EPA "prohibits sex-based wage discrimination between men and women in the same establishment who perform jobs that require substantially equal skill, effort and responsibility under similar working conditions." U.S. EEOC, https://www.eeoc.gov/laws/statutes/epa.cfm. Unlike other federal laws, the EPA applies to employers with at least one (1) employee. *See* U.S. EEOC, https://www.eeoc.gov/employers/small-business/1-do-federal-employment-discrimination-laws-enforced-eeoc-apply-my.

> cause such an employer to discriminate against an employee in violation of paragraph (1) of this subsection.
>
> **(3)** For purposes of administration and enforcement, any amounts owing to any employee which have been withheld in violation of this subsection shall be deemed to be unpaid minimum wages or unpaid overtime compensation under this chapter.
>
> **(4)** As used in this subsection, the term "labor organization" means any organization of any kind, or any agency or employee representation committee or plan, in which employees participate and which exists for the purpose, in whole or in part, of dealing with employers concerning grievances, labor disputes, wages, rates of pay, hours of employment, or conditions of work.[7]

In addition to the Equal Pay Act of 1963, federal law also includes the Lilly Ledbetter Fair Pay Act of 2009.[8] According to the Equal Employment Opportunity Commission, the Lilly Ledbetter Act was signed into law by President Barack Obama on January 29, 2009—the first piece of legislation of his Administration.[9] The Act specifically overturned the Supreme Court's holding in *Ledbetter v. Goodyear Tire & Rubber Co., Inc.*,[10] which had greatly restricted the time periods when a plaintiff filed claims for discrimination in compensation.[11] The late U.S. District Judge Thomas P. Griesa, a former Chief Judge of the Southern District of New York, provided a clear and concise summary of the *Ledbetter* holding:

---

7 29 U.S.C. § 206(d).

8 PL 111-2, § 3, 123 Stat 5 (Jan. 29, 2009) (amending Title VII of the Civil Rights Act of 1964, at 42 U.S.C. § 2000e–5(e)).

9 U.S. EEOC, https://www.eeoc.gov/eeoc/publications/brochure-equal_pay_and_ledbetter_act.cfm.

10 550 U.S. 618 (2007) (Alito, J.; Ginsburg, J., dissenting), *overturned due to legislative action* U.S. Pub. L. No. 111-2 (Jan. 29, 2009).

11 U.S. EEOC, https://www.eeoc.gov/eeoc/publications/brochure-equal_pay_and_ledbetter_act.cfm. *See also* the Findings in Section 2 of the Lilly Ledbetter Act ("(1) The Supreme Court in Ledbetter v. Goodyear Tire & Rubber Co., 550 U.S. 618 (2007), significantly impairs statutory protections against discrimination in compensation that Congress established and that have been bedrock principles of American law for decades. The Ledbetter decision undermines those statutory protections by unduly restricting the time period in which victims of discrimination can challenge and recover for discriminatory compensation decisions or other practices, contrary to the intent of Congress. (2) The limitation imposed by the Court on the filing of discriminatory compensation claims ignores the reality of wage discrimination and is at odds with the robust application of the civil rights laws that Congress intended. . . . ").

> By way of background, the Ledbetter decision will be briefly summarized. In that case, the Court held that a claimant alleging discrimination based on a pay-setting decision must file a charge with the EEOC within 180 days, or 300 days, after the discriminatory decision was made. . . . The Court rejected the plaintiffs [*sic*] claim that she could recover based on a later paycheck she received that would have been larger had the prior discrimination not occurred. . . . The plaintiff conceded that there was no discriminatory intent by the personnel involved in issuing the later paychecks. . . . The Court ruled that the continuing effects of a past employment decision, which was adopted with discriminatory intent, do not transform a subsequent employment act, unaccompanied by discriminatory intent, into a present violation. . . . [12]

In response to the Supreme Court's restrictive holding (issued over the strong dissent of Justice Ginsburg[13]), Congress, in the Lilly Ledbetter Act, amend[ed] Title VII—specifically, 42 U.S.C. § 2000e–5(e)—by adding the following provision:

> (3)(A) . . . [A]n unlawful employment practice occurs, with respect to discrimination in compensation in violation of this subchapter, when a discriminatory compensation decision or other practice is adopted, when an individual becomes subject to a discriminatory compensation decision or other practice, or when an individual is affected by application of a discriminatory compensation decision or other practice, including each time wages,

---

12 *Vuong v. N.Y. Life Ins. Co.*, 2009 WL 306391 at *8 (S.D.N.Y. Feb. 6, 2009) (Griesa, D.J.).

13 Hon. Ruth Bader Ginsburg, an alumna of Columbia University School of Law, and former Rutgers and Columbia law professor, was a lifelong and staunch supporter of women's rights and equal rights for all. She was appointed to the U.S. Court of Appeals for the District of Columbia Circuit by President Jimmy Carter and thereafter elevated to the U.S. Supreme Court by President Bill Clinton. *See Justice Ruth Bader Ginsburg*, The Supreme Court Historical Society, https://www.supremecourthistory.org/history-of-the-court/the-current-court/justice-ruth-bader-ginsburg. The movie biopic, *On the Basis of Sex* (2019), chronicles Justice Ginsburg's legal career. *See* IMDb, https://www.imdb.com/title/tt4669788. Appropriately, the alternative title of the film in Argentina, Mexico, Peru and Uruguay was *La voz de la igualdad* (*The voice of equality*), and in Greece it was Η Αρχή της Ισότητας (*The Principle of Equality*). *Id.*

> benefits, or other compensation is paid, resulting in whole or in part from such a decision or other practice.[14]

The Act was also made retroactive, stating:

> This Act, and the amendments made by this Act, take effect as if enacted on May 28, 2007 and apply to all claims of discrimination in compensation under title VII of the Civil Rights Act of 1964 (42 U.S.C. 2000e et seq.), the Age Discrimination in Employment Act of 1967 (29 U.S.C. 621 et seq.), title I and section 503 of the Americans with Disabilities Act of 1990, and sections 501 and 504 of the Rehabilitation Act of 1973, that are pending on or after that date.[15]

[3.1] II. CASELAW SPEAKING TO BURDENS OF PROOF

Plaintiff employee bears the burden of proving the claim of unequal pay and discrimination. "In order to sustain a claim under the Equal Pay Act, a plaintiff must demonstrate that the jobs at issue require 'equal effort, skill and responsibility, . . . and are performed under similar working conditions,' . . . and that any difference in pay is attributable to sex."[16] Specifically, courts have held that "to establish a prima facie case . . . [plaintiff] has the burden of proving that (1) she was performing work which was substantially equal to that of the male employees considering the skills, duties, supervision, effort and responsibilities of the jobs; (2) the conditions where the work was performed were basically the same; (3) the male employees were paid more under such circumstances."[17]

---

14 42 U.S.C. § 2000e-5(e)(3)(A); *Bush v. Orange Cty. Corrections Dept.*, 597 F.Supp.2d 1293, 1296 (M.D. Fla. 2009); *see also Vuong*, 2009 WL 306391 at *8–9.

15 PL 111-2, § 3, 123 Stat 5 (Jan. 29, 2009); *see Bush*, 597 F.Supp.2d at 1296. Note that this text does not discuss the federal Fair Labor Standards Act (FLSA), 29 U.S.C. § 201, *et seq.*, or the overtime provisions of the New York Labor Law. However, those statutory provisions are sometimes included with claims of discrimination or retaliation with regard to failure to properly pay earned overtime wages. Thus, one should be familiar that the FLSA and New York law on overtime exist. *See also Heisler v. Nationwide Mut. Ins. Co.*, 931 F.3d 786 (8th Cir. 2019).

16 *Fisher v. Vassar College*, 70 F.3d 1420, 1452 (2d Cir. 1995), *on rehearing* 114 F.3d 1332 (1997), *cert. denied* 522 U.S. 1075 (1998), *rehearing denied* 523 U.S. 1041 (1998) (abrogated on other grounds by *Reeves v. Sanderson Plumbing Prods., Inc.*, 530 U.S. 133 (2000), which was superseded on other grounds re. summary judgment standard by 28 U.S.C. § 2254. *See Penton v. Thaler*, 2013 WL 2483244 at *2 (S.D. Tex. June 10, 2013)) (citing *McKee v. McDonnell Douglas Technical Servs.*, 700 F.2d 260, 262 (5th Cir. 1983); *Winkes v. Brown Univ.*, 747 F.2d 792, 793 (1st Cir. 1984)).

Should the plaintiff make her initial *prima facie* showing under the Equal Pay Act, then the burden will shift to the defendant (similar to the *McDonnell Douglas* burden shift), and the defendant "must undertake the burden of persuading the jury that there existed reasons for the wage disparity which are described in the Equal Pay Act.[18] These reasons are: (1) a seniority system; (2) a merit system; (3) a pay system based on quantity or quality of output; (4) a disparity based on any factor other than sex. If the defendant fails to convince the jury with its evidence of one or more of the 'affirmative defenses' listed above the plaintiff will prevail on her prima facie case."[19] The defendant's burden is by a preponderance of the evidence.[20]

The Second Circuit has held that the

> employer bears the burden of proving that a bona fide business-related reason exists for using the gender-neutral factor that results in a wage differential in order to establish the factor-other-than-sex defense. Additionally, we note that the plaintiff may counter the defendant's affirmative defense by offering evidence showing that the reasons sought to be proved are a pretext for sex discrimination. . . . "The appropriate inquiry to determine if the factor put forward is a pretext, is whether the employer has 'use[d] the factor reasonably in light of the

17 *Tidwell v. Fort Howard Corp.*, 989 F.2d 406, 409 (10th Cir. 1993) (citing *Corning Glass Works v. Brennan*, 417 U.S. 188 (1974) (abrogated on other grounds)). *See also Fowler v. Land Mgmt. Groupe, Inc.*, 978 F.2d 158, 161 (4th Cir. 1992) (citing *Keziah v. W.M. Brown & Son, Inc.*, 888 F.2d 322, 324 (4th Cir. 1989)).

18 29 U.S.C. § 206(d)(1).

19 *Tidwell*, 989 F.2d at 409.

20 *Fowler*, 978 F.2d at 161. Note, however, that there are two statutory frameworks under which a plaintiff may seek relief for pay disparities—the EPA and Title VII—and there is a significant difference between the two. The EPA employs a strict liability framework, whereas Title VII requires a plaintiff to demonstrate discriminatory intent (see Chapter 1 for the elements of a Title VII claim). Title VII claims are, therefore, not as limited in scope as EPA claims, and a plaintiff might find an expanded group of pay differential claims under Title VII (for instance, the EPA requires a male comparator earning a greater salary in a similar role; Title VII does not require the EPA's "equal pay for equal work" standard). An EPA plaintiff may file with the EEOC first, but is not required to prior to filing in court, unlike under Title VII; and statutes of limitations and damages provisions, among other things, are different between the two frameworks. It is important to understand the distinctions, and the potential impacts on a claim. For the above, and more, see Christopher R. Dyess, *Second Circuit Clarifies Standard for Gender-Based Pay Disparity Claims*, N.Y.L.J. at p. 4, Mar. 26, 2020; Brian D. Murphy, *Pay Disparity Claims Under the Equal Pay Act and Title VII Of the Civil Rights Act*, N.Y.L.J. at p. 9, Feb. 24, 2020; *Lenzi v. Systemax, Inc.*, 944 F.3d 97 (2d Cir. 2019) (Pooler, J.).

> employer's stated purpose as well as its other practices.'"[21]

There is, however, a Circuit split when it comes to starting pay and the defendant's burden. The Second, Sixth, Ninth and Eleventh Circuits have all addressed the issue of equal pay and the "factor other than sex," holding that the employer must have an acceptable business reason for the factor—meaning that the court would potentially pass judgment on the acceptability or legitimacy of the proffered factor and business reason.[22] However, the Seventh Circuit, in direct contravention, has held:

> Four appellate courts have held that wages in a former job are a "factor other than sex" only if the employer has an "acceptable business reason" for setting the employee's starting pay in this fashion. . . . New employees are supposed to start at the bottom of the range, see 80 Ill. Admin. Code § 310.490(b), with higher salary only if justified by "directly related training and experience", *id.* at § 310.490(b)(A). . . . Yet the Equal Pay Act is not a back-door means to enforce civil-service laws;. . . Section 206(d) does not authorize federal courts to set their own standards of "acceptable" business practices. The statute asks whether the employer has a reason other than sex—not whether it has a "good" reason. . . . Congress has not authorized federal judges to serve as personnel managers for America's employers.[23]

More recently, a panel decision out of the United States Court of Appeals for the Ninth Circuit (based in San Francisco, California), held that when it comes to pay differentials in the workplace and pay decisions by employers, prior salaries may be considered if the pay differential based on prior salary is grounded in any factor other than sex (gender), and it is up to the employer to show that it was the factor other than sex

21 *Aldrich v. Randolph Cent. Sch. Dist.*, 963 F.2d 520 (2d Cir. 1992) (Oakes, C.J.), *cert. denied*, 506 U.S. 965 (1992) (citing *Kouba v. Allstate Ins. Co.*, 691 F.2d 873, 876-77 (9th Cir. 1982); *Maxwell v. City of Tucson*, 803 F.2d 444, 446 (9th Cir. 1986)).

22 *See Aldrich*, 963 F.2d 520; *EEOC v. J.C. Penney Co.*, 843 F.2d 249 (6th Cir. 1992); *Kouba*, 691 F.2d 873 (overruled by *Rizo v. Yovino*, 950 F.3d 1217 (9th Cir. 2020) (*en banc*) (Christen, J.), *cert. denied*, 2020 WL 3578691 (July 2, 2020)); *Glenn v. Gen. Motors Corp.*, 841 F.2d 1567 (11th Cir. 1988) (Johnson, J.).

23 *Wernsing v. Dep't of Human Servs., State of Illinois*, 427 F.3d 466, 468 (7th Cir. 2005) (Easterbrook, J.) (declining to follow, *inter alia*, *Aldrich* 963 F.2d 520).

(gender) that caused the pay differential when there are legal challenges.[24] However, after rehearing *en banc* was granted,[25] the full Ninth Circuit court reversed the panel's holding in 2018, and overruled *Kouba v. Allstate Ins. Co.*, instead sustaining the Eastern District of California magistrate judge's denial of defendant's motion for summary judgment. The full court held that the Equal Pay Act clearly provides an employer cannot justify a pay differential between men and women by relying on prior salary based on any purported reasoning.[26]

The story did not end there, though. The *en banc* decision of the Ninth Circuit was thereafter vacated and remanded by the Supreme Court of the United States in 2019, on a matter of judicial procedure. Circuit Judge Stephen Reinhardt, who authored the *en banc* opinion, passed away before the *en banc* decision had been issued/filed (although the case had been heard and the decision written). Judge Reinhardt's vote had made the majority, but the Supreme Court held that judges' votes are not "inalterably fixed" until the moment a decision is issued.[27] Thus, the case, returned to the Ninth Circuit for further consideration. The court, ruling *en banc* once more in February 2020, held again as follows:

> The question we consider today is whether Aileen Rizo's prior rate of pay is a "factor other than sex" that allows Fresno County's Office of Education to pay her less than male employees who perform the same work. 29 U.S.C. § 206(d)(1)(iv). We conclude it is not.
>
> Congress enacted the Equal Pay Act (EPA) to combat pay disparities caused by sex discrimination, but it allowed employers to justify different pay for employees of the opposite sex based on three enumerated affirmative defenses, or "any *other* factor other than sex." *Id.* (emphasis added). Contrary to Fresno County's argument, we conclude that only job-related factors may serve as affirmative defenses to EPA claims.
>
> The express purpose of the Act was to eradicate the practice of paying women less simply because they are

24 *Rizo v. Yovino*, 854 F.3d 1161 (9th Cir. 2017).

25 869 F.3d 1004 (9th Cir. Aug. 29, 2017).

26 *Rizo v. Yovino*, 887 F.3d 453 (9th Cir. 2018) (*en banc*) (Reinhardt, J.).

27 *Yovino v. Rizo*, 139 S.Ct. 706 (2019) (per curiam).

> women. Allowing employers to escape liability by relying on employees' prior pay would defeat the purpose of the Act and perpetuate the very discrimination the EPA aims to eliminate. Accordingly, we hold that an employee's prior pay cannot serve as an affirmative defense to a prima facie showing of an EPA violation.[28]

Another petition for *certiorari* was subsequently denied by the Supreme Court on July 2, 2020 (2020 WL 3578691).

However, the *en banc* decision of the Ninth Circuit adopted much the same provision as seen in the New York State and New York City legislation. A sea change on this issue in multiple jurisdictions may be in the making.

[3.2] III. CURRENT STATUS OF EQUAL PAY IN THE UNITED STATES

As mentioned above, there has been recent action by courts and legislatures on the issue of Equal Pay. Largely, this is because the matter is one consuming media outlets and news cycles. Such is especially so because athletes and other celebrities have picked up the mantle of chang357e and are advancing the ball, pun intended.

The U.S. Women's National Soccer Team has taken a leading position in ongoing unequal pay between men's and women's teams. Although female soccer players are paid less than male players, we can compare some facts and figures to assess the situation. For instance, the Women's team has won four World Cups (1991, 1999, 2015 and 2019), and four Olympic gold medals (1996 Atlanta, 2004 Athens, 2008 Beijing, and 2012 London) (and a silver medal at the 2000 Sydney Games).[29] In contrast, the U.S. Men's National Soccer Team has never won a World Cup or an Olympic gold medal.[30] Additionally, as of June 2020, the U.S. women's team was ranked Number 1 in the world by FIFA, while the men's team was ranked 22nd in the world.[31]

---

28 *Rizo*, 950 F.3d at 1219–20.

29 *See* U.S. Women's National Team website, https://www.ussoccer.com/teams/uswnt.

30 *See* U.S. Soccer Awards, https://www.ussoccer.com/history/awards/us-soccer-awards.

31 *See* FIFA/Coca-Cola World Ranking (women), https://www.fifa.com/fifa-world-ranking/ranking-table/women/; FIFA/Coca-Cola World Ranking (men), https://www.fifa.com/fifa-world-ranking/ranking-table/men.

Despite the above statistics, a significant pay disparity existed between male and female players on the U.S. national teams as of 2019, an inequality highlighted by members of the women's team immediately after their 2019 World Cup victory, building on a lawsuit they had already filed under both the EPA and Title VII frameworks in U.S. District Court in the Central District of California. Female players emphasized, among other things, the fact that at times they earn 38 percent of what male players earn.[32] Mediation subsequently broke down between the women's team and U.S. Soccer in summer 2019, leaving the issue awaiting resolution in another forum.[33]

It is similarly reported that in the Women's National Basketball Association (WNBA), players start at $50,000 contracts with median salaries of $71,635. For comparison, male players in the National Basketball Association (NBA) earn a minimum of $582,180.[34] April 2 is "Equal Pay Day" in the United States, and occasions annual articles highlighting pay disparities in the larger economy. In April 2019, it was reported that across the U.S. economy, when compared to Caucasian, non-Hispanic males, the ensuing categories of female workers earn the following percentages per dollar paid to those males: Asian women earn 85%; Caucasian women earn 77%; African-American women earn 61%; Native American women

32 Maggie Mertens, *The U.S. National Women's Soccer Team Makes a Really Good Case for Equal Pay*, The Atlantic, Mar. 19, 2019, https://www.theatlantic.com/entertainment/archive/2019/03/why-the-us-national-womens-soccer-team-is-suing/585202.

33 Aimee Lewis, *Talks Break Down Between USWNT and US Soccer Over Equal Pay*, CNN.com, Aug. 15, 2019, https://www.cnn.com/2019/08/15/football/uswnt-us-soccer-equal-pay-spt-intl/index.html. However, in May of 2020, the Women's Team's federal lawsuit was dismissed in part as to the pay differentials by the district court, with only one issue remaining – that of the alleged disparity in working conditions related to amounts spent on travel conditions and personnel/support services, and whether that demonstrated discrimination under Title VII. *See Morgan v. U.S. Soccer Fed., Inc.*, 445 F. Supp. 3d 635 (C.D. Cal. 2020) (Klausner, D.J.).

34 *See* M. Mertens, *The U.S. National Women's Soccer Team Makes a Really Good Case for Equal Pay*, *supra*.

earn 58%; and Latinas earn 53%. Women of all categories combined earn 80% compared to men of all categories combined.[35]

One popular argument to explain the disparity, at least with regard to sports, is that male teams earn more revenue, have larger audiences, and achieve more success—and, thus, in a capitalist, free-market economy the males and females earn what the market will bear. While Adam Smith[36]

35 Dalvin Brown, *Equal Pay Day 2019: Women Still Earn Lower Salaries, Fewer Promotions*, USA Today, Apr. 2, 2019, https://www.usatoday.com/story/money/2019/04/02/national-equal-pay-day-2019-gender-wage-gap/3298020002. Furthermore, it has been reported that black women earn 61 cents for every 1 dollar that white males earn, equating to $946,000.00 less over a 40-year career! Additionally, in order to earn what a white male earns in a 12-month calendar year (January to December), it has been reported that Native American women must work until September of the following calendar year, and Hispanic women must work until November of the following calendar year – working almost 2 years to earn what a white male does in 1 year. *See* Sarah O'Brien, *Here's How the Wage Gap Affects Black Women*, CNBC, Aug. 22, 2019, https://www.cnbc.com/2019/08/22/heres-how-the-gender-wage-gap-affects-this-minority-group.html. It has been further reported that at the 2020 rate, the global wage gap between men and women will not close for another 257 years! Grace Hauck, *When Will Women Get Equal Pay? Not For Another 257 Years, Report Says*, USA Today, Dec. 22, 2019, https://www.usatoday.com/story/news/nation/2019/12/20/gender-pay-gap-equal-wages-expected-257-years-report/2699326001/. *See also U.S. Black-White Inequality in 6 Stark Charts*, CNN, June 3, 2020, https://www.cnn.com/2020/06/03/politics/black-white-us-financial-inequality/index.html (showing, *inter alia*, that white households have higher median incomes and higher median net worths, $71,000 and $171,000, respectively, than black households, $41,000 and $17,600, respectively); Aaron Radford-Wattley, *What is the Average American Salary?*, Fox Business, May 25, 2020, https://www.foxbusiness.com/money/what-is-the-average-american-income (comparing salaries of men and women: in professional/management jobs men earned a median annual salary of $80,912 compared to $59,176 for women; for service workers, men earned a median annual salary of $34,632 compared to $29,068 for women); Valerie Wilson, et al., *Black Women Have to Work 7 Months Into 2017 to Be Paid the Same as White Men in 2016*, Econ. Policy Inst., July 28, 2017, https://www.epi.org/blog/black-women-have-to-work-7-months-into-2017-to-be-paid-the-same-as-white-men-in-2016. Interestingly, discrepancies in perception also exist between genders, as highlighted by a N.Y. Times survey during the COVID-19 pandemic inquiring as to who took care of most of the homeschooling for children in a household. According to the report, 45% of men said they spent more time helping their children with home-schooling and 39% of men said their spouse did so. However, the same report found that 80% of women believed they spent more time on home-schooling their children, and only 3% of women said their spouse did so. *See* Claire Cain Miller, *Nearly Half of Men Say They Do Most of the Home Schooling. 3 Percent of Women Agree*, N.Y. Times, May 6, 2020, https://www.nytimes.com/2020/05/06/upshot/pandemic-chores-homeschooling-gender.html. This illustrates not only real-world discrepancies between men and women, but also the existence of significant differences in perception, and likely psychology.

36 For more on Adam Smith, the Scottish economist and political scientist, and author of the seminal 1776 work *An Inquiry into the Nature and Causes of the Wealth of Nations*, see https://www.biography.com/scholar/adam-smith.

might cheer such an argument, it ultimately does not support the reality in all circumstances. For example, when we return to an evaluation of the arguments in the context of the men's and women's U.S. National Soccer Teams, it has been reported that the women's team in recent years has had much greater tournament success (as highlighted above), has had larger audiences at its matches, and has generated more revenues and profits for the U.S. Soccer Federation.[37] A similar situation existed in the sport of tennis, prior to pay equality being reached at least in the Grand Slam.[38]

Now, the reader may think that pay inequality is an issue for sports, or the general economy, but not the legal profession, which is supposed to be sensitive to and conscious of discriminatory treatment and outcomes. Alas, such a belief would be incorrect, and the situation may actually be *worsening*. For instance, in late 2018 it was reported that when it comes to corporate general counsel, on average women earned $125,000 less than men.[39] Furthermore, the average salary at that time was stated to be $408,000 in the United States, with the disparity existing when one considered that male general counsel earned an average of $453,625 while female general counsel earned $326,477 on average.[40] At that time, even if we compared the top two general counsel in the nation, with regard to compensation, it just so happened that one was a male and one was a female. The male, according to reports, earned a salary of $6.95 million while the female earned $6.7 million.[41] Interestingly, both companies were members of the "Fortune 100,"[42] and yet even at the top, the female general counsel earned $250,000 less than the male general counsel.

In August 2019, the gap was reported to be widening, not narrowing.[43] At that time, it was found that male general counsel earned 18.6% more

37 *See* M. Mertens, *The U.S. National Women's Soccer Team Makes a Really Good Case for Equal Pay*, The Atlantic, *supra*.

38 *See* Peter Bodo, *Follow the Money: How the Pay Gap in Grand Slam Tennis Finally Closed*, ESPN.com, Sept. 7, 2018, https://www.espn.com/tennis/story/_/id/24599816/us-open-follow-money-how-pay-gap-grand-slam-tennis-closed.

39 *See* Melissa Heelan Stanzione, *Women General Counsel Make $125k Less Than Male Colleagues*, Bloomberg Law, Nov. 27, 2018, https://news.bloomberglaw.com/us-law-week/women-general-counsel-make-125k-less-than-male-colleagues.

40 *Id.*

41 *Id.*

42 *See* https://fortune.com/fortune500/2019/search.

43 *See* Phillip Bantz, *Gender Pay Gap for General Counsel Has Grown, Study Says*, Law.com Corporate Counsel, Aug. 28, 2019, https://www.law.com/corpcounsel/2019/08/28/gender-pay-gap-for-general-counsel-has-grown-study-says.

than female general counsel, with the median total pay for males increasing to $2.63 million (from $2.52 million), while median total pay for females *decreased* to $2.21 million (from $2.44 million).[44] The growing gap was aided by another finding: males received $826,131 in average bonus, versus only $285,754 for female general counsel.[45] Furthermore, in 2019, the top six general counsel in terms of earnings were all males, and only four of the top twenty were female.[46]

Additionally, other commentators have observed that attorneys who are women or minorities face barriers at many law firms across the nation.[47]

44 *Id.* (median salary for all general counsel was $565,000, up from the 2018 report).

45 *Id.*

46 *Id.* Worse still, in 2020 the trend was not reversing, with a *Corporate Counsel/Law.com* article finding that at United States corporations with $10 billion or more in revenue, male general counsel were paid 40% more than female general counsel. *See* Phillip Bantz, *Are Gender Pay Gaps Worse for General Counsel at the Largest Corporate Legal Departments?*, Corp. Counsel/Law.com, Apr. 21, 2020, https://www.law.com/corpcounsel/2020/04/21/are-gender-pay-gaps-worse-for-general-counsel-at-the-largest-corporate-legal-departments.

47 *See* Chris Opfer, *Law Firms Warned About Diversity by Contractor Watchdog*, Bloomberg Law, Apr. 10, 2019, https://news.bloomberglaw.com/daily-labor-report/law-firms-warned-about-diversity-by-contractor-watchdog-1.

On the other hand, as we become a more diverse and inclusive society, it seems that a number of businesses (which may or may not be more attuned to the court of public opinion) are placing greater value on opportunities for members of many protected classes and characteristics. Many in-house corporate counsel are advising the outside law firms to promote diversity initiatives or else corporate legal dollars may be re-directed to whatever law firms do make diversity a priority.[48]

Thus, the issue of equality in pay (as well as equality in other employment and educational opportunities, and places of public accommodation, as discussed in other chapters) crosses all professional, economic and

---

48 *See* Debra Cassens Weiss, *170 Top In-House Lawyers Warn They Will Direct Their Dollars to Law Firms Promoting Diversity*, ABA Journal, Jan. 28, 2019, http://www.abajournal.com/news/article/170-top-in-house-lawyers-warn-they-will-direct-their-dollars-to-law-firms-promoting-diversity; Dan Clark, *Discussion Between Firms And Clients Is Key to Diversity*, N.Y.L.J. at p. 9, Feb. 6, 2020. *See also* Tom McParland, *NYSBA Delegates Approve Report Spotlighting Need for Progress on Courtroom Gender Gap*, N.Y.L.J., June 15, 2020, https://www.law.com/newyorklawjournal/2020/06/15/nysba-delegates-approve-report-spotlighting-need-for-progress-on-courtroom-gender-gap (discussing NYSBA Report identifying a persistent lag remaining with regard to opportunities in the courtroom for female and minority attorneys); Debra Cassens Weiss, *These Law Firms Were Named as Top Family- and Female-Friendly Workplaces by Yale Law Women*, ABA Journal, May 21, 2020, https://www.abajournal.com/news/article/which-law-firms-made-yale-law-womens-lists-of-family-and-female-friendly-law-firms; Rachel Silverman, *How to Be an Ally to Women in Law*, ABA Law Practice Today, May 15, 2020, https://www.lawpracticetoday.org/article/ally-women-law; Jack Newsham, *Big NY Firms Increase New Partner Classes, As Female Promotions Steadily Rise*, N.Y.L.J., Apr. 19, 2019, https://www.law.corn/newyorklawjournal/2019/04 /19/big-ny-firms-increase-new- partner-classes-as-female-promotions-steadily-rise (however, only 34% of promoted partners overall were women); Press Release, *Attorney General James Announces Creation of Diversity and Inclusion Office*, Office of the New York State Attorney General, https://ag.ny.gov/press-release/attorney-general-james-announces-creation-diversity-and-inclusion-office.

career borders in the United States, and is one deserving of ongoing attention.[49]

---

49 For instance, it appears that a very grave issue exists in the medical profession, where some medical doctors and other medical professionals tend to discount symptoms and pain complaints expressed by women or minorities versus those complained of by Caucasian males, sometimes with serious consequences. *See Last Week Tonight with John Oliver*, HBO (Season 6, Episode 21, Aug. 18, 2019). Thus, two of the most respected professions—attorneys (doctors of law) and physicians (doctors of medicine)—have more to do in their professions when it comes to diversity, inclusion and respect for differences. *See also* Jane Wester, *New Study Shows Only Minimal Improvement in Women's Representation in NY Courtrooms*, N.Y.L.J. at p. 1, May 29, 2020 (discussing NYSBA report); Shira A. Scheindlin, *Women Still Lag in Courtroom Talk. Here's Why*, N.Y.L.J. at p. 6, June 1, 2020 (same); Debra Cassens Weiss, *Majority of Minority Female Lawyers Consider Leaving Law; ABA Study Explains Why*, ABA Journal, June 22, 2020, https://www.aba-journal.com/news/article/most-minority-female-lawyers-consider-leaving-law-aba-study-explains-why; Rolando T. Acosta, *The State of Diversity in New York's Judiciary*, N.Y. St. Bar Ass'n Journal at 24, May 2020 (discussing the dearth of diversity on the New York bench, particularly amongst the judges sitting on courts outside of New York City); Francine Friedman Griesing, *Women Standing Strong: Strategies for Dealing with Bullying and Bias*, ABA Law Practice Today, May 15, 2020, https://www.lawpracticetoday.org/article/women-standing-strong-strategies-dealing-bullying-bias; Stephanie Russell-Kraft, *Yale Law Women Report Shows Even Best Firms Can Improve Ranks*, Bloomberg Law, Apr. 16, 2019, https://news.bloomberglaw.corn/us-law-week/yale-law-women-names-top-10-firms-for-gender-equity (gains being made; improvement is slow); Dylan Jackson, *Diversity Scorecard: African American Lawyers Are Being Left Out*, The American Lawyer, May 28, 2019, https://www.law.com/americanlawyer/2019/05/28/diversity-scorecard-african-american-lawyers-are-being-left-out. Furthermore, it appears that with the emergence of COVID-19 and the ongoing protests against police brutality in support of the Black Lives Matter movement in the year 2020, the resulting economic, social and biological health of minorities and minority-owned businesses were impacted more significantly than those of Caucasians and Caucasian-owned businesses. *See CBS This Morning: Gayle King, Anthony Mason and Tony Dokoupil*, CBS TV, June 22 & 23, 2020. For instance, it was reported that minorities and diverse communities suffered more serious physical and mental health ailments, including increased incidents of COVID-19 infections and deaths; and minorities experienced a greater number of business failures or were denied government assistance funds more often than Caucasian-owned businesses in 2020. *Id.* Women, especially minority women, also found themselves disproportionately impacted by the employment and business woes created by COVID-19, particularly with regard to unemployment rates (for instance, it was reported that 1 in 6 black women and 1 in 5 Latino women suffered unemployment during the 2020 COVID-19 pandemic; and it was reported that job gains made since the last recession were eliminated -11.1million jobs that had been gained between June 2009 and February 2020 were "wiped out" in April 2020). *See CBS This Morning: Gayle King, Anthony Mason and Tony Dokoupil, Workforce Woes for Women*, CBS TV, May 15, 2020. *See also* Dan Clark, *Don't Forget About Diversity During COV/D-19: A Q&A With NAMWOLF CEO*, N.Y.L.J. at p. 5, Apr. 17, 2020 (discussion with CEO of National Association of Minority & Women Owned Law Firms concerning impacts of COVID-19); Dylan Jackson, *The 2020 Diversity Scorecard Shows Progress, but It's More Precarious Than Ever*, The Am. Lawyer, May 26, 2020, https://www.law.com/americanlawyer/2020/05/26/the-2020-diversity-scorecard-shows-progress-but- its-more-precarious-than-ever.

[3.3] IV. EQUAL PAY ON THE INTERNATIONAL STAGE

The issue of equality in pay is not uniquely American. Since 1961, the Republic of Iceland has had equal pay legislation on the books.[50] In 2017, the Althingi (Icelandic Parliament)[51] passed legislation creating a new standard for equal pay; instead of female employees being required to prove disparate pay, companies must now prove their pay practices are fair and equal.[52] Just as in the United States, it is illegal in Iceland for male and female employees to be paid differently, for the same work and responsibilities, if the differential is based only on gender/sex. However, in Iceland, as well, differential is permitted for other, valid factors.[53]

The Icelandic legislation at issue here was passed in 2017, and went into effect at the beginning of January 2018, because Iceland also found itself facing pay gaps despite other equal pay laws that already existed.[54] Thus, the legislative move forced employers to proactively demonstrate that they pay their employees of different genders equally for the same work, rather than burden employees to prove an employer's practices violate law. As reported, "Iceland's new law applies to companies with 25 employees or more. Every three years, the companies will need to confirm that they are paying men and women equally for jobs of equal value."[55] Any company that does not meet or comply with certification will face a fine, compounded daily.[56] With the two-year anniversary, analysis is nec-

---

50 *See* Camila Domonoske, *Companies In Iceland Now Required To Demonstrate They Pay Men, Women Fairly*, N.P.R., Jan. 3, 2018, https://www.npr.org/sections/thetwo-way/2018/01/03/575403863/companies-in-iceland-now-required-to-demonstrate-they-pay-men-women-fairly.

51 Of interest, the Icelandic Parliament—the Althingi—is the oldest parliament in the world Founded in 930A.D.(C.E.), at Thingvellir (Parliament Plains), it was briefly suspended by Danish royal decree between 1800 and 1845. *See* Althingi Introduction Brochure, https://www.althingi.is/pdf/Althingi2018_enska.pdf. The oldest parliament in the world in continuous operation is the Tynwald, Parliament of the Isle of Man, which has been in existence and operating since 976 A.D. (C.E.). *See* Tynwald, the Parliament of the Isle of Man, http://www.tynwald.org.im/education/history/Pages/default.aspx. However, the Tynwald was not always democratic or responsible for legislation, and it currently concerns internal governance since the Isle of Man is a Crown Dependency of the United Kingdom, and the Monarch of Great Britain is the Lord of the Isle of Man and Head of State. *See* https://www.isleofman.com/parliament/the-queen.

52 *See* Domonoske, *supra.*

53 *Id.*

54 *Id.*

55 *Id.*

56 *Id.*

essary to see if the legislation, with its concomitant "teeth" of fines to encourage compliance, will accomplish the goal of ultimately creating equality in wages not previously accomplished by earlier legislation.

In Australia, we can evaluate equal pay for women in a high-profile area, by examining sports—just as in the United States. As in other nations, female athletes in Australia have not been paid on an equal basis when compared to male athletes.[57] This often results in female athletes not having the ability to work as full-time athletes because they cannot earn enough to do so.[58] In 2016-17, this started to change. Funding for women's salaries almost doubled, from AUS$2.36 million to AUS$4.23 million, with an increase in maximum "retainers" (contracts) from AUS$49,000 to AUS$65,000, and the best cricket players saw an increase to AUS$80,000.[59] Minimum retainers in other leagues also at least doubled for female players.[60] However, while hourly pay may have been increased for female players, women play less than then men, meaning they will still earn less overall.[61] Nonetheless, cricket and tennis (with the Australian Open, as part of the Grand Slam, equalizing prize money) have been identified as leaders in the movement for equal pay; and with a historic equal pay plan now in place as of 2019, involving every Australian sport, there is hope that Australia will become a world model.[62]

It was reported that the CEO of Cricket Australia, a governing body, stated that female cricketers deserved to be compensated commensurate with the fact that they included some of the most successful athletes in the nation. The CEO stated: "Cricket is a sport for all Australians and Cricket Australia will continue to invest heavily in the women's game in the com-

---

57 *See* Ian Ransom, *Australian Sports Sign Up to Gender Pay Equality Scheme*, Reuters, Feb. 17, 2019, https://www.reuters.com/article/us-sport-australia-equality/australian-sports-sign-up-to-gender-pay-equality-scheme-idUSKCN1Q704T; *Australia's Sporting Chief Executives Join Forces to Push for Equal Pay for Elite Women Athletes*, ABC News Australia, Feb. 17, 2019, https://www.abc.net.au/news/2019-02-18/sports-team-up-to-close-the-gender-pay-gap/10821018.

58 *See* Gaby Alejandro, *Australian Sports Historic Equal Pay Plan*, Girls Soccer Network, Mar. 6, 2019, https://girlssoccernetwork.com/news/australian-sports-historic-equal-pay-plan/.

59 *See WBBL Contracting Period Opens, Pay Increase Confirmed*, Sydney Sixers, 6 Apr. 2016, https://www.sydneysixers.com.au/news/wbbl-contracting-period-opens-southern-stars-wage-increase-womens-cricket-contract-earnings-wbbl02/2016-04-06. *See also* I. Ransom, *supra*.

60 *Id.*

61 *See* I. Ransom, *supra*.

62 *See* I. Ransom, *supra*; ABC News Australia, *supra*; G. Alejandro, *supra*.

ing years."[63] Indeed, population demographics have become one of the largest impetuses for an increase in investment in the women's cricket teams in Australia; apparently 25% of the 1.2 million Australians who played cricket as of 2016 were females of all ages.[64] Furthermore, just as in the United States, some argue that female teams in Australia have many times achieved greater success than male teams in competition.[65]

Finally, keep in mind that a disparity in pay is noted not just between male and female players, but also across corporate and administrative roles in Australian sports: a 27% pay gap, compared to the average of 21.3% across all Australian industries.[66] So far, efforts at equalizing pay seem to be meeting with success. Although salaries between male and female athletes have not yet quite reached parity, plans are in place, and minds are opening to change.

[3.4] V. CONCLUSION

There are equal pay laws in effect, and court decisions that interpret and apply the laws and regulations. We have administrative agencies responsible for enforcement. Yet, we still fall short on the issue of equal pay in most industries within our society. The issue, though, is not purely a legal one. These matters also impact potential violations of ethical rules for attorneys, which could carry with them professional discipline. "In what way would this be possible?" you may ask. In those jurisdictions having adopted the specific language of ABA Model Rule of Professional Conduct 8.4(g), it is a violation of ethical rules for attorneys to act in a manner that would be discriminatory or harassing in the practice of law.[67] Although N.Y.'s Rule 8.4(g) appears to have slightly altered the wording from ABA Model Rule 8.4(g) to specifically address discrimination in the practice of law and employment contexts, N.Y. Rule 8.4(h) speaks to an

63 *See* Sydney Sixers, *supra.*

64 *Id.*

65 *See* G. Alejandro, *supra.*

66 *See* I. Ransom, *supra.*

67 *See* Am. Bar Assoc. Model Rule of Prof'l Conduct 8.4(g) ("It is professional misconduct for a lawyer to: … (g) engage in conduct that the lawyer knows or reasonably should know is harassment or discrimination on the basis of race, sex, religion, national origin, ethnicity, disability, age, sexual orientation, gender identity, marital status or socioeconomic status in conduct related to the practice of law. This paragraph does not limit the ability of a lawyer to accept, decline or withdraw from a representation in accordance with Rule 1.16. This paragraph does not preclude legitimate advice or advocacy consistent with these Rules."). *See also* ABA Formal Op. 493 (July 15, 2020) (addressing Model Rule 8.4(g) and its "Purpose, Scope, and Application").

attorney engaging "in any other conduct that adversely reflects on the lawyer's fitness as a lawyer."[68] Clear discrimination by attorneys against those in protected classes, when related to an attorney's practice of law or operation of an ongoing firm or business, may fall dangerously close to that line, if not over it. A cautionary tale can be found in the case of *Attorney Grievance Commission of Maryland v. Markey*.[69] In *Markey*, Maryland's highest court indefinitely suspended two attorneys who were barred in the state—one an administrative law judge and the other an attorney-advisor, both at the Board of Veterans' Appeals of the United States Department of Veterans Affairs. The opening paragraph of the decision set the stage:

> This attorney discipline proceeding involves two lawyers who, for approximately seven years, while working for the federal government, participated in an exchange of e-mails **among a group of federal government employees, who were also lawyers, using their official government e-mail addresses during work hours** to make disturbingly inappropriate and offensive statements that demonstrated "bias or prejudice based upon race, sex, . . . national origin, . . . sexual orientation[,] or socioeconomic status," Maryland Lawyers' Rules of Professional Conduct ("MLRPC") 8.4(e) (Bias or Prejudice), about Hispanic, Asian, and African American people, and people whom they referred to as gay men, who were their colleagues.[70]

In *Markey*, the emails included derogatory, disparaging and sexist remarks about others, such as female administrative judges and homosexual Board employees. Due to the violations of Maryland's MLRPC 8.4, severe sanctions were imposed by the Court.[71]

There is little doubt, however, that more will be accomplished in the coming months and years, and indeed more should be done until one's education, experience, training and skills—together with legitimate busi-

---

68 N.Y. Rule of Prof'l Conduct 8.4(g), (h)).

69 469 Md. 485, 230 A.3d 942 (Md. 2020) (Watts, J.).

70 *Id.* at 488 (emphasis added).

71 *Id.*

ness reasons and geographic locations—are among the only factors to impact wages/salaries, pushing protected class characteristics (such as sex) to the sidelines.

CHAPTER FOUR

CURRENT STATUS OF FEDERAL EQUAL RIGHTS AMENDMENT

[4.0] I. A BRIEF HISTORY OF WOMEN'S RIGHTS AND THE RIGHT TO VOTE

Internationally, the nation officially recognized as the first to have granted women the right to vote is New Zealand, in 1893, followed by Australia in 1902 after its independence from Great Britain[1] (although both are still Commonwealth Nations[2]). By contrast, the United Kingdom (its constituent countries being England, Scotland, Wales, and Northern Ireland) did not follow until 1928, and even then, restrictions existed.[3] Comparatively on the World stage, the United States as a nation was the twelfth to grant women the right to vote with the ratification of the 19th Amendment to the Constitution in 1920[4] (Australia and Canada, who technically acted before the United States, excluded their first peoples—*male and female* Aborigines and Canadian First Nation, respectively—until the 1960's[5]; but, frankly, so did the United States until the Voting Rights Act of 1965[6]). The most recent nation to take action was Saudi Arabia, in 2011.[7] Interestingly, four other nations actually led the way, but do not receive credit on official lists because they were colonized: Corsican Republic (right to vote in 1755), Pitcairn Island (1838), Isle of Man (1881, although it excluded married women[8]), and Cook Islands (1893, the same year as New Zealand).[9]

1 *See* Kim Hjelmgaard, Voting Rights for Women: How Countries Stack Up, USA Today, Feb. 5, 2018, https://www.usatoday.com/story/news/2018/02/05/voting-rights-women-how-countries-stack-up/306238002/; *Which Country First Gave Women The Right To Vote?*, World Atlas, https://www.worldatlas.com/articles/first-15-countries-to-grant-women-s-suffrage.html.

2 *See* https://commonwealthfoundation.com/about-us/where-we-work.

3 *See* Hjelmgaard, *supra*; World Atlas, *supra*.

4 *See* Hjelmgaard, *supra*. It is of note that the Law Day 2020 theme (celebrated on May 1, 2020 in the United States) was "Your Vote, Your Voice, Our Democracy: The 19th Amendment at 100." *See* Am. Bar Ass'n, https://www.americanbar.org/groups/public_education/law-day. *See also Law Day Supplement*, N.Y.L.J. at p. 9, May 1, 2020 (including a timeline of the "Battle for the 19th Amendment"); Janet DiFiore, *Women Have Made Many Strides, But Dangerous Voting Trends Remain*, N.Y.L.J. at p. 9, May 1, 2020.

5 *See* Hjelmgaard, *supra*.

6 https://www.ourdocuments.gov/doc.php?flash=false&doc=100).

7 *See* Hjelmgaard, *supra*.

8 *See* Tynwald, Parliament of the Isle of Man, *Women in Tynwald*, http://www.tynwald.org.im/education/women/Pages/VotesForWomen.aspx.

9 *See* World Atlas, *supra*; Hjelmgaard, *supra*.

Within the United States of America, the State of Wyoming was the first to grant women full voting rights—well ahead of sister States. Wyoming first granted the right as a Territory in 1869, and thereafter as a state in 1890.[10] The State of New York has a proud history when it comes to equal rights, and the rights of women. In 1917, New York became just the twelfth State to grant women the right to vote, before the 19th Amendment to the United States Constitution.[11] Of course, voting rights are just one set of rights with which we are concerned.

The first Women's Rights Convention was held in Seneca Falls, New York, in 1848, and led by Elizabeth Cady Stanton and Lucretia Mott.[12] Thereafter, again in Seneca Falls in 1923—on the occasion of the 75th anniversary of the first convention—Alice Stokes Paul introduced the Equal Rights Amendment to the United States Constitution (first named the Lucretia Mott Amendment, until 1943).[13]

The Amendment as proposed in 1923 was simple, but powerful:

> Men and women shall have equal rights throughout the United States and every place subject to its jurisdiction. Congress shall have power to enforce this article by appropriate legislation.[14]

The 1943 Amendment (Alice Paul Amendment) was changed slightly, and read:

> Section 1: Equality of rights under the law shall not be denied or abridged by the United States or by any state on account of sex.
>
> Section 2: The Congress shall have the power to enforce, by appropriate legislation, the provisions of this article.

10 *See* National Constitution Center, https://constitutioncenter.org/timeline/html/cw08_12159. html.

11 *See id.*

12 *See* https://www.equalrightsamendment.org/history ("ERA History").

13 *See* ERA History, https://www.equalrightsamendment.org/history; Alice Paul Institute, *The History of the Equal Rights Amendment*, https://www.alicepaul.org/era.

14 https://www.equalrightsamendment.org/faq.

> Section 3: This amendment shall take effect two years after the date of ratification.[15]

The Equal Rights Amendment (ERA) was introduced during every session of Congress from 1923 until 1972, when it finally won the required passage by two-thirds of each House.[16] In 1972, when the Amendment was finally passed by the Senate, and thereafter moved to the States for ratification, the language of the Amendment still stated: "equality of rights under the law shall not be denied or abridged by the United States or any State on account of sex."[17]

The Amendment had a seven-year window for ratification by the States, and although there were extensions until 1982, the Amendment fell three States shy of ratification[18], and has yet to become part of the United States Constitution.

[4.1] II. WHERE DOES THE EQUAL RIGHTS AMENDMENT CURRENTLY STAND?

New York was among the 35 States that voted for ratification of the Equal Rights Amendment following its passage by Congress.[19] Since the failure of the Amendment to achieve ratification in 1982, numerous efforts have been undertaken to push forward a renewed campaign. Members of Congress have introduced bills aimed at extending or removing the 1982 deadline for the Amendment so that ratification votes could continue; while others have introduced new ERAs (called "fresh start amendments").[20] It is of note that since 1982, the final three states ostensibly needed for ratification have voted to ratify the Amendment, despite the passage of the deadline: Nevada in 2017, Illinois in 2018, and Virginia in

---

15 *Id.*

16 *See* Alice Paul Institute, *supra*; U.S Const. Art. V.

17 Thomas H. Neale, The Proposed Equal Rights Amendment: Contemporary Ratification Issues, Congressional Research Service, July 18, 2018, https://fas.org/sgp/crs/misc/R42979.pdf.

18 *Id.*

19 Hawai'i was the first state to ratify, doing so the same day the Senate took final action and the Amendment went to the States for ratification votes: March 22, 1972. *See* T. Neale, *supra*, at 17. The 15 states that did not ratify the Amendment by the 1982 deadline were: Alabama, Arizona, Arkansas, Florida, Georgia, Illinois, Louisiana, Mississippi, Missouri, Nevada, North Carolina, Oklahoma, South Carolina, Utah, and Virginia. *See* https://www.equalrightsamendment.org/faq.

20 *See* T. Neale, *supra*.

2020.[21] Although these ratification votes are powerfully symbolic, they are of little legal authority absent further Congressional action. However, if Congress were to somehow pass deadline extensions for the Amendment, and re-open ratification voting, the ERA could potentially be ratified.[22]

Given that history, and prior to Virginia's ratification vote, advocates for the ERA redoubled efforts, and reignited the flame for ratification. On April 30, 2019, the U.S. House of Representatives' Judiciary Committee held hearings on the ERA for the first time since 1982.[23]

Furthermore, the American Bar Association directly addressed the ERA in the 21st Century. The ABA has approximately 400,000 members,[24] and represents the interests of attorneys and society across the United States and its territories, and around the World.[25] The governing

---

21 *Id. See also Virginia Ratifies The Equal Rights Amendment, Decades After The Deadline*, NPR, Jan. 15, 2020, https://www.npr.org/2020/01/15/796754345/virginia-ratifies-the-equal-rights-amendment-decades-after-deadline; Timothy Williams, *Virginia Approves the E.R.A., Becoming the 38th State to Back It*, N.Y. Times, Jan. 16, 2020, https://www.nytimes.com/2020/01/15/us/era-virginia-vote.html.

22 *See* T. Neale, *supra*. Point of fact, the U.S. House of Representatives passed H.J. Res. 79 on February 13, 2020, removing any deadlines for ratification of the ERA. The Resolution passed by a vote of 232-183. Its text was as follows: "*Resolved by the Senate and House of Representatives of the United States of America in Congress assembled*, That notwithstanding any time limit contained in House Joint Resolution 208, 92d Congress, as agreed to in the Senate on March 22, 1972, the article of amendment proposed to the States in that joint resolution shall be valid to all intents and purposes as part of the United States Constitution whenever ratified by the legislatures of three-fourths of the several States." Following receipt in the U.S. Senate, it was referred to the Committee on the Judiciary, but as of the time of this writing no further action was taken. *See* https://www.congress.gov/bill/116th-congress/house-joint-resolution/79/all-actions. The Senate also referred S.J. Res 6 to the Committee on the Judiciary on January 25, 2019, a resolution having similar language to H.J. Res. 79. *See* https://www.congress.gov/bill/116th-congress/senate-joint-resolution/6/actions.

23 *See* U.S. House Committee on the Judiciary, Equal Rights Amendment hearing summary, at https://judiciary.house.gov/legislation/hearings/equal-rights-amendment; Aimee Sala, *Equal Rights Amendment Will Get a Hearing Before House Judiciary Committee Next Week*, ABA Journal, Apr. 25, 2019, http://www.abajournal.com/news/article/equal-rights-amendment-will-get-a-hearing-next-week.

24 *See ABA President Urges Unity, Diversity and Equal Justice for All*, American Bar Association, Aug. 12, 2019, https://www.americanbar.org/news/abanews/aba-news-archives/2019/08/aba-president-urges-unity--diversity-and-equal-justice-for-all/.

25 "Our mission is to serve equally our members, our profession and the public by defending liberty and delivering justice as the national representative of the legal profession." ABA Mission Statement, https://www.americanbar.org/about_the_aba.

body of the ABA is the House of Delegates,[26] and at the House's Midyear Meeting in February 2016 (held in San Diego, California), the Delegates debated and passed Resolution 10B, proposed by the New Jersey State Bar Association. The Resolution stated:

> RESOLVED, That the American Bar Association supports constitutional equality for women, and urges the extension of legal rights, privileges and responsibilities to all persons, regardless of sex.
>
> FURTHER RESOLVED, That the American Bar Association reaffirm its support of and affirmatively act toward the goal of the ratification of the Equal Rights Amendment to the U.S. Constitution.
>
> FURTHER RESOLVED, That the American Bar Association calls on all bar associations to support and take up the pursuit of ratification of the Equal Rights Amendment to the United States Constitution.[27]

Since then, former ABA President Bob Carlson, during his tenure leading the Association, wrote to the political leaders of the Commonwealth of Virginia in January 2019, urging them to make Virginia the 38th State to ratify the ERA,[28] which, as discussed above, the State did in January 2020. Of course, 38 would be the number of States needed for final ratification, again if Congress remedies the issue of the expired deadline[29] (such as by the Senate approving H.J. Res. 79 (2020), or approving and sending S.J. Res. 6 (2020) (having similar wording) to the House, before the expiration of the 116th Congress on January 3, 2021). Being in the vanguard of this issue is quite fitting for the ABA, given its Diversity &

---

26 *See* ABA House of Delegates, https://www.americanbar.org/groups/leadership/house_of_delegates.

27 ABA House of Delegates, Daily Journal, Feb. 8, 2016, https://www.americanbar.org/content/dam/aba/administrative/house_of_delegates/daily-journals/2016_hod_midyear_meeting_daily_journal.pdf. The author of this book, while attending the 2016 Midyear Meeting of the ABA House as an Alternate Delegate from the New York State Bar Association (following seven years of service as a NYSBA Delegate), spoke in favor of Resolution 10B during debate on the House floor, and voted in favor of the Resolution.

28 *See* Debra Cassens Weiss, *ABA President Urges Virginia Lawmakers to Ratify Equal Rights Amendment*, ABA Journal, Jan. 3, 2019, http://www.abajournal.com/news/article/aba-president-urges-virginia-lawmakers-to-ratify-the-equal-rights-amendment.

29 *See* U.S. Const. Art. V (with 50 States in the Union, three-quarters would be 37.5, thus the need for 38 States to vote in the affirmative).

Inclusion Center, and pride in advancing the cause of justice and equality.[30]

According to legal commentators, if the ERA can eventually succeed in ratification and addition to the Constitution of the United States, it would result in several vital societal impacts, such as embedding equality between and among genders as "fundamental and irrevocable," while "require[ing] judges to apply [strict] scrutiny in deciding sex discrimination," and "protect[ing] and reinforce[ing]. . . gender equality" under the laws of the United States and the several states.[31]

Certainly, all are laudable and important goals, and all would be vital with regard to the subject matter of this book on diversity and inclusion in American society and business.

[4.2] III. NEW YORK HAS HELD FOR MANY YEARS THAT WOMEN ARE ENTITLED TO INDIVIDUAL RIGHTS SEPARATE FROM MEN

Let us reflect on an issue related to property rights. Consider the New York case of *Walpole v. State Liquor Authority*,[32] from 1974. The facts are generally the following: A wife applies for a state liquor license, pursuant to New York Alcoholic Beverage Control Law § 128, so that she might complete a purchase contract for a going liquor store concern. The statutory provision, however, did not allow certain stated police officials or police officers in the state to have an interest (direct or indirect) in the manufacturing or sale of alcoholic beverages.[33] The issue was that while wife, the person seeking the liquor license, was not a police officer, her husband was. On that basis, despite the recommendation of the County Alcoholic Beverage Control Board that the license be granted, the State Liquor Authority denied wife's license. The Authority had but one reason, as stated by the Court: "APPLICANT, WIFE OF STATE POLICEMAN, DISQUALIFIED—SECTION 128 ALCOHOLIC BEVERAGE CONTROL LAW."[34]

30 *See* https://www.americanbar.org/groups/diversity.

31 *See* A. Sala, *supra*.

32 78 Misc.2d 372, 356 N.Y.S.2d 462 (Sup. Ct., Erie Co. 1974).

33 *Id.*

34 *Id.* at 373, 463.

The facts of the case were clear, however, that the husband did not have a financial interest in the business or license and had not invested or contributed any funds. Wife was denied the license purely because she was a woman, married to a police officer, and therefore was treated by the Authority as though she was not a separate person with individual rights.

Wife sought review by the full Authority, which denied the license on the same grounds, and also added the inherent discretion of the Authority as further justification.[35]

Wife thereafter brought an Article 78 proceeding under the New York Civil Procedure Law & Rules, to challenge the Authority's denial, and alleged "that the disapproval at issue based upon her marital status and the exercise by respondent of its discretion [was] a violation of lawful procedures, arbitrary, capricious, discriminatory and a violation of her civil rights."[36]

The Supreme Court[37] agreed with the plaintiff wife in all respects, annulled the denial of the license, and ordered the Authority to grant the license forthwith. Of interest for this particular chapter of this book, is that the Court cited to and quoted directly from a prior decision on a similar matter:

> On the present record it is the ultimate in arbitrariness for the State Liquor Authority, as an arm of the State, to effectively sabotage the duly enacted law of the State (Domestic Relations Law, s 50; General Obligations Law, s 3-305). *These laws have vested women with Individual property rights.* If the State Liquor Authority in fact believes that public policy or interest requires a statutory provision that marriage between a licensee and a police officer should be grounds, per se, for a refusal to issue a license, then the Court suggests (without commenting on the constitutionality thereof) that the State Liquor

35 *Id.* at 373, 464.

36 *Id.*

37 For those not familiar with New York law and court structure, the Supreme Court is New York's court of general jurisdiction—a trial court. The highest court in the State of New York is the Court of Appeals. For more information, see http://www.courts.state.ny.us/courts.

> Authority undertake to have the Alcoholic Beverage Control Statute so amended.[38]

Despite holdings like those in *Walpole*, and the statutory protections discussed therein, however, it has been argued by some that New York is technically lagging behind other jurisdictions in providing full and equal rights for women under the law. Although statutes and regulations provide protection based on sex (as discussed in earlier chapters), the New York State Constitution does not.[39]

Statutory protection is certainly important, but statutes can be repealed or amended more easily than constitutional provisions, they can be interpreted in various ways by courts, and they can be declared unconstitutional,[40] which is why there is a push for New York to join other States in providing an Equal Rights Amendment to the State Constitution, mirroring efforts on the federal level. At this time, 25 States provide either partial or complete protection based on gender/sex in their state constitutions.[41] The question is whether New York will become the 26th state, and whether those provisions will provide the full panoply of guarantees for protection sought by the proponents.

The New York State Bar Association, and its Women in the Law Section, is itself at the forefront of this matter. In January 2019, during the State Bar Annual Meeting in New York City, the Women in the Law Section held a full-day meeting and continuing legal education program, at which one of the panels specifically addressed "recent efforts to secure passage of an Equal Rights Amendment to the U.S. and New York State Constitution and related changes to New York employment laws, and how

38 *Walpole*, 78 Misc. 2d at 374-375, 356 N.Y.S.2d at 465 (citing and quoting *Sanspar Rest. Corp. v. Ring*, (65 Misc.2d 847, 319 N.Y.S.2d 230 (Sup. Ct., Nassau Co. 1971), *aff'd* 39 A.D.2d 595, 332 N.Y.S.2d 608 (2d Dep't 1972), *lv. to app. denied*) (emphasis added). It is also noted that the Walpole Court specifically mentioned that it was not considering a tangential issue related to § 128 of the Alcoholic Beverage Control Law – namely that the law excluded certain police officials and officers, but did not in its language appear to include N.Y. State Police officers, of which plaintiff's husband was one.

39 *See* Rachel Silberstein, *New York Lags as Equal Rights Amendment on Verge of Ratification*, Albany Times Union, Dec. 3, 2018, https://www.timesunion.com/news/article/With-federal-ERA-on-verge-of-ratification-New-13440152.php.

40 *See, e.g.*, https://www.equalrightsamendment.org/faq.

41 *See* https://www.equalrightsamendment.org/faq (those 25 states are: Alaska, California, Colorado, Connecticut, Delaware, Florida, Hawaii, Illinois, Iowa, Louisiana, Maryland, Massachusetts, Montana, Nebraska, New Hampshire, New Jersey, New Mexico, Oregon, Pennsylvania, Rhode Island, Texas, Utah, Virginia, Washington, and Wyoming).

other states are advancing women through legislative efforts and policy changes."[42]

[4.3] IV. CONCLUSION

Given the many thousands of years of recorded human history, not all that much time has passed comparatively since women were considered subservient to men, or little better than property of their husbands. But, in the last hundred years, many evolutions in law have occurred to advance the cause for equal rights. That being said, we have not necessarily reached the end of the road. The ERA did fail to pass by its original and extended deadlines—by three States' ratification votes—because a significant anti-ratification movement succeeded in stoking fear and animus against the Amendment.[43] However, it appears that although inequality remains ever present, momentum—previously stalled—has picked up again, possibly in a final push to get the ERA over the goal line. We will see in the coming years if Congress chooses to extend or eliminate the

42 New York State Bar Association, Women in the Law Section Meeting, Jan. 15, 2019, http://www.nysba.org/am2019wils/. The NYSBA, founded in 1876, is the largest voluntary bar association in the United States, with more than 70,000 members; and its membership spans the United States and the World. See NYSBA Member Profile, at https://www.nysbamediaplanner.org/member-profile.

43 Among the early fears: that the ERA would actually result in the loss of protection for women in the labor force with regard to working conditions, hours and wages. Prominent female leaders, including former First Lady Eleanor Roosevelt and former Secretary of Labor Frances Perkins (the first female member of a President's Cabinet, that of President Franklin Delano Roosevelt), opposed the ERA because of the perceived threat. Later, in opposition to final ratification, the anti-Amendment groups reignited the earlier arguments, even though some labor organizations supported the ERA, and overall public support was generally strong. *See* T. Neale, *supra*, at 17.

original ratification deadline, given the 38th and final ratification vote was finally accomplished in Virginia in January 2020.[44]

---

44 In such circumstance, if the ratification votes of Virginia, Illinois and Nevada, made since 1982, are deemed valid by some renewed action of Congress, then Virginia's vote would serve to ratify the Amendment (with the State's legislature having heeded the calls of former ABA President Carlson, among countless others). Although there have been arguments advanced cutting the other way—that the most recent ratification votes are invalid because they took place after the deadlines established by Congress. *See* CBS News Sunday Morning, Apr. 19, 2020; NPR, *Virginia Ratifies The Equal Rights Amendment, supra*. The U.S. Department of Justice's Office of Legal Counsel issued an opinion on January 6, 2020 stating that the ERA had expired, and votes to ratify by additional states would be ineffective under 1 U.S.C. § 106b. *See* Memorandum for the General Counsel National Archives and Records Administration, Office of Legal Counsel, U.S. Dep't Justice, Jan. 6, 2020, https://www.justice.gov/olc/file/1232501/download. Three states (Alabama, Louisiana and South Dakota), in addition, filed suit in court to block addition of the ERA to the Constitution. *See* NPR, *Virginia Ratifies The Equal Rights Amendment, supra*. Finally, creating further complication, several States have, since their initial votes in favor of ratification, passed measures rescinding their approval. While it appears that the rescission measures are constitutionally suspect, the issue is moot at this time given the expiration of the ratification deadlines, as well as beyond the scope of this text. If interest exists for further exploration and assessment, the reader may wish to start with discussions in T. Neale, *supra*, and the Alice Paul Institute's Frequently Asked Questions webpage ("Can a state withdraw, or rescind, its ratification of a constitutional amendment that is still in the process of being ratified?"), at https://www.equalrightsamendment.org/faq.

CHAPTER FIVE

ADMINISTRATIVE PROCEEDINGS: THE U.S. EEOC AND N.Y.S. DHR, AND THE IMPORTANCE OF POLICIES AND PAPERWORK

[5.0] I. OVERVIEW OF THE U.S. EEOC AND N.Y.S. DHR

Federally, the Equal Employment Opportunity Commission (EEOC) is an independent federal agency, separate from the U.S. Department of Labor.[1] The Department of Labor, however, has its own agencies to review and enforce equal employment opportunities: "Equal Employment Opportunity (EEO) laws prohibit specific types of job discrimination in certain workplaces. The Department of Labor has two agencies which deal with EEO monitoring and enforcement, the Civil Rights Center and the Office of Federal Contract Compliance Programs."[2] For purposes of this chapter, though, on the federal level we will examine and evaluate the EEOC and its procedures.

Pursuant to the EEOC's website:

> **Overview**
>
> The U.S. Equal Employment Opportunity Commission (EEOC) is responsible for enforcing federal laws that make it illegal to discriminate against a job applicant or an employee because of the person's race, color, religion, sex (including pregnancy, gender identity, and sexual orientation), national origin, age (40 or older), disability or genetic information. It is also illegal to discriminate against a person because the person complained about discrimination, filed a charge of discrimination, or participated in an employment discrimination investigation or lawsuit.
>
> Most employers with at least 15 employees are covered by EEOC laws (20 employees in age discrimination cases). Most labor unions and employment agencies are also covered.
>
> The laws apply to all types of work situations, including hiring, firing, promotions, harassment, training, wages, and benefits.

---

1 *Equal Employment Opportunity*, U.S. Dep't of Labor, https://www.dol.gov/general/topic/discrimination.

2 *Id.*

Authority & Role

The EEOC has the authority to investigate charges of discrimination against employers who are covered by the law. Our role in an investigation is to fairly and accurately assess the allegations in the charge and then make a finding. If we find that discrimination has occurred, we will try to settle the charge. If we aren't successful, we have the authority to file a lawsuit to protect the rights of individuals and the interests of the public and litigates a small percentage of these cases. When deciding to file a lawsuit, the EEOC considers several factors such as the strength of the evidence, the issues in the case, and the wider impact the lawsuit could have on the EEOC's efforts to combat workplace discrimination.

We also work to prevent discrimination before it occurs through outreach, education and technical assistance programs.

The EEOC provides leadership and guidance to federal agencies on all aspects of the federal government's equal employment opportunity program. EEOC assures federal agency and department compliance with EEOC regulations, provides technical assistance to federal agencies concerning EEO complaint adjudication, monitors and evaluates federal agencies' affirmative employment programs, develops and distributes federal sector educational materials and conducts training for stakeholders, provides guidance and assistance to our Administrative Judges who conduct hearings on EEO complaints, and adjudicates appeals from administrative decisions made by federal agencies on EEO complaints.

Location

We carry out our work through our headquarters offices in Washington, D.C. and through 53 field offices serving every part of the nation.[3]

3 *About*, U.S. EEOC, https://www.eeoc.gov/overview.

In New York State, the governmental agency responsible for equal rights and opportunities is the Division of Human Rights (DHR).

> New York has the proud distinction of being the first state in the nation to enact a Human Rights Law, which affords every citizen "an equal opportunity to enjoy a full and productive life." This law prohibits discrimination in employment, housing, credit, places of public accommodations, and non-sectarian educational institutions, based on age, race, national origin, sex, sexual orientation, gender identity or expression, marital status, disability, military status, and other specified classes.
>
> The New York State Division of Human Rights was created to enforce th[e] important [Human Rights Law]. The mission of the agency is to ensure that "every individual… has an equal opportunity to participate fully in the economic, cultural and intellectual life of the State." It does so in many ways, including the following:

- Through the vigorous prosecution of unlawful discriminatory practices;
- Through the receipt, investigation, and resolution of complaints of discrimination;
- Through the creation of studies, programs, and campaigns designed to, among other things, inform and educate the public on the effects of discrimination and the rights and obligations under the law; and
- Through the development of human rights policies and proposed legislation for the State.[4]

[5.1] II. PROCEDURES IN THE EEOC AND DHR

When it comes to a complaint alleging discrimination, harassment or retaliation in any of the fields in society covered by the federal and state laws, complainants (plaintiffs) have several options.

4 *Mission Statement*, N.Y.S. Division of Human Rights, https://dhr.ny.gov/mission-statement.

[5.2] A. Federal EEOC Procedure

It should be understood that filing with one of the agencies, either the N.Y.S DHR or EEOC is considered a joint filing with the other, because they have worksharing agreements.[5] Just be certain your local jurisdiction's agency has a worksharing (joint filing) agreement because, if not, filings should be made individually with each agency on a claim.[6] However, even with worksharing, generally the agency with which the original charging document is filed is the lead agency, and keeps the filing for determination.[7] If the state/local agency makes a determination on matters of federal law, and there is a worksharing agreement with the EEOC, an appeal/request for review can be made to the EEOC (within 15 days of the state/local agency's determination).[8]

Under federal law, before a complainant may file their claim in U.S. District Court (or state court having concurrent jurisdiction, for that matter) under certain specific statutory provisions, a filing must first be made with the EEOC (or the local agency under a worksharing), and administrative remedies must be exhausted. Absent exhaustion, claims will be dismissed if filed in federal court.[9] However, this exhaustion requirement does not exist for all federal claims.[10] The EEOC filing requirement exists for claims under Title VII, the Americans with Disabilities Act (ADA), the Age Discrimination in Employment Act (ADEA), the Genetic Infor-

---

5 *See Fair Employment Practices Agencies (FEPAs) and Dual Filing*, U.S. EEOC, https://www.eeoc.gov/employees/fepa.cfm; *see, generally*, *Benardo v. Am. Idol Prods., Inc.*, 2011 WL 2565489 at *4 (S.D.N.Y. June 21, 2011) (McMahon, D.J.); *Parekh v. Swissport Cargo Servs., Inc.*, 2009 WL 290465 at *2 (E.D.N.Y. Feb. 5, 2009) (Sifton, Senior D.J.).

6 *Id.*

7 *Id.*

8 *Id.*

9 *See McIver v. Mattis*, 318 F.Supp.3d 245, 249-251 (D.D.C. 2018) (Friedrich, D.J.); *Batchelor v. Rose Tree Media Sch. Dist.*, 759 F.3d 266 (3d Cir. 2014) (Greenaway, J.) (discussing similar exhaustion requirement related to Individuals with Disabilities Education Act (IDEA), and interplay with claims of discrimination under the ADA and Rehabilitation Act).

10 For instance, there is no exhaustion requirement for Section 1981 claims. *See Williams v. Waste Mgmt., Inc.*, 2020 WL 3250980 at *9 (5th Cir. June 15, 2020) (*per curiam*) (citing *Scarlett v. Seaboard Coast Line R. Co.*, 676 F.2d 1043, 1050 (5th Cir. 1982)).

mation Nondiscrimination Act (GINA), the Rehabilitation Act,[11] and claims alleging retaliation thereunder.[12] A similar administrative exhaustion requirement, through a procedure other than EEOC (i.e. through an impartial hearing procedure set out by statute), is also required for claims under the Individuals with Disabilities Education Act (IDEA), including claims brought under the ADA and Rehabilitation Act *if* those claims relate to allegations of denial of a free appropriate public education (FAPE); if not, then the IDEA's exhaustion requirements do not apply.[13]

Federally, a filing must be made within 180 days of the act complained of, or if the state or local jurisdiction has its own Human Rights Law and agency, then a filing must be made within 300 days.[14] Failure to exhaust the administrative remedies on the federal level results in dismissal of the relevant federal claims; and failure to file within 300 days of actions that

11 Note, however, that claims filed under the Rehabilitation Act, 29 U.S.C. § 701, *et seq.*, must be filed first with the EEOC only if against the federal government or agencies thereof. Exhaustion/filing with the EEOC is not required if claims are against private employers or state or local public entities. *See Employment Rights: Who has Them and Who Enforces Them*, Office of Disability Employment Policy, U.S. Dep't of Labor, https://www.dol.gov/odep/pubs/fact/rights.htm.

12 *See Filing a Lawsuit*, U.S. EEOC, https://www.eeoc.gov/employees/lawsuit.cfm; 42 U.S.C. § 2000e-5, *et seq.*, 42 U.S.C. §§ 12112(a), 12117(a); 29 U.S.C. § 621, *et seq.*; *Fowlkes v. Ironworkers Local 40*, 790 F.3d 378, 384 (2d Cir. 2015) (Carney, J.); *Ogalo v. N.Y. State Thruway Auth.*, 972 F.Supp.2d 301, 305 (N.D.N.Y. 2013) (Hurd, D.J.). While the EEOC also administers/enforces the EPA (Equal Pay Act) (*see What Laws Does EEOC Enforce?*, U.S. EEOC, https://www.eeoc.gov/youth/what-laws-does-eeoc-enforce), there is no exhaustion requirement under the EPA, and a plaintiff may choose to file a claim under that statutory framework directly in court so long as within the requisite statute of limitations for the claim. *See Equal Pay/Compensation Discrimination*, U.S. EEOC, https://www.eeoc.gov/equal-paycompensation-discrimination.

13 *See Fry v. Napoleon Community Schs.*, 137 S.Ct. 743 (2017) (Kagan, J.); *see also* 20 U.S.C. § 1415(f), (g), (l); *Rose Tree Media Sch. Dist.*, 759 F.3d 266.

14 *See* 42 U.S.C. § 2000e-5; *McGullam v. Cedar Graphics, Inc.*, 609 F.3d 70 (2d Cir. 2010) (Jacobs, C.J.); *Ikossi-Anastasiou v. Bd. of Supervisors of Louisiana State Univ.*, 579 F.3d 546 (5th Cir. 2009) (Owen, J.), *cert. denied* 130 S.Ct. 1285, 559 U.S. 904; *Bowers v. District of Columbia*, 883 F.Supp.2d 1 (D.D.C. 2011) (Huvelle, D.J.) (charge needs to be initially filed with the state/local agency to qualify for a 300-day deadline, otherwise the deadline is 180 days for a filing with EEOC; filings beyond that are deemed untimely and a failure to exhaust administrative remedies); *but cf. Chambers v. District of Columbia*, 2019 WL 3323608 (D.D.C. July 24, 2019) (Walton, D.J.), appeal filed, No. 19-7098 (D.C. Cir. Aug. 28, 2019) (distinguishing *Bowers*, and holding that a worksharing agreement automatically extends the time for filing to 300 days from 180 days, regardless of whether a filing is initially made with the local agency or EEOC, since the filing would be joint/cross-filed in any event) (extensively citing *Carter v. George Wash. Univ.*, 387 F.3d 872, 877, 879 (D.C. Cir. 2004)).

are discrete acts—and not continuing violations[15]—results in dismissal of claims as time-barred.[16] Senior U.S. District Judge Lawrence E. Kahn held just that in *Dacier*, evaluating plaintiff's claims to determine whether plaintiff raised continuing violations or discrete acts in the complaint, since plaintiff missed the 300-day filing deadline for several claims. The *Dacier* plaintiff sought relief under Title VII for alleged "unlawfully discriminatory hiring pattern" and discrimination following several failure to promote instances in the years 2010, 2012 and 2016.[17] Plaintiff missed the filing deadlines for the 2010 and 2012 claims, filing with the EEOC only once, sometime in 2016 after the third failure to promote instance complained of.[18] Judge Kahn held that each act of alleged failure to promote was a discrete act, not a continuing violation. Therefore, the 2010 and 2012 claims were dismissed, with the court further holding that the time-barred claims (2010 and 2012 claims) remained barred even if they related to timely filed charges (the 2016 claim in this particular case).[19]

The EEOC procedural process starts with a filing similar to a complaint in a court of law, although the complainant's filing (charge) is usually made *ex parte*, meaning that the filing is submitted to the EEOC without a copy being sent by the complainant or complainant's counsel to the

15 "The continuing-violation exception 'extends the limitations period for all claims of discriminatory acts committed under an ongoing policy of discrimination even if those acts, standing alone, would have been barred by the statute of limitations.'... The exception 'applies to cases involving specific discriminatory policies or mechanisms such as discriminatory seniority lists, or discriminatory employment tests. However, multiple incidents of discrimination, even similar ones, that are not the result of a discriminatory policy or mechanism do not amount to a continuing violation.'" *Collins v. Christopher*, 48 F. Supp. 2d 397, 406 (S.D.N.Y. 1999) (B. Parker, D.J.) (some internal quotation marks omitted) (citing *Quinn v. Green Tree Credit Corp.*, 159 F.3d 759, 765 (2d Cir. 1998); *Lambert v. Genesee Hosp.*, 10 F.3d 46, 53 (2d Cir. 1993)).

16 *See Dacier v. Reardon*, 2018 WL 2022610 (N.D.N.Y. Apr. 27, 2018) (Kahn, D.J.). *See also Sauveur v. Fed. of Org.*, 2019 WL 2994449 (E.D.N.Y. July 9, 2019) (Donnelly, D.J.) (claim dismissed as untimely, equitable tolling denied).

17 *Dacier*, 2018 WL 2022610 at *1.

18 *Id.*

19 *Id.* at *2-3 (citing cases). Note, courts have addressed different methods for calculating the 300-day time frame, often dependent on the claim and surrounding facts. For instance, "when the adverse employment action is a constructive discharge, the employee holds the key to when his claim accrues for purposes of the 300-day period. In *Green v. Brennan* . . . , the Supreme Court held that it was the act of 'resignation [that] triggers the limitations period for a constructive-discharge claim.' An employee does not resign until he provides notice of his intent to end his employment, regardless of when he last worked for his employer." *Kornmann v. City of N.Y. Bus. Integrity Comm'n*, 2020 WL 3165537 at *3-4 (E.D.N.Y. June 15, 2020) (Cogan, D.J.) (citing 136 S. Ct. 1769, 1782 (2016)).

opposing/respondent organization.[20] The EEOC will provide a copy of the charging documents to the respondent, and seek a response position statement. That response is also usually submitted *ex parte*. The EEOC will thereafter provide the response position statement to the complainant, and ask for a rebuttal. Among other authority, the EEOC and its investigators are empowered to speak with witnesses, make site visits, and call the complainant and counsel into the EEOC's offices for questioning.[21]

If either party requires additional time to gather materials or provide response statements, the party (or their legal counsel if they are represented), should request more time from the Investigator and explain why it is needed. Depending on the nature of the case, sometimes only a few weeks is provided, other times more or less than that may be allowed. Regardless, never ignore charges that are received. The agency can and will proceed without a party's participation.

At the beginning of the case, the EEOC may inquire if the parties wish to mediate and attempt resolution, or the parties may make this request of the EEOC.[22] The mediation attempt must be mutually agreeable; one party cannot force the other to mediate. If mediation is attempted but not successful, the matter will be reassigned from ADR to Investigation. Investigation is the division that will make a determination whether there is probable cause to believe discrimination occurred on the charge.

If cause is found by the EEOC, then the EEOC will attempt conciliation (mediation after a finding of probable cause)—a process required by

---

20 Although, if legal counsel for the complainant have been communicating with or otherwise attempting to resolve a dispute with respondent's legal counsel prior to the EEOC/DHR filing, complainant's counsel sometimes chooses to exercise professional courtesy and provide a copy to respondent's counsel when the filing occurs.

21 *See What You Can Expect After a Charge is Filed*, U.S. EEOC, https://www.eeoc.gov/employers/process.cfm. Note, however, that nothing in this process is made public, and indeed if any individual makes information about the EEOC investigation/proceedings public, they could face up to a $1,000.00 fine or up to 1 year in federal prison as a misdemeanor offense, or both. *See* 42 U.S.C. § 2000e-5(b).

22 *See What You Can Expect After a Charge is Filed*, U.S. EEOC, https://www.eeoc.gov/employers/process.cfm.

law.[23] However, again, this process must be mutually agreeable, and if conciliation does not resolve the matter then the EEOC will close its investigation and issue a "Right to Sue" notice/letter to complainant.[24] The Right to Sue is a notice from the EEOC advising complainant that the agency has closed its investigation, and clears the way for the matter to proceed to a filing in federal or state court under the federal statutes.[25]

Should probable cause be found by the EEOC, and conciliation fail, the agency could also choose to bring a lawsuit on behalf of the complainant, although that only happens in a small percentage of cases. Most of the time, the parties will receive the Letter of Determination, and thereafter the Notice of Right to Sue if conciliation either fails or is not pursued by the parties, clearing the way for complainant to proceed to court either *pro se* (representing themselves) or represented by an attorney. Should the EEOC not find probable cause that discrimination occurred as alleged by the complainant, the EEOC simply issues a Dismissal and Notice of Rights, which includes the Right to Sue.[26] Interestingly, even if the EEOC does not find cause, the complainant may still proceed to court as a plaintiff on the same federal claims.

Once the Right to Sue is issued, the complainant has 90 days from the date of receipt to file a complaint on the federal charges in federal or state court, or they are *forever barred* on the claims arising out of the facts and circumstances presented to the EEOC.[27] The 90-day period has been

23 *See* 42 U.S.C. § 2000e-5(b); https://www.eeoc.gov/employers/resolving.cfm; *Mach Mining, LLC v. E.E.O.C.*, 135 S.Ct. 1645, 1651 (2015) (Kagan, J.). Although judicial review of conciliation in EEOC is very limited, and there is no "reciprocal duty to negotiate in good faith." *See Mach Mining, LLC*, 135 S.Ct. 1645; *E.E.O.C. v. Wal-Mart Stores Texas, LLC*, 2019 WL 6877175 (S.D. Tex. Dec. 17, 2019) (Lake, Senior D.J.) (citing, and declining to extend, *Mach Mining*). Note that in the United States District Courts for the Southern and Eastern Districts of New York, Local Rule 83.8 (Eastern District only) and 83.9 (Southern District only) provide the rules for the Courts' mediation programs. Furthermore, in the Southern District, the rule states: "The Board of Judges may, by Administrative Order, direct that certain specified categories of cases shall automatically be submitted to the mediation program. The assigned District Judge or Magistrate Judge may issue a written order exempting a particular case with or without the request of the parties. . . . Judicial settlement conferences may be ordered by District Judges or Magistrate Judges with or without the request or consent of the parties." Southern District of NY Rule 83.9(e)(2), (f). In years past, the Board of Judges had mandated mediation at the start of employment discrimination cases.

24 *See What You Can Expect After a Charge Is Filed*, U.S. EEOC, https://www.eeoc.gov/employers/process.cfm.

25 *Id.*

26 *Id.*

27 *Romney v. N.Y.C. Transit Auth.*, 294 A.D.2d 481, 742 N.Y.S.2d 651 (2d Dep't 2002).

determined a statute of limitations for these purposes,[28] therefore watch the clock! Such 90-day limit also applies to arbitration. If the arbitration agreement does not refer to any other statutes of limitations, the 90-day limit applies the same as it would for a filing in court.[29] Further, as a statute of limitations, the court will only toll the time for extraordinary circumstances.[30]

One should also be cautious to observe that although New York State law speaks of elections of remedies (i.e., choosing either the administrative agency route or the court of law route), such is only the case for state law claims. Federal law claims, like those under Title VII, the Rehabilitation Act, the ADA, the ADEA, or GINA (as discussed earlier), must first go through the EEOC as required by federal law, as mentioned earlier. A complainant/plaintiff *cannot* attempt to circumvent the agency filing requirement by instead filing a complaint initially in state court for both federal and state claims. Doing so is a failure to exhaust remedies under federal law and will result in dismissal of the federal statutory claims, even if filed in a state court—and the same is true for missing the 90-day deadline following issuance of the Right to Sue, and thereafter attempting to file in state court.[31]

Furthermore, if a complainant files a charge with the DHR or EEOC, and only alleges violations of certain statutory frameworks, such that the agency is not aware of other violations to investigate, then the remaining unasserted or unidentified claims are not "reasonably related" to the previous administrative complaint and will be dismissed for "failure to exhaust available administrative remedies." This was the holding, as set

---

28 *Virgil v. Wells Fargo Bank N.A.*, 2018 WL 5289494 (D. Or. Mar. 20, 2018) (Simon, D.J.) (citing *Nelmida v. Shelly Eurocars, Inc.*, 112 F.3d 380, 383 (9th Cir. 1997); 42 U.S.C. § 2000e-5(f)(1)); *Williams v. Raymond & Assoc., LLC*, 2014 WL 2215872 (S.D. Ala. May 29, 2014) (Granade, D.J.) (90-day statute of limitations under both Title VII and the ADA).

29 *See Hagan v. Katz Comm'n, Inc.*, 200 F.Supp.3d 435 (S.D.N.Y. 2016) (Abrams, D.J.).

30 *See Grant v. Dep't of Treasury*, 272 F.Supp.3d 182, 189 (D.D.C. 2017) (Collyer, D.J.); *Dyson v. Hagel*, 2014 WL 2959108 (D.D.C. July 2, 2014) (Jackson, D.J.) ("A federal employee may file a civil action in district court under Title VII and ADEA 'within 90 days of receipt of notice of final action taken by a department, agency ... or the [EEOC].' 42 U.S.C. § 2000e–16(c); *see also* 29 C.F.R. § 1614.408. The 90–day time limit 'functions like a statute of limitations[,]' ... and although a court has the power to toll this limitations period, it can only exercise that power in 'extraordinary circumstances.'") (some citations omitted).

31 *See, e.g., Romney*, 294 A.D.2d 481, 742 N.Y.S.2d 651; *Meadows v. Robert Flemings, Inc.*, 290 A.D.2d 386, 737 N.Y.S.2d 272 (Mem) (1st Dep't 2002); *Patrowich v. Chemical Bank*, 98 A.D.2d 318, 323-324 (1st Dep't 1984).

forth in the Southern District of New York case of *Clarke v. White Plains Hospital*,[32] decided by U.S. District Judge Cathy Seibel.

Additionally, be aware that although the complainant/plaintiff must usually exhaust administrative remedies, there are procedures whereby the complainant/plaintiff may proceed to court prior to the EEOC completing its review. According to the EEOC's website:

> **Exceptions When Filing a Lawsuit**
>
> Age Discrimination Lawsuits (ADEA)
>
> If you plan to file an age discrimination lawsuit, you must have filed a charge but you don't need a Notice of Right to Sue to file a lawsuit in court. You can file a lawsuit in court any time after 60 days have passed from the day you filed your charge (but no later than 90 days after you receive notice that our investigation is concluded).
>
> Equal Pay Lawsuits (EPA)
>
> If you plan to file a lawsuit under the Equal Pay Act, you don't have to file a charge or obtain a Notice of Right to Sue before filing. Rather, you can go directly to court, provided you file your suit within two years from the day the pay discrimination took place (3 years if the discrimination was willful).
>
> Title VII also makes it illegal to discriminate based on sex in the payment of wages and benefits. If you have an Equal Pay Act claim, there may be advantages to also filing under Title VII. To file a Title VII lawsuit in court, you must have filed a charge with EEOC and received a Notice of Right to Sue.
>
> **Filing a Lawsuit Before the Investigation Is Completed**
>
> If you want to file a lawsuit before we have finished our investigation, you can request a Notice of Right to Sue.
>
> **How to Request a Notice of Right to Sue:**

32 2015 WL 13022510 *4 (S.D.N.Y. Apr. 22, 2015) (Seibel, D.J.).

> If you have a registered in EEOC's Public Portal, you can submit your request by logging in to your charge account and uploading your request. If you don't have an online charge account, send your request for a Notice of Right to Sue to the EEOC office responsible for investigating your charge and include your EEOC charge number and the names of the parties.

- *After 180 days have passed from the date your charge was filed.* If more than 180 days have passed from the day you filed your charge, we are required by law to give you the notice if you ask for it.

- *Before 180 days have passed form the date your charge was filed.* If fewer than 180 days have passed, we will only give you the notice if we will be unable to finish our investigation within 180 days.

> If you want the EEOC to continue investigating your charge, don't request a Notice of Right to Sue.[33]

One should also note that rare, extenuating circumstances *might* further excuse a complainant/plaintiff's failure to file with the EEOC and exhaust remedies; circumstances such as: futility,[34] EEOC failure to properly pro-

33 *Filing a Lawsuit*, U.S. EEOC, https://www.eeoc.gov/employees/lawsuit.cfm. However, note that if a complainant files before the 180 days have passed, a District Court is *not* deprived of subject matter jurisdiction, despite 42 U.S.C. § 2000e-16(c) and 29 C.F.R. § 1614.407(b), at least according to one federal Circuit. Therefore, a Rule 12(b)(1) motion may fail, but a 12(b)(6) motion might not. *See Stewart v. Iancu*, 912 F.3d 693 (4th Cir. 2019) (Wynn, J.). A respondent/defendant, though, must raise a timely objection and motion based on failure to exhaust under Title VII, or the defense is waivable since the Supreme Court of the United States has held it is not a jurisdictional requirement. *See Fort Bend Cty. v. Davis*, 139 S.Ct. 1843 (2019) (Ginsburg, J.). The charge filing requirement with the EEOC is not jurisdictional (and thus cannot be raised at any stage of a proceeding to deprive a court of the authority to hear a claim). Rather, it is a mandatory processing rule, and waiver will result if the defending party does not raise a failure to exhaust defense in a timely fashion as with other waivable defenses. *Id. See also Jamiel v. Viveros*, 2020 WL 1847566 at *3 (S.D.N.Y. Apr. 13, 2020) (Daniels, D.J.) ("relief may be granted on a Rule 12(b)(6) motion only when 'failure to exhaust appears on the face of the complaint.'... Construing the face of the pleadings in a light most favorable to Plaintiff, it is not clear that he failed to exhaust the administrative remedies available to him. Therefore, Defendants' argument is rejected without prejudice") (citations omitted).

34 Note, however, that federal courts have held futility not to excuse a failure to exhaust. *See Talbot v. U.S. Foodservice, Inc.*, 191 F. Supp. 2d 637 (D.Md. 2002) (Motz, D.J.); *Nuss v. Central Iowa Binding Corp.*, 284 F.Supp.2d 1187, 1197–98 (S.D. Iowa 2003) (Gritzner, D.J.) (citing *Talbot* with approval, and collecting cases from around the nation concerning other reasons not to excuse exhaustion).

cess a complaint or amendment after it is filed, mistakes by the EEOC interviewer who fails to include claims in a charge, or the claims raised are "reasonably related" to a timely filed charge. In order for unasserted/unexhausted claims to survive, they must be "reasonably related" to claims already asserted and filed with the investigating agency (i.e., EEOC or DHR). For instance, a decision out of the Northern District of New York in October 2019 noted:

> [T]he Second Circuit has "long recognized that in certain circumstances, it may be unfair, inefficient, or contrary to the purposes of the statute to require a party to separately re-exhaust new violations that are 'reasonably related' to the initial claim." . . . Title VII claims are considered r*easonably related* to a previous administrative complaint in three instances: (1) where the claims concern conduct that falls within the scope of an EEOC investigation that can reasonably be expected to grow out of the charge; (2) where the claims allege retaliation for filing the charge; or (3) where the claims concern further incidents of discrimination carried out in precisely the same manner alleged in the charge.[35]

Finally, the reader may wonder, after reading the next subchapter section on DHR procedures, if the EEOC ever holds its own hearings. That would be a good question. There are instances where the EEOC may also hold hearings, which are binding, with administrative law judges conducting the hearings. The process looks similar to that in the N.Y.S. DHR, discussed below.[36] These are usually cases of EEO—federal government

---

35 *Robinson v. Med. Answering Serv.*, 2019 WL 5653378 at *4 (N.D.N.Y. Oct. 31, 2019) (Suddaby, C.J.) (emphasis by court) (citing, *inter alia*, *Duplan v. City of New York*, 888 F.3d 612, 622 (2d Cir. 2018); *Gittens-Bridges v. City of N.Y.*, 2020 WL 3100213 at *9 (S.D.N.Y. June 11, 2020) (Ramos, D.J.) ("Recognizing that EEOC complaints are frequently filed by lay people, the Second Circuit has said that '[t]he central question is whether the complaint filed with the EEOC gave that agency adequate notice to investigate discrimination on both bases'"); *Malarkey v. Texaco, Inc.*, 983 F.2d 1204, 1208 (2d Cir. 1993); *Ogalo v. N.Y.S. Thruway Auth.*, 972 F. Supp. 2d 301, 306 (N.D.N.Y. 2013)). *See also Angotti v. Kenyon & Kenyon*, 929 F.Supp. 651, 658 (S.D.N.Y. 1996) (Koeltl, D.J.); *Fowlkes v. Ironworkers Local 40*, 790 F.3d 378; *Butts v. City of New York Dep't of Housing Preservation & Dev.*, 990 F.2d 1397, 1401-1402 (2d Cir. 1993) (superseded by statute on other grounds, *Duplan v. City of New York*, 888 F.3d 612 (2d Cir. 2018)); *Early v. Bankers Life & Cas. Co.*, 959 F.2d 75 (7th Cir. 1992) (Posner, J.). Although some courts have brought "special circumstances" excusal of exhaustion and equitable relief into question when there is a statutory exhaustion requirement. *See U.S. v. McIndoo*, 2020 WL 2201970 at *6 (W.D.N.Y. May 6, 2020) (Wolford, D.J.) (questioning *Fowlkes*; citing *Ross v. Blake*, 136 S.Ct. 1850 (2016)).

36 *See* 29 C.F.R. § 1614.109.

employers and labor claims. If the reader is on staff at a federal agency, or represents federal agencies or employees of federal agencies, the cited regulations should be investigated in more detail.

[5.3] B. New York DHR Procedure

In New York State, claimants must file a complaint or charging document with the DHR within one year, pursuant to DHR Rule of Practice 465.3(e), although claimants of sexual harassment will have three years to file with the DHR given the Governor's signing of the Amendments Act on August 12, 2019 (see Chapter 1, *supra*). That change took effect one year from August 12, 2019 (or on August 12, 2020), while the time frame remains one year for other claims of discrimination or harassment.

However, in New York State, a complainant/plaintiff has the option to elect remedies—meaning in New York there is no requirement to first file with an administrative agency. The complainant/plaintiff may choose to file either with the DHR or State Supreme Court (a trial court in New York) under the Human Rights Law. If the avenue chosen is a complaint filed in Supreme Court, then a three-year statute of limitation applies for the state law claims, pursuant to CPLR 214(2). But the complainant cannot file in both New York Supreme Court and the DHR; they must choose one or the other. Once the election of remedies is made, if the selection is a filing in DHR the only avenue to Supreme Court thereafter on the state charges (whether complainant prevails or is dismissed in DHR) is through an appeals process—Article 78 of the Civil Practice Law and Rules—not through a plenary action in court starting the case over from scratch.[37] The same is true in New York City.[38]

Furthermore, be aware that in New York City, Mayor Bill DeBlasio signed the "Stop Sexual Harassment in NYC Act" into law on May 9, 2018, thereby amending certain time frames for filing within the City of New York—complainants have three years, not one year, to file with the N.Y.C. Commission on Human Rights in cases of discriminatory practices, including gender-based harassment.[39]

---

37 *See* N.Y. Exec. Law §§ 297(9), 298; N.Y.C. Admin. Code § 8-101(a), *et seq.*; *York v. Ass'n of Bar of City of New York*, 286 F.3d 122, 127 (2d Cir. 2002) (Garaufis, D.J., by designation).

38 *Id.*

39 *See Stop Sexual Harassment Act*, NYC Human Rights, https://www1.nyc.gov/site/cchr/law/stop-sexual-harassment-act.page. *See also* N.Y.C. Admin. Code § 8-502.

The procedure in DHR is similar to that in the EEOC with regard to the initial filings, investigations, and attempts at mediation/conciliation (although in DHR conciliation is the term before a determination),[40] while a significant divergence from the federal procedure takes place if the agency makes the determination that there is probable cause that discrimination, harassment, or retaliation occurred. In the DHR, administrative law judges are empowered to hold trials (bench trials, non-jury), and issue awards to prevailing complainants. Their power to issue awards is very similar to that of state supreme court justices under the statutes.[41]

If probable cause is found, then prior to the hearing a separate proceeding is conducted, with an administrative law judge other than the one who will conduct the hearing, for settlement purposes to see if the case can be resolved.[42] If the case is not resolved, the DHR hearing is held in the same manner as a bench trial in state court. Sworn witnesses may be called by each party, evidence is taken, and arguments are made by counsel/the litigants.[43]

There are, however, some unique features of a DHR hearing, similar to some arbitrations. For instance, the rules of evidence are more relaxed, and provide in part at § 465.12:

> *Form and content of proof.* The administrative law judge, in conducting the hearing, should utilize any procedures consonant with due process to elicit evidence concerning the ultimate issues. The following guidelines shall govern.
>
> (1) Hearsay evidence is fully admissible.
>
> . . .
>
> (3) Documentary evidence may be admitted without testamentary foundation, where reasonable.
>
> (4) Witness information need not be introduced in the form of question and answer testimony.

40 *See N.Y.S. DHR Rules of Practice* §§ 465.3, 465.6, 465.7, 465.8.

41 *See N.Y.S. DHR Rule of Practice* § 465.17.

42 *See N.Y.S. DHR Rule of Practice* § 465.10.

43 *See N.Y.S. DHR Rules of Practice* §§ 465.11-465.17.

> (5) Information from witnesses may be introduced in the form of affidavits, without oralexamination and cross examination.
>
> . . .
>
> (9) Written stipulations may be introduced in evidence if signed by the person sought to be bound thereby or by that person's attorney-at-law. Oral stipulations may be made on the record at open hearing. The entire record may be in the form of a stipulation, submitted to the chief administrative law judge without the convening of a hearing before an administrative law judge.
>
> . . .
>
> (11) Where reasonable and convenient, the administrative law judge may permit the testimony of a witness to be taken by telephone, subject to the following conditions:
>
> (i) a person within the hearing room can testify that the voice of the witness is recognized, or identity can otherwise be established;
>
> (ii) the administrative law judge, reporter and respective attorneys can hear the questions and answers;
>
> (iii) the witness is placed under oath and testifies that he or she is not being coached by any other person.[44]

The DHR Rules also differ from those in courts of law when it comes to the ALJ's determination after hearing. While the ALJ issues a written decision, the draft proposed order, with findings of fact and a decision, is first circulated to the parties/counsel, and they may make objections to same before the Commissioner makes the final determination and order.[45] The objections have to be in writing, and filed within 21 days of the service of the proposed order.[46] Once objections are filed, if any, that is the close of the hearing.[47] The decision may then be appealed, in limited fash-

44 *See N.Y.S. DHR Rule of Practice* § 465.12(e).

45 *See N.Y.S. DHR Rule of Practice* § 465.17.

46 *Id.*

47 *Id.*

ion. Furthermore, the DHR Commissioner and the Division may thereafter, within one year, investigate to ensure that respondent is complying.[48] Additional proceedings may be brought if there are violations.[49]

[5.4] III. THE IMPORTANCE OF POLICIES AND PAPERWORK/RECORDS

"Paper" (which may include "documentation," such as electronic files that are appropriately backed-up and accessible) can be your friend. Generally speaking, an employer or businessperson is very much benefited by maintaining an adequate paper file, including a thorough personnel file for all employees. If or when claims of discrimination are filed, the employer may immediately turn to the file for material potentially relevant to the claim. Therefore, it is vital that the employer or businessperson maintain a good, thorough and up-to-date filing system.

One should retain all copies of signed handbooks and policies, any contracts pertaining to employees, any non-compete agreements, any non-disclosure agreements, any periodic reviews, write-ups, complaints or disciplines against an employee, as well as any commendations received by the employee, which can also be useful in litigation. For instance, as support for a legitimate, non-discriminatory reason behind a termination, i.e., the employee claims that the employer routinely treated them poorly, but the files show the employee was recognized as a terrific worker, until subsequent termination due to economic constraints, a documented violation of rules, or a subsequent documented reduction in their workplace productivity or performance.[50] For places of public accommodation, maintain records of modifications or responses to complaints, construction records, and records of attempts to resolve any issues of access. Of course, all record-keeping must be done accurately and contemporaneously to be more effective.

Finally, documentation from any meeting with an employee or business customer should include the names of all of those present, and, when an employee, management should ensure that at least two persons are present representing the company; a meeting for reprimand or commendation should not be attended by only one manager and the employee. An

48 *See N.Y.S. DHR Rule of Practice* § 465.18.

49 *Id.*

50 *See, e.g., Flynn v. Mid-Atl. Mari-Time Acad.*, 2019 WL 7859409 at *19 (E.D. Va. July 30, 2019) (Leonard, M.J.) (citing, *inter alia*, *Kalola v. IBM*, 2017 WL 3394115 at *11–12 (S.D.N.Y. Feb. 28, 2017)).

employee should be asked to sign an acknowledgment of receipt of all paperwork, and all reviews, write-ups or commendations, and notations should be made if an employee refuses to sign. Of course, if the workplace is unionized, a union representative must accompany the employee, and the collective bargaining agreement will govern the interactions between management and the employee.

Always keep in mind that membership in a protected class, or protection against retaliation provided to those making claims under the law, does not mean that someone—particularly an employee—is thereafter immune from workplace rules and job expectations. Protection under the statutes and caselaw does not trump misconduct.

Take the case of *Fanelli v. New York.*[51] In applying the *McDonnell Douglas* burden shifting test (*see* Chapter 1, *supra*), and finding in employer's favor, dismissing the case, the Court evaluated the proffered, non-discriminatory reasons advanced by the employer as to why the employee/plaintiff experienced adverse treatment in the workplace. Plaintiff alleged the adverse treatment was close in time to her EEOC filing so as to constitute retaliation.[52] The Court accepted the employer/defendant's proffered reasons that the employee had engaged in misconduct, and the employer had begun an investigation prior to the EEOC charge. Plaintiff failed to produce any evidence in rebuttal that another investigation or mistreatment took place *after* the EEOC charge.[53] Additionally, notation of Internet misconduct/misuse, even if included in the employee's review or addressed with the plaintiff, would have been proper absent evidence that it was against the employer's policy or was used in a manner inconsistent with how other employees received reviews (and, plaintiff produced no such evidence).[54] The employer's paperwork and records, no doubt, aided in the defense.[55]

When it comes to anti-harassment and anti-discrimination policies, particularly in a workplace, in New York State one can first look to the model policies created by the DOL and DHR (*see* Chapter 1, and Appendices A, B and C). Furthermore, these can be stand-alone or incorporated

51 200 F.Supp.3d 363 (E.D.N.Y. 2016) (Hurley, D.J.).

52 *Id.*

53 *Id.*

54 *Id.*

55 *See also Hui-Wen Chang v. N.Y.C. Dep't of Educ.*, 412 F.Supp.3d 229 (E.D.N.Y. 2019) (Matsumoto, D.J.).

into handbooks. The policies should state that the business is an equal opportunity employer, and that no actions or activities in violation of the law or discriminatory toward any groups will be tolerated. The policies could then spell out the particular laws, and specify the types of activities that are prohibited: sexual harassment, hostile work environment, discrimination based on race or disability. The policies can be as detailed as the employer would like, restricting e-mails of off-color jokes, sexual touching, suggestive language, etc. But it would be good to include language such as "including, but not limited to," so it is clear that examples are not exclusive.

The policies should make explicitly clear that no retaliation will occur against employees who report or make a complaint in good faith, or those who aid such a complainant, so that there is no fear of reprisal. The policies should specify penalties that will exist if someone is found to have violated the policy; this can include a tiered discipline policy, or conditions for immediate termination. Obviously, if the employees are unionized, the policy and discipline provisions must first be discussed with the union. Each employee should be provided with a copy of the policy. They should sign and date, indicating receipt, and that should be kept in the personnel file, as discussed a moment ago when talking about paperwork. These are just some suggestions, a few of what could be myriad provisions that an employer chooses to create, so long as consistent with law.

Regardless of the policy wording, the key is to provide clear guidance under the applicable laws.

[5.5] IV. CONCLUSION

The goal of this chapter was to provide particularized and specific information concerning administrative procedures, and paperwork policies. Many cases today have their genesis in the administrative process, particularly those alleging discrimination, harassment or retaliation under the federal statutory provisions of Title VII, the Rehabilitation Act, the ADA, the ADEA and GINA. As the well-known saying goes: Knowledge is power.

CHAPTER SIX

DISABILITIES LAW AND LEAVE ISSUES

[6.0] I. INTRODUCTION

As mentioned in prior chapters, while New York State and New York City's protections for those with qualifying disabilities can be found under their respective Human Rights Laws[1] (*see* Chapter 1), Congress created a separate statutory framework for different protected classes. Protections for those with qualifying disabilities, and for those who qualify for protected, unpaid leave from the workplace, are not found under Title VII of the Civil Rights Act. Instead, those protections are found under the Americans with Disabilities Act[2] or the Family and Medical Leave Act,[3] respectively. Take note, however, that while this chapter largely addresses these statutes in the employment context, the ADA also applies in other fields, such as access to services and public accommodations (*see also* Chapter 7, *infra*), and access to government programs.[4] Courts have stated:

> The scope of the ADA covers not only intentional discrimination, but also the discriminatory effects of facially neutral practices and barriers. . . . Title III of the ADA prohibits discrimination against individuals in any place of public accommodation. . . . Liability is imposed upon "any person who owns, leases (or leases to), or operates a place of public accommodation" that discriminates against an individual on the basis of disability. . . . Discrimination includes the failure to remove "architectural barriers" in existing facilities where such removal is "readily achievable.". . . If a place of public accommodation fails to remove architectural barriers, the enforcement provisions of the ADA provide a private right of

---

1 *See* N.Y. Exec. Law § 296; N.Y.C Admin. Code § 8-107.

2 42 U.S.C. §§ 12101, *et seq.*

3 29 U.S.C. §§ 2601, *et seq.*

4 *See Tennessee v. Lane*, 541 U.S. 509, 516–17 (2004) (Stevens, J.) (The ADA "forbids discrimination against persons with disabilities in three major areas of public life: employment, which is covered by Title I of the statute; public services, programs, and activities, which are the subject of Title II; and public accommodations, which are covered by Title III"). *See also Helping Patients with HIV Infection Who Need Accommodations at Work*, at 1, U.S. EEOC, https://www.eeoc.gov/eeoc/publications/hiv_doctors.cfm. It is unclear if a plaintiff can bring an action under one Title for claims belonging under another, i.e., an employment claim under Title II. *See Brumfield v. City of Chicago*, 735 F.3d 619, 625 (7th Cir. 2013) (Sykes, J.); *Whitfield v. Tennessee*, 639 F.3d 253, 258 (6th Cir, 2011) (Boggs, J.). *See also* Appendix E (*Revised Guidelines Aim to Facilitate Swifter Provision of Appropriate Accommodations for Court Users with Special Needs*, State of New York Unified Court System (June 29 2020)).

> action. . . . Further, the Court may order injunctive relief which includes an order to make a facility "readily accessible."[5]

Always remember that the ADA was created "to provide 'a clear and comprehensive national mandate for the elimination of discrimination against individuals with disabilities.'"[6] But, understand that nothing in the ADA requires an employer to hire unqualified individuals, utilize hiring preferences for those with disabilities, or provide very expensive accommodations.[7] Let us now examine the provisions of law in more detail.

[6.1] II. THE PROVISIONS OF THE AMERICANS WITH DISABILITIES ACT (ADA)

The reader's first question may be: What is the ADA? According to the United States Department of Justice's Civil Rights Division:

> The Americans with Disabilities Act (ADA) was signed into law on July 26, 1990, by President George H.W. Bush. The ADA is one of America's most comprehensive pieces of civil rights legislation that prohibits discrimination and guarantees that people with disabilities have the same opportunities as everyone else to participate in the mainstream of American life—to enjoy employment opportunities, to purchase goods and services, and to participate in State and local government programs and services. Modeled after the Civil Rights Act of 1964, which prohibits discrimination on the basis of race, color, reli-

5 *Grove v. De La Cruz*, 407 F.Supp.2d 1126, 1130 (C.D. Cal. 2005) (Snyder, D.J.) (citing *Crowder v. Kitagawa*, 81 F.3d 1480, 1483 (9th Cir. 1996); 42 U.S.C. §§ 12182, 12188)). Note that Title III of the ADA, concerning places of public accommodation, applies to any place of public accommodation, i.e., businesses of any size. *See* Tia Benjamin, *Does the ADA Affect Small Businesses?*, Chron, https://smallbusiness.chron.com/ada-affect-small-businesses-36227.html; *see also* Katie Truesdell, *Here's How to Make Sure Your Small Business Is ADA Compliant*, NFIB, Feb. 13, 2017, https://www.nfib.com/content/resources/labor/heres-how-to-make-sure-your-small-business-is-ada-compliant; https://www.ada.gov/ADA_TITLE_III.HTM. *See also United States. v. Asare*, 2020 WL 4496319 (S.D.N.Y. Aug. 5, 2020) (Torres, D.J.) (surgeon violated Title III of the ADA by denying services to individuals with disabilities, including HIV).

6 *Grove*, 407 F. Supp. 2d at 1129–30. According to the last decennial U.S. Census, and estimates since then, 8.6% of Americans under the age of 65 have a disability in some form. *See Understanding the Census, What the Numbers Mean*, Times Herald-Record Supplement at 15, Mar. 15, 2020.

7 *Employers and the ADA: Myths and Facts*, U.S. Dep't of Labor, https://www.dol.gov/odep/pubs/fact/ada.htm.

> gion, sex, or national origin—and Section 504 of the Rehabilitation Act of 1973—the ADA is an "equal opportunity" law for people with disabilities.
>
> To be protected by the ADA, one must have a disability, which is defined by the ADA as a physical or mental impairment that substantially limits one or more major life activities, a person who has a history or record of such an impairment, or a person who is perceived by others as having such an impairment. The ADA does not specifically name all of the impairments that are covered.[8]

A disability as determined under the current version of the Americans with Disabilities Act, is defined as follows:

> **(1) Disability**
>
> The term "disability" means, with respect to an individual—
>
> (A) a physical or mental impairment that substantially limits one or more major life activities of such individual;
>
> (B) a record of such an impairment; or
>
> (C) being regarded as having such an impairment (as described in paragraph (3)).
>
> **(2) Major life activities**
>
> **(A) In general**
>
> For purposes of paragraph (1), major life activities include, but are not limited to, caring for oneself, performing manual tasks, seeing, hearing, eating, sleeping, walking, standing, lifting, bending, speaking, breathing, learning, reading, concentrating, thinking, communicating, and working.
>
> **(B) Major bodily functions**

8 *Introduction to the ADA*, Civil Rights Division, U.S. Dep't of Justice, https://www.ada.gov/ada_intro.htm.

> For purposes of paragraph (1), a major life activity also includes the operation of a major bodily function, including but not limited to, functions of the immune system, normal cell growth, digestive, bowel, bladder, neurological, brain, respiratory, circulatory, endocrine, and reproductive functions.[9]

When one looks to the protections of the ADA, it should be understood that the ADA (just like most of the other protections discussed elsewhere in this book) applies to the entire "life cycle" of employment: from the advertising of a position, to collecting résumés, to interviewing, hiring, training and promotion decisions, and termination/retirement/death.[10] Indeed, the ADA's purpose or general rule is stated in the statutory language:

> **(a) General rule**
>
> No covered entity shall discriminate against a qualified individual on the basis of disability in regard to job application procedures, the hiring, advancement, or discharge

9 42 U.S.C. § 12102(1), (2).

10 *See* 42 U.S.C. § 12112(b); *Whitfield v. Tennessee*, 639 F.3d 253, 258–59 (6th Cir, 2011). Additionally, commentators have written articles and dedicated valuable time and print space to advising employers how to, *inter alia*, effectively, and lawfully, terminate employees. *See* Brian Arbetter and Maria Biaggi, *Employer Tips for Lawfully Ending the Employment Relationship*, N.Y.L.J. at p. 4, Aug. 13, 2019.

> of employees, employee compensation, job training, and other terms, conditions, and privileges of employment.[11]

In addition, the ADA applies to companies doing business in, or controlling a corporation in, a foreign country, unless complying with the provisions of the ADA would result in violation of the laws of that foreign jurisdiction.[12] Thus, if the provisions of the ADA, as complied with, would not violate the laws of a nation in which the reader operates a business, take care to comply with the U.S. law, or face potential litigation at your peril.

To qualify as a business with employees covered by the ADA, the business must employ at least 15 employees.[13] That is but a shorthand measure for convenience, however. The actual calculation to determine the number of employees to qualify for coverage is a little more complicated,

---

11 42 U.S.C. § 12112(a). After the emergence of the COVID-19 pandemic, the EEOC addressed a series of questions under the ADA, including whether employers could take employee temperatures, administer COVID-19 tests (for virus detection) to employees, require employees to stay home if ill, and require a physician's note before an employee returned to work. The answer to all of the foregoing was "yes". However, given guidance from the U.S. Centers for Disease Control and Prevention, the EEOC stated it was not permissible for employers to make employment decisions based upon, or to administer to employees, COVID-19 antibody tests. *See What You Should Know About COVID-19 and the ADA, the Rehabilitation Act, and Other EEO Laws*, U.S. EEOC, June 17, 2020, https://www.eeoc.gov/wysk/what-you-should-know-about-covid-19-and-ada-rehabilitation-act-and-other-eeo-laws. EEOC also stated that employers could not exclude from the workplace employees deemed "higher risk", because of age, pregnancy, or other conditions. That would be discriminatory, unless employer showed there was some "direct threat" posed to the worker, the workplace or co-workers. Although, employer and employee could engage in an interactive process (see later in this chapter) to determine, for example, if a reasonable accommodation would allow the employee to perform the essential functions of the job outside of the workplace. *See id.* Guidance on "reasonable accommodations" and related matters was likewise provided by EEOC to guide employers and employees during the health pandemic. *Id.* Additionally, a virtual landslide of articles by attorneys and legal commentators issued forth in the spring and summer of 2020, discussing potential employee workplace safety claims, discrimination claims, wage and hour claims, and others, all while the COVID-19 pandemic continued to rage. *See, e.g.*, Christopher R. Dyess, *The Coming Tsunami of Employment-Related COVID-19 Litigation*, N.Y.L.J. at p. 4, Apr. 22, 2020; David E. Schwartz & Risa M. Salins, *Return to Work: Testing and Tracing?*, N.Y.L.J. at p. 3, June 5, 2020; Jeffrey S. Klein & Nicholas J. Pappas, *Challenges for Employers Reopening During the COVID-19 Pandemic*, N.Y.L.J. at p. 3, June 3, 2020; Justin T. Kelton, *Employers Should Brace for an Influx Of Disability Discrimination Lawsuits*, N.Y.L.J. at p. 4, May 26, 2020; Frances Kulka Browne & Erika Ghaly, *Employers' Options Under Employment Agreements in Light of COVID-19*, N.Y.L.J. at p. 4, May 21, 2020; Randi B. May, *Your Doors Are Open, Now What? Top 10 Tips for Employers*, N.Y.L.J. at p. 6, May 18, 2020; Debbie Kaminer, *Discrimination Against Employees Without COVID-19 Antibodies*, N.Y.L.J. at p. 6, May 5, 2020.

12 42 U.S.C. § 12112(c).

13 *Clackamas Gastroenterology Assoc., P.C. v. Wells*, 538 U.S. 440, 446-47 & n.6 (2003) (Stevens, J.).

and requires assessment of the number of employees in 20 or more weeks of the current or preceding calendar year (and has been reduced from an original number of 25 employees in 20 or more calendar weeks):

> **(4) Employee**
>
> The term "employee" means an individual employed by an employer. With respect to employment in a foreign country, such term includes an individual who is a citizen of the United States.
>
> **(5) Employer**
>
> **(A) In general**
>
> The term "employer" means a person engaged in an industry affecting commerce who has 15 or more employees for each working day in each of 20 or more calendar weeks in the current or preceding calendar year, and any agent of such person, except that, for two years following the effective date of this subchapter, an employer means a person engaged in an industry affecting commerce who has 25 or more employees for each working day in each of 20 or more calendar weeks in the current or preceding year, and any agent of such person.
>
> **(B) Exceptions**
>
> The term "employer" does not include—
>
> **(i)** the United States, a corporation wholly owned by the government of the United States, or an Indian tribe; or
>
> **(ii)** a bona fide privatc membership club (other than a labor organization) that is exempt from taxation under section 501(c) of Title 26.[14]

Should disputes arise under the ADA, such that a claim is made, employers and employees must be certain to break down the number of employees per week, to ensure that the business either was or was not a covered entity for the time period of the claim. If the number of employees cannot be verified such that the employer falls under the ADA, claims

14 42 U.S.C. § 12111(4), (5).

are dismissed.[15] The "current year" referred to is the year in which the alleged claim occurred.[16] An employment agency can, if acting as an employer, meet the definition and be sued as an employer under the ADA.[17] Furthermore, reading the cases on the matter, it appears that the 20 calendar weeks need not be consecutive for measurement purposes.[18] However, partners/shareholders of a business, those "most able to control" the operations of the business, are not included in the count for number of employees.[19]

One may ask why such a high threshold for the number of employees, considering that a good number of businesses will have less than 15 employees. The answer is that Congress made the decision "to limit the coverage of the legislation to firms with 15 or more employees . . . namely, [to ease] entry into the market and preserv[e] the competitive position of smaller firms."[20]

After being signed into law in 1990 by President George H.W. Bush, the ADA was read and interpreted more and more narrowly in application of the "terms 'substantially limits' and 'major life activity'"[21] when determining qualifying disabilities, as well as application of the ADA to those "regarded as"[22] having a disability. Congress, however, had intended for the ADA to be interpreted broadly, applying greater protections in the workplace. The "narrow interpretations resulted in the denial of the ADA's protection for many individuals with impairments that Congress

15 *Clements v. Housing Auth. of the Borough of Princeton*, 532 F.Supp.2d 700, 704-07 (D.N.J. 2007) (Wolfson, D.J.).

16 *Binns v. Primary Group, Inc.*, 23 F.Supp.2d 1363, 1366 (M.D. Fla. 1998) (Conway, D.J.).

17 *Id.*

18 *See Clements*, 532 F.Supp.2d 700; *Binns*, 23 F.Supp.2d 1363.

19 *Clackamas*, 538 U.S. at 454 (Ginsburg, J., dissenting).

20 *Id.*, at 446-47.

21 *See E.E.O.C. v. AutoZone, Inc.*, 630 F.3d 635, 641 & n.3 (7th Cir. 2010) (Hamilton, J.).

22 The "regarded as" qualification applies to those who may not have an actual disability, but who may be mistakenly perceived by others as disabled and as having an impairment limiting a major life activity, and who thereafter suffers discrimination due to being "regarded as" having a disability qualifying under the ADA. *See* 42 U.S.C. §12102(3); *Murphy v. United Parcel Serv., Inc.*, 527 U.S. 516, 521-22 (1999) (O'Connor, J.), *superseded by statute on other grounds* as noted in *Kemp v. Holder*, 610 F.3d 231, 235 (5th Cir. 2010) (per curiam); *Wooten v. Farmland Foods*, 58 F.3d 382, 385-86 (8th Cir. 1995) (Hansen, J.); *Cox v. Civista Med. Ctr.*, 16 Fed.Appx. 185 (4th Cir. 2001) (per curiam).

intended to cover under the law, such as cancer, diabetes, and epilepsy."[23] Additionally, the Supreme Court had required consideration of ameliorative or mitigating devices or effects (such as hearing aids or medications) before determining a plaintiff had a qualifying disability.[24] As a result, following a series of narrowing interpretations by the U.S. Supreme Court—in decisions including *Sutton v. United Air Lines, Inc.*[25] and *Toyota Motor Mfg., Kentucky, Inc. v. Williams*[26]—Congress passed the Americans with Disabilities Act Amendments Act (ADAAA), which was subsequently signed into law by President George W. Bush on September 25, 2008.[27] "The ADA Amendments Act provides clear direction about what 'disability' means under the ADA and how it should be interpreted so that covered individuals seeking the protection of the ADA can establish that they have a disability."[28]

New York-based ADA claims are subject to a three-year statute of limitations.[29] To state a claim for relief under the ADA, alleging discrimination on the basis of disability or perception of/regarded as disability, the

---

23 *Questions and Answers about the Department of Justice's Final Rule Implementing the ADA Amendments Act of 2008*, ADA.gov, https://www.ada.gov/regs2016/adaaa_qa.html.

24 *Kemp*, 610 F.3d at 235. Post the ADA Amendments Act, discussed *infra*, ameliorative effects or mitigating measures are not to be considered when determining disability. *See* 42 U.S.C. § 12102(4)(E).

25 527 U.S. 471 (1999) (O'Connor, J.), *overturned due to legislative action* U.S. Pub. L. 110-325 (Jan. 1, 2009).

26 534 U.S. 184 (2002) (O'Connor, J.), *overturned due to legislative action* U.S. Pub. L. 110-325 (Jan. 1, 2009).

27 *See Mercado v. Puerto Rico*, 814 F.3d 581, 589 (1st Cir. 2016) (Barron, J.); *Canavan v. City of El Paso*, 2010 WL 2228496 at *3 & n.2 (W.D. Tex. Jan. 27, 2010) (Cardone, D.J.).

28 ADA.gov, *supra*, *at* https://www.ada.gov/regs2016/adaaa_qa.html. Courts determined that the ADAAA did not apply retroactively, *see, e.g.*, *Kemp*, 610 F.3d at 236, but those determinations have less or no relevance today, more than 10 years since the ADAAA went into effect. Furthermore, "Congress indicated that the ADA Amendments Act was meant to reinstate a broad scope of protection under the ADA. Therefore, the Department's regulation retains the three-prong definition of 'disability' as: (1) a physical or mental impairment that substantially limits one or more major life activities; (2) a record (or past history) of such an impairment; or (3) being regarded as having a disability. The ADA Amendments Act regulations specify how that definition should be interpreted and applied." ADA.gov, *supra*.

29 *Purcell v. N.Y. Instit. of Tech.–Coll. of Osteopathic Med.*, 931 F.3d 59 (2d Cir. 2019) (Walker, J.) (claims against medical college under Title IX of the Education Amendments Act, Title II of the ADA, and N.Y.S. Human Rights Law; four-month statute of limitations under Article 78 of the NY CPLR was not the sole governing limitations period, given the federal claims; these cases are like personal injury actions, and thus 3-year limitations period applied).

plaintiff bears the initial burden. Thereafter the *McDonnell Douglas* burden shift is applied to ADA cases, as well.[30]

> To make out a prima facie case of employment discrimination through indirect evidence under Title I, a plaintiff must show that "1) he or she is disabled; 2) otherwise qualified for the position, with or without reasonable accommodation; 3) suffered an adverse employment decision; 4) the employer knew or had reason to know of the plaintiff's disability; and 5) the position remained open while the employer sought other applicants or the disabled individual was replaced."[31]

It is observed that the Sixth Circuit applies the five-prong test mentioned above (called the "*Monette* formulation" in Sixth Circuit caselaw).[32] However, other courts have applied a three-prong test, which may be more familiar to some, requiring the plaintiff show "(1) that he or she is an individual with a disability; (2) who was otherwise qualified to perform a job's requirements, with or without reasonable accommodation, and (3) who was discharged solely by reason of the disability" (the "*Mahon* formulation" in the Sixth Circuit).[33] Still others, such as those in New York, utilize a four-prong test: "To establish a prima facie ADA discrimination claim, a plaintiff must show that: (1) his employer is subject to the ADA; (2) he was disabled within the meaning of the ADA; (3) he was otherwise qualified to perform the essential functions of the job, with

30 *Hernandez v. Int'l Shoppes, LLC*, 100 F.Supp.3d 232, 255 (E.D.N.Y. 2015) (Weinstein, Senior D.J.) (citing *McBride v. BIC Consumer Prods. Mfg. Co., Inc.*, 583 F.3d 92, 96 (2d Cir. 2009)).

31 *Whitfield v. Tennessee*, 639 F.3d 253, 258–59 (6th Cir, 2011) (citing *Macy v. Hopkins Cnty. Sch. Bd. of Educ.*, 484 F.3d 357, 365 (6th Cir. 2007) (quoting *Monette v. Elec. Data Sys. Corp.*, 90 F.3d 1173, 1186 (6th Cir. 1996)). *See also Williams v. MTA Bus Co.*, 2020 WL 1922911 (S.D.N.Y. Apr. 20, 2020) (Freeman, M.J.) (granting summary judgment to defendant and dismissing claims under Section 504 of the Rehabilitation Act, as well as under state law, since plaintiff failed, *inter alia*, to demonstrate a material issue of fact regarding whether he was qualified for the position sought).

32 *Id.*

33 *Whitfield*, 639 F.3d at 259 (citing *Mahon v. Crowell*, 295 F.3d 585, 589 (6th Cir. 2002)).

or without reasonable accommodation; and (4) he suffered an adverse employment action because of his disability."[34]

A plaintiff must show that they were rejected from a position for which they were otherwise qualified, or the claim will fail.[35] A plaintiff must also identify the disability(s) at issue, and which qualifies them for protection, or the claim will fail.[36] Courts hold that "establishing a prima facie case 'is not a demanding burden.'… 'Courts—not juries—should deter-

34 *Hernandez*, 100 F.Supp.3d at 256 (citing *McMillan v. City of N.Y.*, 711 F.3d 120, 125 (2d Cir. 2013)). Bear in mind that the pleading threshold is reduced under ADA and Title VII claims, such that the plaintiff is not pleading a *prima facie* case, they are making a *prima facie* showing—on its face—that they can surpass the first prong of the *McDonnell Douglas* burden shift. It is a lower standard "because 'a temporary "presumption" of discriminatory motivation' is created under the first prong of the *McDonnell Douglas* analysis, [so] a plaintiff 'need only give plausible support to a minimal inference of discriminatory motivation.'" *See Vega v. Hempstead Union Free Sch. Dist.*, 801 F.3d 72, 84 (2d Cir. 2015) (Chin, J.); *Bussa v. St. John's Univ.*, 2019 WL 136641 at *2 (E.D.N.Y. Jan. 8, 2019) (Matsumoto, J.) (citing *Dooley v. JetBlue Airways Corp.*, 636 F. App'x 16, 21 (2d Cir. 2015); *Vega*, 801 F.3d at 84).

35 *See Bussa*, 2019 WL 136641; *Rios v. Dep't of Educ.*, 351 Fed.Appx. 503, 505 (2d Cir. 2009); *Sirota v. N.Y.C. Bd. of Educ.*, 283 A.D.2d 369, 370, 725 N.Y.S.2d 332, 333 (1st Dep't 2001) ("Moreover, assuming plaintiff does have a disability, her chronic absenteeism, tardiness and unsatisfactory performance evaluations establish that she was unable to perform the essential functions of her job as a special education teacher, and thus was not otherwise qualified therefor as required by the discrimination statutes…, and that defendants did not retaliate against her for requesting accommodation on account of her cancer") (citing *McLee v. Chrysler Corp.*, 109 F.3d 130, 135 (2d Cir. 1997)); *but see Leonard F. v. Israel Discount Bank of N.Y.*, 1996 WL 634860 (S.D.N.Y. Sept. 24, 1996) (Brieant, D.J.).

36 *McCarrick v. Corning, Inc.*, 2019 WL 2106506 at *2-3 (W.D.N.Y. May 14, 2019) (Geraci, C.J.).

mine whether the initial McDonnell Douglas burdens of production have been met.'"[37]

The legal standard applied on disability discrimination claims is the same, whether under federal law (ADA) or New York State law.[38] It

---

37 *Id.* at 256 (citations omitted). While the elements stated above are for an employment action, note that they are very similar to the elements needed for a claim under Title III of the ADA concerning places of public accommodation and services. *Bebry v. ALJAC LLC*, 954 F.Supp.2d 173, 177 (E.D.N.Y. 2013) (Spatt, D.J.) ("To state a claim under Title III, '[a plaintiff] must allege (1) that [he] is disabled within the meaning of the ADA; (2) that [the] defendants own, lease, or operate a place of public accommodation; and (3) that [the] defendants discriminated against [him] by denying [him] a full and equal opportunity to enjoy the services [that the] defendants provide'") (citing *Camarillo v. Carrols Corp.*, 518 F.3d 153, 156 (2d Cir. 2008)). Furthermore, a disabled patron of businesses (places of public accommodation) as "'an ADA plaintiff can establish standing to sue for injunctive relief either by demonstrating deterrence, or by demonstrating injury-in-fact coupled with an intent to return to a noncompliant facility.'... A plaintiff suing under the ADA must demonstrate that 'he personally suffered discrimination as defined by the ADA as to the encountered barriers on account of his [particular] disability.'... Indeed, to prevail on a claim for a violation of the ADA, a plaintiff must show the barrier 'interfere[d] with the plaintiff's "full and equal enjoyment" of the facility.'" *Feezor v. Patterson*, 896 F.Supp.2d 895, 900 (E.D. Cal. 2012) (Mueller, D.J.) (citing *Chapman v. Pier 1 Imports*, 631 F.3d 939, 944 (9th Cir. 2011); 42 U.S.C. § 12182(a)). There is a slight difference between the elements necessary to state a claim under Title II versus Title III. "To state a claim under Title II, a plaintiff must allege: '(1) that he is a "qualified individual with a disability;" (2) that he was "excluded from participation in or . . . denied the benefits of the services, programs, or activities of a public entity" or otherwise "discriminated [against] by such entity;" (3) "by reason of such disability."...'" *Price v. City of Ocala,* 375 F. Supp. 3d 1264, 1269 (M.D. Fla. 2019) (citing, *inter alia*, *Shotz v. Cates*, 256 F.3d 1077, 1079 (11th Cir. 2001); 42 U.S.C. § 12132). Courts also look to future injury when evaluating Title II and III claims. *See Price*, 375 F.Supp.3d at 1269-1270 ("In considering the future injury element of standing in Title III cases, district courts in this Circuit apply a four-factor test that this Court will refer to as the *Houston* factors. The *Houston* factors are: '(1) the proximity of the defendant's business to the plaintiff's residence; (2) the plaintiff's past patronage of the defendant's business; (3) the definiteness of the plaintiff's plan to return; and (4) the frequency of the plaintiff's travel near the defendant's business.'") (citing, *inter alia*, *Houston v. Marod Supermarkets, Inc.*, 733 F.3d 1323, 1328 (11th Cir. 2013)). *See also Ctr. for Indep. of Disabled, N.Y. v. Metro. Trans. Auth.*, 2020 WL 1503454 (S.D.N.Y. Mar. 30, 2020) (Daniels, D.J.), appeal filed No. 20-1433 (2d Cir. May 1, 2020) (granting defendants' motion for summary judgment and dismissing plaintiffs' Title II claim arising from alleged violation of the ADA, as well as alleged violations of the Rehabilitation Act, where plaintiffs failed, *inter alia*, to demonstrate "systematic failure" of the NYC Subway System to provide "meaningful access" to "individuals with mobility issues"; NYCHRL claims, although required to be analyzed "separately and independently from any federal and state law claims", were also dismissed because plaintiffs were not "entirely exclude[ed]" from accessing the public accommodation—the NYC Subway System).

38 *See Bebry*, 954 F.Supp.2d at 176; *McEniry v. Landi*, 84 N.Y.2d 554, 558 (1994) (Ciparick, J); *Garcia v. City Univ. of N.Y.*, 136 A.D.3d 577, 578, 26 N.Y.S.3d 36, 37 (1st Dep't 2016); *Morse v. JetBlue Airways Corp.*, 941 F.Supp.2d 274, 292 (E.D.N.Y. 2013) (Matsumoto, D.J.).

should also be recognized that while the federal Rehabilitation Act[39] was enacted before the ADA was enacted, claims under the two frameworks utilize basically the same standards.[40] Furthermore, retaliation claims under the ADA apply the same standard as those under Title VII and Section 1981, although anti-retaliation protection is recognized to be broader than anti-discrimination protection under the same statutes.[41]

Employers and employees alike should recognize that workers must be "qualifying individuals" who are able to perform the essential functions of their job with or without a reasonable accommodation or modification in order to be covered by the ADA and have standing to sue for relief

39 29 U.S.C. §§ 701, *et seq.*

40 *See Mahon v. Crowell*, 295 F.3d 585, 588–89 (6th Cir. 2002); *Natofsky v. City of N.Y.*, 921 F.3d 337 (2d Cir. 2019) (Keenan, D.J. by designation) (requiring that Rehabilitation Act claims meet the same causation standard as those under the ADA); *Butterfield v. N.Y.S.*, 1998 WL 401533 at *7 (July 15, 1998) (L. Smith, M.J.) ("The ADA, and the RHA upon which it was modeled, are very similar. Because of this similarity, we look to case law interpreting one statute to assist us in interpreting the other.... The RHA, in slightly different wording, prohibits the same type of discrimination, and defines disability in the same way, but applies only to federally funded programs") (citing *Francis v. City of Meriden*, 129 F.3d 281, 283, 284 n. 4 (2d Cir. 1997); 29 U.S.C. § 794(a); 29 U.S.C. § 706(8)(B)). *See also Williams*, 2020 WL 1922911 at *5 ("To establish a *prima facie* case of disability discrimination in employment under the Rehab Act, a plaintiff must demonstrate that (1) he or she is disabled under the Act, (2) he or she was '"otherwise qualified" for the position' sought, (3) he or she was 'excluded from the position solely because of [his or her disability],' and (4) 'the program sponsoring the position received federal funding.'... More specifically, where a Rehab Act claim for employment discrimination turns on an alleged failure to provide a reasonable accommodation, a plaintiff must demonstrate that (1) he or she is disabled; (2) the employer was on notice of his or her disability; (3) 'with reasonable accommodation, plaintiff could perform the essential functions of the job at issue'; and (4) the employer has refused to provide a reasonable accommodation.... The same prima facie requirements apply to claims of failure to accommodate brought pursuant to the NYSHRL or NYCHRL.... The NYSHRL is interpreted coextensively with the Rehab Act,... and, although it has been held that 'claims under the [NYCHRL] must be given "an independent liberal construction,"'... courts in this Circuit have nonetheless continued to apply the *McDonnell Douglas* burden-shifting framework to claims under the NYCHRL") (citations omitted).

41 *See Sosa v. N.Y.C. Dep't of Educ.*, 368 F.Supp.3d 489 (E.D.N.Y. 2019) (Chen, D.J.); *Flowers v. So. Reg. Physician Servs. Inc.*, 247 F.3d 229, 234 (5th Cir. 2001) (King, C.J.). However, "[t]o survive a motion to dismiss, a complaint for retaliation under the ADA must allege facts plausibly showing that: (1) the plaintiff participated in a protected activity; (2) the defendant knew of the protected activity; (3) an adverse employment action; and (4) a causal connection between the protected activity and the adverse employment action." *Durant v. Friends of Crown Heights Educ. Ctrs, Inc.*, 2020 WL 1957449 at *4 (E.D.N.Y. Apr. 23, 2020) (Cogan, D.J.) (citing *Treglia v. Town of Manlius*, 313 F.3d 713, 719 (2d Cir. 2002) (dismissing retaliation claim under ADA, but allowing ADA discrimination claim to survive motion to dismiss).

under Title I,[42] and the employer and employee must engage in the "Interactive Process." There is a lot to unpack in that one sentence: What are the essential functions of a job? What is a reasonable accommodation or modification? What is the "Interactive Process?" Let's address each in order.

When it comes to the "essential functions" of one's job, the statute provides that the term impacts the determination of a "qualified individual" requiring protection under the Act.

> The term "qualified individual" means an individual who, with or without reasonable accommodation, can perform the essential functions of the employment position that such individual holds or desires. For the purposes of this subchapter, consideration shall be given to the employer's judgment as to what functions of a job are essential, and if an employer has prepared a written description before advertising or interviewing applicants for the job, this description shall be considered evidence of the essential functions of the job.[43]

The essential functions of a person's job, as one might expect, are not tangential duties that someone might perform once in a while or which someone might be asked to perform on a specific occasion. No, the essential functions of the job are those that in essence define the job or position and are integral to it.[44] Therefore, essential functions are determined on a case-by-case basis, and it is important to consider what the employer considers an essential function, and what, if anything, is mentioned in the job description created by the employer for the position[45] (and a knowledgeable employer, recalling the discussion of paperwork and policies in Chapter 5, *supra*, will have a documented policy that includes specific job descriptions).

---

42 *See Weyer v. Twentieth Century Fox Film Corp.*, 198 F.3d 1104, 1108-1109, 1112 (9th Cir. 2000) (Kleinfeld, J.) (also noting that needing to be a "qualifying individual" for Title I relief in the employment context is an intentional distinction in the statute, since Title III applying to public accommodations does not require a plaintiff to be a "qualifying individual" but rather just "any 'individual'").

43 42 U.S.C. § 12111(8).

44 *See Heise v. Genuine Parts Co.*, 900 F.Supp. 1137, 1152 (D. Minn. 1995) (Doty, D.J.); *White v. York Intern. Corp.*, 45 F.3d 357, 361-62 (10th Cir. 1995) (Anderson, J.) (citing *Chandler v. City of Dallas*, 2 F.3d 1385 (5th Cir. 1993), *cert. denied*, 511 U.S. 1011 (1994)).

45 *Id.*

Once it is determined that a disability exists, the employer and employee then must evaluate whether a reasonable accommodation exists to permit the employee to perform essential functions, thus advancing the determination concerning whether they are a qualifying individual under the Act. A reasonable accommodation is defined by statute as:

> **(9) Reasonable accommodation**
>
> The term "reasonable accommodation" may include—
>
> **(A)** making existing facilities used by employees readily accessible to and usable by individuals with disabilities; and
>
> **(B)** job restructuring, part-time or modified work schedules, reassignment to a vacant position, acquisition or modification of equipment or devices, appropriate adjustment or modifications of examinations, training materials or policies, the provision of qualified readers or interpreters, and other similar accommodations for individuals with disabilities.[46]

Reasonable accommodation is further defined by the EEOC as:

> any change or adjustment to a job or work environment that permits a qualified applicant or employee with a disability to participate in the job application process, to perform the essential functions of a job, or to enjoy benefits and privileges of employment equal to those enjoyed by employees without disabilities. For example, reasonable accommodation may include:

- acquiring or modifying equipment or devices,
- job restructuring,
- part-time or modified work schedules,
- reassignment to a vacant position,
- adjusting or modifying examinations, training materials or policies,

46 42 U.S.C. § 12111(9).

- providing readers and interpreters, and
- making the workplace readily accessible to and usable by people with disabilities.

> Reasonable accommodation also must be made to enable an individual with a disability to participate in the application process, and to enjoy benefits and privileges of employment equal to those available to other employees.[47]

Such accommodations may include protections for those employees suffering from depression.[48]

A reasonable modification is sometimes included under the heading of "reasonable accommodation," though on occasion it refers to separate items. A reasonable modification may refer to a physical alteration or construction affecting a dwelling/housing, building or workplace, while a reasonable accommodation may refer to a change in work conditions, job assignment, duties, or hours. However, despite the fact that Titles I, II and III of the ADA utilize one term or the other, there is truly no fundamental or functional difference between modification and accommodation, and they may be used interchangeably.[49]

In situations where an employee is unable to perform essential functions of a position, even with a reasonable accommodation, they are not a qualified person for a particular position, and there is no protection for them under the ADA.[50] That includes individuals who cannot complete or

---

47 *What Are My Obligations to Provide Reasonable Accommodations?*, U.S. EEOC, https://www.eeoc.gov/eeoc/publications/ada17.cfm.

48 *See* Klein & Pappas, *Reasonable Accommodations for Employees Suffering from Depression*, N.Y.L.J. at p. 3, Dec. 5, 2018.

49 *See Higgins v. Comm'n, Soc. Sec. Admin.*, 898 F.3d 793, 796 (8th Cir. 2018) (Smith, C.J.); *Holcomb v. Comm'n of Soc. Sec.*, 2019 WL 1102250 at *10 (N.D. Ohio Jan. 14, 2019) (Ruiz, M.J.); *Heinzl v. Cracker Barrel Old Country Stores, Inc.*, 2016 WL 2347367 at *21 (W.D. Pa. Jan. 27, 2016) (Mitchell, M.J.); *Swenson v. Lincoln Cty. Sch. Dist. No. 2*, 260 F.Supp.2d 1136, 1144 & n.10 (D. Wyo. 2003) (Brimmer, D.J.); *Powers v. MJB Acquisition Corp.*, 993 F.Supp. 861, 868 (D. Wyo. 1998) (Brimmer, D.J.). *But cf. Wygle v. Saul*, 2020 WL 3120352 (N.D. Iowa Feb. 27, 2020) (Roberts, M.J.) (distinguishing *Higgins*).

50 *See Weyer*, 198 F.3d at 1108-1109, 1112.

are prevented from completing the essential functions specifically because of the disability they have, which cannot be accommodated reasonably.[51]

Keep in mind that the law does not require an employer or business to accommodate a disabled individual at all costs. Rather, the accommodation must be "reasonable." That word is a term of art that is intentionally and specifically used in the above discussion. If the accommodation sought under any Title of the ADA is not reasonable due to "undue burden" or "undue hardship" created[52] or, say, because in the employment context under Title I an employee seeks a work-from-home accommodation when regular attendance in the workplace is essential, then the employer or business is not required to consider or provide the accommodation at issue.[53]

Finally, when an employee approaches the employer's representative concerning a qualifying disability, or when the employer believes that an employee has a qualifying disability that concerns the workplace, the employer and employee must engage in what is called the "interactive process." The interactive process is required by law and involves discussions between the employer and employee concerning disability and reasonable accommodations. Courts have held, however, that technically

> [a]lthough the ADA "envisions an 'interactive process' by which employers and employees work together to assess whether an employee's disability can be reasonably accommodated"... an "employer's failure to engage in a sufficient interactive process does not form the basis

---

51 *See Brown v. Milwaukee Bd. of Sch. Dir.*, 855 F.3d 818 (7th Cir. 2017) (Hamilton, J.); *Kieffer v. CPR Restoration & Cleaning Service, LLC*, 200 F.Supp.3d 520 (E.D. Pa. 2016) (Beetlestone, D.J.), *aff'd* 733 Fed.Appx. 632 (3d Cir. 2018) (Roth, J).

52 *See McGann v. Cinemark USA, Inc.*, 873 F.3d 218 (3d Cir. 2017) (Restrepo, J.) (Chief Magistrate Judge of the U.S. District Court, on remand, was to consider whether provision of tactile interpreter for movie theatre patron presented undue burden (hardship) prior to permitting defendant to prevail on argument that accommodation requested was unreasonable).

53 *Samper v. Providence St. Vincent Med. Ctr.*, 675 F.3d 1233 (9th Cir. 2012) (McKeown, J) (regular attendance at work was essential for neo-natal nurse, such that absences from work and unplanned absences accommodation were not reasonable; grant of employer's motion to dismiss ADA claim affirmed); *see also* 42 U.S.C. § 12111(10) ("(10) Undue hardship (A) In general The term "undue hardship" means an action requiring significant difficulty or expense, when considered in light of the factors set forth in subparagraph (B)...." Specific factors to be considered thereafter spelled out in subparagraph B thereof); 42 U.S.C. § 12182(b)(2)(A)(iii); *When Does a Reasonable Accommodation Become An Undue Hardship?*, U.S. EEOC, https://www.eeoc.gov/eeoc/publications/ada17.cfm.

> of a claim under the ADA and evidence thereof does not allow a plaintiff to avoid summary judgment unless [he or] she also establishes that, at least with the aid of some identified accommodation, [he or] she was qualified for the position at issue."[54]

Employers beware, though, because while it may appear from the above that you are free to refuse an interactive process unless plaintiff can meet certain requirements, it has also been held by courts that "[n]evertheless, 'an employer's failure to engage in a good faith interactive process can be introduced as evidence tending to show disability discrimination, and that "the employer has refused to make [a reasonable] accommodation,"'"[55] and defendants have lost motions for summary judgment due to the existence of material issues of fact regarding whether a proper interactive process was utilized.[56] It may be better, at the end of the day, to hold an interactive process, and document the process in accurate and contemporaneous notes for potential later use.

---

54 *Kalola v. Int'l Bus. Mach. Corp.*, 2017 WL 3394115 at *14 (S.D.N.Y. Feb. 28, 2017) (L. Smith, M.J.), *adopted* 2017 WL 3381896 (S.D.N.Y. Aug. 4, 2017) (Briccetti, D.J.), *appeal dismissed* 2018 WL 894064 (2d Cir. Jan. 24, 2018) (citing *Sheng v. M&T Bank Corp.*, 2017 WL 443641 at *6 (2d Cir. Feb. 2, 2017); *McBride v. BIC Consumer Prods. Mfg. Co., Inc.*, 583 F.3d 92, 97, 99 (2d Cir. 2009)). *But see* N.Y.C. Admin. Code §§ 8-101 to 8-131, as amended by Local Law 59 of 2018, whereby the New York City Council made failure to engage in a proper interactive process a new stand-alone claim under the New York City Human Rights Law.

55 *Kalola v. Int'l Bus. Mach. Corp.*, 2017 WL 3394115 at *15.

56 *See Hosking v. Memorial Sloan–Kettering Cancer Ctr.*, 126 N.Y.S.3d 98, 101–03 (Sup. Ct. App. Div. 1st Dep't June 18, 2020) (Acosta, P.J.) (citing and discussing, *inter alia*, N.Y.C. Local Law 59 of 2018; also noting a distinction between New York State and New York City law: "Notably, the State and City HRL define 'disability' in the employment context differently. The State HRL limits the term to 'disabilities which, upon the provision of reasonable accommodations, do not prevent the complainant from performing in a reasonable manner the activities involved in the job or occupation ... held'... 'Reasonable accommodation,' in turn, means actions which permit an employee or prospective employee with a disability 'to perform in a reasonable manner the activities involved in the job or occupation sought or held and include, but are not limited to, provision of an accessible worksite, acquisition or modification of equipment, ... [or] job restructuring and modified work schedules,' with the additional proviso that the accommodation does 'not impose an undue hardship on the business, program or enterprise of the entity from which action is requested'... In contrast to the State HRL, 'the City HRL's definition of "disability" does not include "reasonable accommodation" or the ability to perform a job in a reasonable manner. Rather, the City HRL defines "disability" solely in terms of impairments'.... The City HRL shifts the burden to the employer to show as an 'affirmative defense that the person aggrieved by the alleged discriminatory practice could not, with reasonable accommodation, satisfy the essential requisites of the job ... provided that the disability is known or should have been known by the [employer]'....Moreover, such 'reasonable accommodation' should not 'cause undue hardship in the conduct of the [employer's] business'") (citing, *inter alia*, N.Y. Exec. Law § 292(21), (21-e); *Romanello v. Intesa Sanpaolo, S.p.A.*, 22 N.Y.3d 881, 885, 998 N.E.2d 1050 (2013); N.Y.C. Admin. Code §§ 8-102, 8–107(15)(b)).

If the interactive process once engaged in does not result in a resolution of the matter between employer and employee (or if the employer simply rejects any request by the employee out of hand during the process without consideration), the result may be a claim of failure to accommodate. But this does not necessarily mean plaintiff will prevail because:

> "[t]o establish a *prima facie* case of discrimination based on failure to accommodate, a plaintiff must establish that (1) he [or she] is a person with a disability; (2) defendant had notice of his [or her] disability; (3) plaintiff could perform the essential functions of the job at issue with reasonable accommodation; and (4) defendant refused to make such accommodations.". . . "A claim based on a failure to make reasonable accommodations does not require the plaintiff to show a discriminatory animus.". . . "Rather, it is sufficient to establish that a covered entity failed to fulfill its affirmative duty to make a reasonable accommodation for the known physical or mental limitations of a disabled employee."[57]

Be aware, there is no legal requirement that an employer create or even identify a position for an employee.[58] The employee will have to identify a reasonable accommodation allowing them to perform essential job functions, or identify a position that exists and is vacant at the time the accommodation is sought, for which the plaintiff is qualified and to which the plaintiff could be assigned by the employer.[59] Absent that, the ADA claim will fail.[60] However, "[t]he scope of the interactive process required is not defined in detail by the statutes, regulations, or case law, but is generally understood to mean that at a minimum, the employer must engage in an informal conversation with the employee to uncover 'potential reasonable

57 *Kalola*, 2017 WL 3394115 at *14 (citing *Howard v. United Parcel Serv., Inc.*, 101 F.Supp.3d 343, 352 (S.D.N.Y. 2015) (citing *Graves v. Finch Pruyn & Co., Inc.*, 457 F.3d 181, 184 (2d Cir. 2006)); *Craddock v. Little Flower Children & Family Servs. of N.Y.*, 2016 WL 755631 at *10 (E.D.N.Y. Feb. 25, 2016)).

58 *Kalola*, 2017 WL 3394115 at *15.

59 *Id.* (citing cases).

60 *See Schmeichel v. Installed Bldg. Prods., LLC*, 2018 WL 6171750 (W.D.N.Y. Nov. 26, 2018) (Geraci, C.J.). Additionally, "'[t]he plaintiff bears the burdens of both production and persuasion as to the existence of some accommodation that would allow [him or] her to perform the essential functions of [his or] her employment, including the existence of a vacant position for which [he or] she is qualified.'" *Kalola*, 2017 WL 3394115 at *7-*8 (citing *McBride*, 583 F.3d at 97).

accommodations' that could address the employee's needs."[61] Note that here, again, an employer might also show, as a defense, that the requested accommodation(s) "would impose an undue hardship,"[62] if that is indeed the case. Simply failing to accommodate without a legitimate reason or hardship, when plaintiff otherwise meets his or her burden of identifying a vacant position for which they are qualified, would smack of discriminatory animus and demonstrate a lack of respect for diversity and inclusion in such workplace.

Thus, given the guidance of the statutes, regulations and caselaw, the employer and employee should discuss the needs of the employer and employee, and what if any reasonable accommodation(s) could allow the employee to continue to perform his or her essential job functions. If the employer fails to engage in the interactive process, and thereafter discharges the employee by stating that the employer has no jobs that the employee could continue to perform, the employee might use that as a basis to show discriminatory animus in a discrimination lawsuit. If the employee refuses the interactive process, and states that no accommodation is necessary, the employer should document everything (see "The Importance of Policies and Paperwork/Records," Chapter 5, *supra*). If the employee does not perform essential job functions as required, is a danger to others, or commits misconduct, the employer, upon properly documenting all issues, may be able to discharge the employee.

Training of employees and supervisors is of vital importance in the workplace. Supervisors and decision-makers must be aware that their decisions and liability for the employer hinge on how they address known conditions. This will not necessarily excuse failure to engage in the interactive process, however. Simply put: decisions must be made in a legal, non-discriminatory, non-pretextual way. Additionally, an important point to remember is that

61 *Kahriman v. Wal–Mart Stores, Inc.*, 115 F.Supp.3d 153, 162 (D. Mass. 2015) (Woodlock, D.J.) (citing *Tobin v. Liberty Mut. Ins. Co.*, 433 F.3d 100, 109 (1st Cir. 2005); *EEOC v. Kohl's Dep't Stores Inc.*, 774 F.3d 127, 132 n.4 (1st Cir. 2014) ("an employer's participation in the interactive process [is not] an absolute requirement under the ADA"; rather, employer must "initiate... a dialogue" with employee, and court will review adequacy "on a case-by-case-basis" (citation omitted); 29 C.F.R. § 1630.2(o)(3) ("This process should identify the precise limitations resulting from the disability and potential reasonable accommodations that could overcome those limitations")).

62 *Morse v. JetBlue Airways Corp.*, 941 F.Supp.2d 274, 292 (E.D.N.Y. 2013) (internal quotation marks omitted) (citing *Jackan v. N.Y.S. Dep't of Labor*, 205 F.3d 562, 566 (2d Cir.2000); 42 U.S.C. § 12112(b)(5)(A)).

> [u]nder Second Circuit law, a plaintiff alleging discrimination on account of his protected status must offer evidence that a decision-maker was personally aware of his protected status to establish a prima facie case of discrimination.... In order to avoid summary judgment, therefore, Plaintiff must do more than offer evidence that someone at HR knew he had [protected status] before he was suspended and terminated. He must offer some evidence that either Ms. [ ] or Ms. [ ] knew he had [the particular protected status/condition] before they decided to suspend him, and that either Ms. [ ], Ms. [ ], or Mr. [ ] knew he had [the particular protected status/condition] before they decided to terminate him.[63]

Additionally, employers should recognize that the actions—or inaction—of management can result in employees believing it acceptable to belittle, make fun of or become cruel toward a co-worker with a qualifying disability. In such circumstances, when the activities become pervasive, courts have recognized that plaintiffs may maintain a claim of hostile work environment under the ADA. In the case of *Fox v. Costco Wholesale Corporation*,[64] the Second Circuit, for the first time, joined sister courts in just such a holding. Reversing the district court's holding that granted employer defendant's summary judgment motion on the hostile work environment claim, the court reiterated the following, from plaintiff's testimony in the matter:

> Fox testified that once he began his position as an Assistant Cashier, other Costco employees mocked him for his Tourette's and OCD. In his deposition, Fox described how certain Costco employees would make "hut-hut-hike" remarks to mimic Fox's verbal and physical tics. Fox also testified that these comments "were audible to the managers of the Holbrook warehouse from their position on the warehouse's podium," and "happened in plain

63 *Murray v. Cerebal Palsy Assoc. of N.Y., Inc.*, 2018 WL 264112 at *7 S.D.N.Y. Jan. 2, 2018) (Ramos, D.J.) (citing *Woodman v. WWOR-TV, Inc.*, 411 F.3d 69, 87–88 (2d Cir. 2005) ("To defeat summary judgment, [plaintiff] was obliged to do more than produce evidence that someone at [the employer] knew her age. She was obliged to offer evidence indicating that persons who actually participated in her termination decision had such knowledge"); *Lambert v. McCann Erickson*, 543 F.Supp.2d 265, 278 n.12 (S.D.N.Y. 2008) ("[A] plaintiff must offer evidence that a decision-maker was aware of her protected status to establish a prima facie case of discrimination")).

64 918 F.3d 65 (2d Cir. 2019) (Hall, J.).

> view of the Supervisors and the Front End Managers and nothing was ever said." . . . Fox testified further that these types of comments happened for "months and months" and "whenever" he would experience tics.[65]

Thereafter, the court stated that it joined its sister Circuits in explicitly recognizing that a plaintiff can maintain a cognizable hostile work environment claim pursuant to the protections of the ADA.[66] Just as under Title VII, "[t]o prevail on a hostile work environment claim, [plaintiff] must show '(1) that the harassment was "sufficiently severe or pervasive to alter the conditions of [his] employment and create an abusive working environment," and (2) that a specific basis exists for imputing the objectionable conduct to the employer.'"[67] In *Fox*, plaintiff introduced evidence sufficient to warrant a remand to the district court on the hostile work environment claim.

Observe that the protections provided under the ADA in the employment field very much follow a parabolic curve. If the employee has no disability, they are on the one end of the spectrum, having no claim or protection under the ADA. However, if the employee has a disability such that no reasonable accommodation will enable the employee to perform the essential functions of their job, they fall on the other end of the spectrum, and are outside of the protection of the ADA. Thus, protected employees fall under the "bell" of the parabolic curve.

It is worth the reminder that the ADA and state disability laws do not only apply in the employment context. Those who need accommodations for public services, such as emotional support animals, also fall under the laws, although agencies may seek to create reasonable limitations.[68] Others protected include those with disabilities utilizing the services of places of public accommodation. For instance, an individual with Crohn's dis-

---

65 *Id.* at 70 (omitting citations).

66 *Id.* at 73-74 (citing *Lanman v. Johnson Cty.*, 393 F.3d 1151, 1155–56 (10th Cir. 2004); *Shaver v. Indep. Stave Co.*, 350 F.3d 716, 720 (8th Cir. 2003); *Flowers v. S. Reg'l Physician Servs., Inc.*, 247 F.3d 229, 232–35 (5th Cir. 2001); *Fox v. Gen. Motors Corp.*, 247 F.3d 169, 175–76 (4th Cir. 2001)).

67 *Id.* at 74 (citations omitted).

68 *See* Mina Kaji, David Kerley & Samantha Spitz, *Feds Release New Airline Guidance on Emotional Support Animals*, ABC News, Aug. 9, 2019, https://abcnews.go.com/Politics/feds-release-airline-guidance-emotional-support-animals/story?id=64883549.

ease (an inflammatory bowel disease) is permitted under the laws of some states to demand access to employee-only bathrooms in a business during an emergency situation.[69] Finally, it is not only one's own qualifying disability that may result in protection under, or a claim pursuant to, the ADA. "Associational discrimination" is another cognizable claim, which arises from adverse action taken against an individual because of their relationship or association with, or support of claims made by, another who has a known disability.[70]

[6.2] III. FAMILY AND MEDICAL LEAVE ACT (FMLA) AND NEW YORK PAID LEAVE

[6.3] A. FMLA

When Congress enacted the FMLA, as with many statutes, it provided a series of findings, as well as the purposes of the Act. Thus, according to Congress:

> [i]t is the purpose of this Act—
>
> (1) to balance the demands of the workplace with the needs of families, to promote the stability and economic security of families, and to promote national interests in preserving family integrity;
>
> (2) to entitle employees to take reasonable leave for medical reasons, for the birth or adoption of a child, and for the care of a child, spouse, or parent who has a serious health condition;

---

69 *See* Debra Cassens Weiss, *Lawyer with Crohn's Disease Goes Public with Starbucks Story to Publicize Bathroom-Access Laws*, ABA Journal, Aug. 22, 2019, http://www.abajournal.com/news/article/lawyer-with-crohns-disease-goes-public-with-starbucks-story-to-publicize-bathroom-access-law.

70 *Simmons v. Woodycrest Ctr. for Human Dev., Inc.*, 2011 WL 855942 at *3 (S.D.N.Y. Mar. 9, 2011) (Rakoff, D.J.) ("in order to establish any claim for associational discrimination, [plaintiff] must demonstrate, *inter alia* that: (1) at the time of [plaintiff's] termination, [defendant] knew she had a relative or associate with a disability; and (2) that [plaintiff's] termination occurred under circumstances raising a reasonable inference that the disability of the relative or associate was a determining factor in the termination") (citing *Dollinger v. State Ins. Fund*, 44 F.Supp.2d 467 (N.D.N.Y. 1999); 42 U.S.C. § 12112(b)(4)). *See* 42 U.S.C. § 12112(b)(4) ("As used in subsection (a), the term 'discriminate against a qualified individual on the basis of disability' includes— . . . (4) excluding or otherwise denying equal jobs or benefits to a qualified individual because of the known disability of an individual with whom the qualified individual is known to have a relationship or association").

> (3) to accomplish the purposes described in paragraphs (1) and (2) in a manner that accommodates the legitimate interests of employers;
>
> (4) to accomplish the purposes described in paragraphs (1) and (2) in a manner that, consistent with the Equal Protection Clause of the Fourteenth Amendment, minimizes the potential for employment discrimination on the basis of sex by ensuring generally that leave is available for eligible medical reasons (including maternity-related disability) and for compelling family reasons, on a gender-neutral basis; and
>
> (5) to promote the goal of equal employment opportunity for women and men, pursuant to such clause.[71]

According to the United States Department of Labor, the federal law known as the Family and Medical Leave Act:

> applies to all:

- public agencies, including local, State, and Federal employers, and local education agencies (schools); and
- private sector employers who employ 50 or more employees for at least 20 workweeks in the current or preceding calendar year—including joint employers and successors of covered employers.[72]

Furthermore,

> [i]n order to be eligible to take leave under the FMLA, an employee must:

- work for a covered employer;
- have worked 1,250 hours during the 12 months prior to the start of leave; (special hours of service rules apply to airline flight crew members)

71 29 U.S.C. § 2601(b).

72 *FMLA Frequently Asked Questions*, U.S. Dep't of Labor, https://www.dol.gov/whd/fmla/fmla-faqs.htm#2.

- work at a location where the employer has 50 or more employees within 75 miles; and
- have worked for the employer for 12 months. The 12 months of employment are not required to be consecutive in order for the employee to qualify for FMLA leave. In general, only employment within seven years is counted unless the break in service is (1) due to an employee's fulfillment of military obligations, or (2) governed by a collective bargaining agreement or other written agreement.[73]

Employees and employers who may otherwise qualify under FMLA should take great care in calculating the requisite hours of work time. Paid leave and unpaid leave do not count in the 1,250 hours calculation for eligibility.[74]

FMLA provides not only entitlement to leave for a qualifying employee, it also contains return to work protections. The statute specifically provides:

> **Restoration to position**
>
> **(1) In general**
>
> Except as provided in subsection (b), any eligible employee who takes leave under section 2612 of this title for the intended purpose of the leave shall be entitled, on return from such leave—
>
> **(A)** to be restored by the employer to the position of employment held by the employee when the leave commenced; or

---

73 *Id.* The FMLA, where applicable, is, of course, in addition to any other leave policies an employer may institute, such as parental leave policies, or generous vacation or sick leave policies. *See, e.g.,* Dylan Jackson, *Are Parental Leave Policies Innovative or Just Expected Now*, N.Y.L.J. at p. 5, Aug. 9, 2019. But the United States is still lagging when it comes to paid sick leave for most workers in general. *See* Chris Lu, M. Patricia Smith & David Weil, *Why Americans Don't Know About Their Right to Paid Sick Leave / Opinion*, Newsweek, May 4, 2020, https://www.newsweek.com/why-americans-dont-know-about-their-right-paid-sick-leave-opinion-1501532.

74 *Id.*

> **(B)** to be restored to an equivalent position with equivalent employment benefits, pay, and other terms and conditions of employment.[75]

It is vital for employers and employees to understand that the leave is "protected," and when the leave period is over an employee must be allowed to return to their same job (or a comparable job) with the same pay and benefits, and seniority, so long as the employee can perform the essential functions with or without a reasonable accommodation.[76] There are some exceptions to the return to work provisions, and they are spelled out in the statute.[77] The protections and provisions of the ADA and New York Human Rights Law also still apply.

Although FMLA leave is unpaid, an employer may require, an employee may elect, or they may agree, that the employee will use any accrued paid time off—sick, vacation, or personal time—during the FMLA period; and if there is less accrued paid time off than the qualifying leave period, the unpaid time under FMLA will make up the difference. This is not for avoidance of FMLA obligations, it is simply an allowance to use a sequence of paid leave followed by FMLA leave.[78] This will often be governed by an employer's applicable policy and should be applied equally to all employees. Keep in mind, though, that the employee's leave, if under FMLA, is still protected leave, even if paid time off is used during the leave period.[79]

---

75 29 U.S.C. § 2614.

76 *FMLA Frequently Asked Questions*, U.S. Dep't of Labor, https://www.dol.gov/whd/fmla/fmlafaqs.htm#2 ("On return from FMLA leave (whether after a block of leave or an instance of intermittent leave), the FMLA requires that the employer return the employee to the same job, or one that is nearly identical (equivalent). If not returned to the same job, a nearly identical job must: offer the same shift or general work schedule, and be at a geographically proximate worksite (i.e., one that does not involve a significant increase in commuting time or distance); involve the same or substantially similar duties, responsibilities, and status; include the same general level of skill, effort, responsibility and authority; offer identical pay, including equivalent premium pay, overtime and bonus opportunities, profit-sharing, or other payments, and any unconditional pay increases that occurred during FMLA leave; and offer identical benefits (such as life insurance, health insurance, disability insurance, sick leave, vacation, educational benefits, pensions, etc.)").

77 29 U.S.C. § 2614(b) ("Exemption concerning certain highly compensated employees").

78 *Strickland v. Water Works & Sewer Bd. of City of Birmingham*, 239 F.3d 1199, 1204 (11th Cir. 2001) (Tjoflat, J.); *Crites v. City of Haysville*, 2018 WL 2236855 at *10 (D. Kan. May 16, 2018) (Broomes, D.J.); 29 C.F.R. § 825.207.

79 *See Crites*, 2018 WL 2236855 at *10.

According to the U.S. Department of Labor:

> A covered employer must grant an eligible employee up to a total of 12 workweeks of unpaid, job-protected leave in a 12 month period for one or more of the following reasons:

- for the birth of a son or daughter, and to bond with the newborn child;
- for the placement with the employee of a child for adoption or foster care, and to bond with that child;
- to care for an immediate family member (spouse, child, or parent – but not a parent "in-law") with a serious health condition;
- to take medical leave when the employee is unable to work because of a serious health condition; or
- for qualifying exigencies arising out of the fact that the employee's spouse, son, daughter, or parent is on covered active duty or call to covered active duty status as a member of the National Guard, Reserves, or Regular Armed Forces.

> The FMLA also allows eligible employees to take up to 26 workweeks of unpaid, job-protected leave in a "single 12-month period" to care for a covered servicemember with a serious injury or illness.[80]

An employee who has recurrent issues, or requires periodic medical care, or has periodic family matters, all of which otherwise qualify for FMLA leave, may then qualify for what is known as intermittent leave under the FMLA, which means that the equivalent of up to 12 workweeks of leave may be taken periodically, rather than all at once.[81]

The employee must notify the employer, and complete and return appropriate and specific paperwork and forms, with medical physician

80 *FMLA Frequently Asked Questions*, U.S. Dep't of Labor, https://www.dol.gov/whd/fmla/fmla-faqs.htm#11.

81 29 U.S.C. § 2612 (held unconstitutional as to suits against States, in violation of sovereign immunity, by *Coleman v. Court of Appeals of Maryland*, 566 U.S. 30 (2012) (Kennedy, J.)), and as amended by Families First Coronavirus Response Act (FFCRA), PL 116-127, March 18, 2020, 134 Stat 178 (effective until December 31, 2020).

documentation, to request FMLA leave.[82] If the reason and documentation provided is not sufficient or not qualifying, the leave may be denied. The employer bears the ultimate decision whether to approve the leave, and can request that the employee furnish necessary information related thereto within a reasonable time before the leave requested (or within days after, if there is an unforeseen or sudden need for leave).[83] However, the employee bears the burden of demonstrating entitlement to leave, and providing necessary information, including anticipated timing and duration of qualifying condition and leave, as part of the Certification for FMLA. Absent that, the employee has not sufficiently submitted for FMLA leave, and there is no claim if denied.[84] The employer should be cautious, though, and ensure they request all possible information to make a determination.[85] The employer is also permitted to request recertification by an employee who is out on leave, but generally not more often than every 30 days.[86]

If, however, the employer unlawfully prevents an employee from taking leave, or retaliates against an employee on the basis of their qualified leave, that will provide the employee with claims for interference with FMLA rights.[87] When such claims arise, the burden on the plaintiff differs

---

82 *FMLA Frequently Asked Questions, Employee notice*, U.S. Dep't of Labor, https://www.dol.gov/whd/fmla/fmla-faqs.htm#11.

83 *See* 29 U.S.C. § 2613(a); 29 C.F.R. § 825.305(a).

84 *See Horsting v. St. John's Riverside Hosp.*, 2018 WL 1918617 at *4–5 (S.D.N.Y. Apr. 18, 2018) (Seibel, D.J.).

85 *See Coutard v. Mun. Credit Union*, 848 F.3d 102 (2d Cir. 2017) (Kearse, J.) (employer has obligation to obtain/request more information if needed; denial of FMLA leave when lack of full information existed and was not requested by employer before decision made, could subject employer to liability).

86 *Graham v. BlueCross BlueShield of Tennessee, Inc.*, 521 Fed.Appx. 419, 423 (6th Cir. 2013) (Stranch, J.); *Geromanos v. Columbia Univ.*, 322 F.Supp.2d 420, 431 (S.D.N.Y. 2004) (McMahon, D.J.); 29 U.S.C. § 2613; 29 C.F.R. § 825.308(a). However, certain factors, such as a significant change in circumstances or a request for extension of leave by the employee (if eligible and time remaining), might result in a recertification request being made more frequently than every 30 days. *See Geromanos*, 322 F.Supp.2d at 431; *Jurczyk v. Coxcom, LLC*, 191 F.Supp.3d 1256, 1264 (N.D. Okla. 2016) (Kern, D.J.); 29 C.F.R. § 825.308(c).

87 *See* 29 U.S.C. §§ 2615, 2617; *Bearley v. Friendly Ice Cream Corp.*, 322 F.Supp.2d 563, 570-71 (M.D. Pa. 2004) (Caputo, D.J.) (identifying two types of claims under FMLA; "Courts have recognized two distinct causes of action under the [FMLA].... First, a plaintiff may pursue recovery under an 'interference' theory. This claim arises under 29 U.S.C. § 2615(a)(1), which makes it unlawful for an employer 'to interfere with, restrain, or deny' an employee's rights under the FMLA.... The second type of recovery under the FMLA is the 'retaliation' theory. This claim arises under 29 U.S.C. § 2615(a)(2), which makes it unlawful for an employer to discriminate against an employee who has taken FMLA leave.") (some citations omitted).

depending on the claim. For an FMLA interference claim, "[t]o plead a *prima facie* case for FMLA interference, a plaintiff must plausibly plead that: (1) he is an eligible employee under the FMLA, (2) the defendant is an employer as defined by the FMLA, (3) he was entitled to leave under the FMLA, (4) he gave notice to the defendant of his intention to take leave, and (5) he was denied benefits to which he was entitled under the FMLA."[88] Additionally, "it is plaintiff's burden to demonstrate that she was entitled to a benefit under the FMLA, but was denied that entitlement. . . . The FMLA entitles eligible employees to reinstatement at the end of their FMLA leave to the position held before taking leave or an equivalent position. . . . If the plaintiff meets this burden, then it is defendant's burden to demonstrate that she would have been denied reinstatement even if she had not taken FMLA leave."[89]

On the other hand, for a FMLA retaliation claim plaintiff can either prove their case by direct evidence, or by indirect/circumstantial evidence under application of the *McDonnell Douglas* burden shift.[90] The plaintiff bears the following burden:

> To establish a prima facie case of retaliation under the FMLA, a plaintiff must show: (1) she engaged in a statutorily protected activity; (2) she suffered an adverse employment action; and (3) a causal connection exists between the adverse action and Plaintiff's exercise of her FMLA rights…. After establishing a prima facie case, the burden shifts to the employer to articulate a legitimate, nondiscriminatory reason for its adverse employment action…. If the employer offers a legitimate, nondiscrim-

88 *Horsting*, 2018 WL 1918617 at *4 (citing, *inter alia*, *Graziadio v. Culinary Inst. of Am.*, 817 F.3d 415, 424 (2d Cir. 2016)); *see also Robles v. Medisys Health Network, Inc.*, 2020 WL 3403191 at *13-14 (E.D.N.Y. June 19, 2020) (Ross, D.J.).

89 *Id.* (citing *Parker v. Hahnemann Univ. Hosp.*, 234 F.Supp.2d 478, 485 (D.N.J. 2002)).

90 *Dotson v. Pfizer, Inc.*, 2006 WL 8438668 at *8 (E.D.N.C. Mar. 10, 2006) (Britt, Senior D.J.); *Dotson v. Pfizer, Inc.*, 558 F.3d 284, 296 (4th Cir. 2009) (Cacheris, Senior D.J., by designation) ("In order to prevail on a FMLA retaliation claim, Dotson must have shown evidence linking the adverse employment action taken against him to a 'protected activity,' in this case his adoption-related leave) (citing *Yashenko v. Harrah's NC Casino Co.*, 446 F.3d 541, 551 (4th Cir. 2006) (analyzing FMLA retaliation claim under Title VII framework)).

inatory reason, the burden is shifted back to plaintiff to establish that the employer's reasons are pretextual.[91]

The plaintiff must ultimately meet the proof requirements on the final shift of the burden, or the claim will fail.[92]

91 *Id.* (citing *Callison v. City of Phila.*, 2004 WL 765479 at *4 (E.D. Pa. Mar. 31, 2004)). *See also Horsting*, 2018 WL 1918617 at *5 ("To make out a *prima facie* case for FMLA retaliation, a plaintiff must establish: (1) he exercised rights protected under the FMLA; (2) he was qualified for his position; (3) he suffered an adverse employment action; and (4) the adverse employment action occurred under circumstances giving rise to an inference of retaliatory intent") (citations and internal quotation marks omitted).

92 *Clemens v. Moody's Analytics, Inc.*, 770 Fed.Appx. 10, 11 (2d Cir. 2019) ("'In short,' at step three, 'the question becomes whether the evidence, taken as a whole, supports a sufficient rational inference of discrimination.') (citing *Weinstock v. Columbia Univ.*, 224 F.3d 33, 42 (2d Cir. 2000)).

Be aware, failure to meet the time requirements under the statutory framework will result in dismissal of a claim for discrimination or interference under the FMLA.[93]

[6.4] B. New York Paid Leave

A new era began in New York as of January 1, 2018—not one created by the presidential election, but rather one created by the votes of the State Assembly and Senate, and the stroke of the Governor's pen. On January 1, 2018, New York's law creating paid family leave went into effect.[94] At that moment, New York joined only a handful of other states in blazing that path—a path that has met with little success in the United States Congress.[95]

93 *See King v. Clarke County, Ala.*, 2012 WL 5287040 at *6 (S.D. Ala. Sept. 27, 2012) (Cassady, M.J.), *adopted* 2012 WL 5265954 (S.D. Ala. Oct. 24, 2012) (Granade, D.J.). Note further that, following the emergence of the COVID-19 pandemic, the U.S. Department of Labor issued guidance that parents could take federal coronavirus leave in the summer of 2020 if their children could not attend camp as otherwise planned because of COVID closures. The protection fell under the Families First Coronavirus Response Act (FFCRA), PL 116-127, March 18, 2020, 134 Stat. 178. *See* Braden Campbell, *DOL Says COVID Leave OK If Virus Sinks Kids' Summer Plans*, Law360, June 26, 2020. The FFCRA also provided, among other things, sick leave/pay for independent contractors affected by COVID. *See Rogers v. Lyft, Inc.*, 2020 WL 1684151 at *2 (N.D. Cal. Apr. 7, 2020). "The FFCRA, which applies to private sector employers that employ fewer than 500 employees and some public sector employers, provides up to 80 hours of paid sick leave to workers who are ill, quarantined, or seeking treatment as a result of COVID-19, or caring for those who are sick or quarantined as a result of COVID-19. These provisions will be in effect until December 31, 2020." *ESI/Employee Solutions, L.P. v. City of Dallas*, 2020 WL 1532373 at *27 & n.19 (E.D. Tex. Mar. 3, 2020) (Jordan, D.J.). The FFCRA also provides, effective through December 31, 2020 (as of the time of this writing): "Two weeks (up to 80 hours) of paid sick leave at the employee's regular rate of pay where the employee is unable to work because the employee is quarantined (pursuant to Federal, State, or local government order or advice of a health care provider), and/or experiencing COVID-19 symptoms and seeking a medical diagnosis; or Two weeks (up to 80 hours) of paid sick leave at two-thirds the employee's regular rate of pay because the employee is unable to work because of a bona fide need to care for an individual subject to quarantine (pursuant to Federal, State, or local government order or advice of a health care provider), or to care for a child (under 18 years of age) whose school or child care provider is closed or unavailable for reasons related to COVID-19, and/or the employee is experiencing a substantially similar condition as specified by the Secretary of Health and Human Services, in consultation with the Secretaries of the Treasury and Labor; and Up to an additional 10 weeks of paid expanded family and medical leave at two-thirds the employee's regular rate of pay where an employee, who has been employed for at least 30 calendar days, is unable to work due to a bona fide need for leave to care for a child whose school or child care provider is closed or unavailable for reasons related to COVID-19." *Families First Coronavirus Response Act: Employee Paid Leave Rights*, Wage & Hour Division, U.S. Dep't of Labor, https://www.dol.gov/agencies/whd/pandemic/ffcra-employee-paid-leave.

94 N.Y. Workers Compensation Law § 204 (Work. Comp. Law).

95 *See* Sheryl B. Galler, *Know New York State's New Paid Family Leave Benefits Law*, 89 N.Y. St. Bar J. 43 (May 2017).

New York Paid Leave is only mentioned herein so that the reader is aware of its existence, as compared with FMLA. Ultimately, once fully implemented in 2021, the New York law will provide employees with up to 12 weeks of paid leave from their jobs, and although not entitled to receive their usual full paycheck, they will receive up to 67 percent of the State's average weekly wage.[96] Sections 202 and 203 of the New York Workers' Compensation Law provide the categories of covered employers and workers, and when employees qualify for benefits.[97] Those who qualify for leave (including, potentially, part-time workers, self-employed individuals and independent contractors who opt in as self-employed) may take the leave upon the birth or adoption of a child, or to care for an ill family member. The leave runs concurrently with FMLA, if applicable. There is also the potential that leave can be used when a spouse is called to military service if there are other familial obligations in the home, as provided in the FMLA (which is specifically referenced in the applicable New York Workers' Compensation Law section).[98] The paid leave law applies to male and female employees alike, and similar to the FMLA, employers must understand that the leave is a "protected" leave.[99] An employee, however, cannot take Paid Family Leave under New York law for their own medical or health condition.[100]

With the emergence of the COVID-19 pandemic in early 2020, though, Governor Cuomo signed into law Senate Bill 8091[101] on March 18, 2020, which law provided for protected leave—and in some cases paid sick leave—for New York workers affected by COVID-19 mandatory quarantine orders. The law divided employers into groups, based on number of employees, and then granted protections to said employees depending on the category into which the employer fell:

> (a) For employers with ten or fewer employees as of January 1, 2020, each employee who is subject to a mandatory or precautionary order of quarantine or isolation

96 Work. Comp. Law § 204.

97 Work. Comp. Law §§ 202, 203.

98 Work. Comp. Law § 201(15). *See also Eligibility, Who is eligible for Paid Family Leave?*, N.Y.S. Paid Family Leave, https://paidfamilyleave.ny.gov/eligibility.

99 Work. Comp. Law §§ 120, 203-a, 203-b.

100 *Paid Family Leave and Other Benefits*, N.Y.S. Paid Family Leave, https://paidfamilyleave.ny.gov/paid-family-leave-and-other-benefits.

101 2020 Sess. Law News of N.Y. Ch. 25 (S. 8091) (2020), https://legislation.nysenate.gov/pdf/bills/2019/S8091.

issued by the state of New York, the department of health, local board of health, or any governmental entity duly authorized to issue such order due to COVID–19, shall be provided with unpaid sick leave until the termination of any mandatory or precautionary order of quarantine or isolation due to COVID–19 and any other benefit as provided by any other provision of law.

. . .

(b) For employers with between eleven and ninety-nine employees as of January 1, 2020, each employee who is subject to a mandatory or precautionary order of quarantine or isolation issued by the state of New York, the department of health, local board of health, or any governmental entity duly authorized to issue such order due to COVID–19, shall be provided with at least five days of paid sick leave and unpaid leave until the termination of any mandatory or precautionary order of quarantine or isolation. After such five days of paid sick leave, an employee shall be eligible for paid family leave benefits and benefits due pursuant to disability pursuant to this act.

(c) For employers with one hundred or more employees as of January 1, 2020, each employee who is subject to a mandatory or precautionary order of quarantine or isolation issued by the state of New York, the department of health, local board of health, or any governmental entity duly authorized to issue such order due to COVID–19, shall be provided with at least fourteen days of paid sick leave during any mandatory or precautionary order of quarantine or isolation.

(d) For public employers, each officer or employee who is subject to a mandatory or precautionary order of quarantine or isolation issued by the state of New York, the department of health, local board of health, or any governmental entity duly authorized to issue such order due to COVID–19 shall be provided with at least fourteen days of paid sick leave during any mandatory or precautionary order of quarantine or isolation.[102]

This was created as potentially paid sick leave, but also universal protected leave for those who qualify, and workers return to their same positions, with no loss of accrued benefits. The State Department of Labor and Commissioner of Labor regulate actions under the law.[103] It is also worth noting, that among other provisions in the law, it stated:

> [a]n employee shall not receive paid sick leave benefits or any other paid benefits provided by any provisions of this section if the employee is subject to a mandatory or precautionary order of quarantine because the employee has returned to the United States after traveling to a country for which the Centers for Disease Control and Prevention has a level two or three travel health notice and the travel to that country was not taken as part of the employee's employment or at the direction of the employee's employer, and if the employee was provided notice of the travel health notice and the limitations of this subdivision prior to such travel.[104]

Thus, the government of the State of New York, similar to the actions taken by the Congress of the United States, provided for workers (even if only temporarily) in the face of a *sui generis* health pandemic.[105]

[6.5] IV. CONCLUSION

The purpose of this chapter was to highlight certain provisions in the law protecting those with qualifying disabilities, or other exigencies or circumstances that require accommodations. As our society and its legal system strive to increase inclusiveness, tolerance and respect for diversity, statutes and caselaw such as those addressed in this chapter will continue to hold a place of prominence, and will be an important source of knowledge and information for attorneys and their clients, employers and employees, business owners and their customers, and general citizens alike.

---

102 *Id.*

103 *Id.*

104 *Id.*

105 For more on the New York law, see Eve I. Klein & Rebecca S. Ruffer, *New York's New Job Protected Paid Leave Law*, N.Y.L.J. at p. 4, Mar. 27, 2020 (article compares provisions of the NYPFL with the federal FMLA, and provisions of the state law S. 8091 with the federal FFCRA).

CHAPTER SEVEN

WEBSITES AND REQUIREMENTS FOR ACCESSIBILITY*

* This chapter previously appeared as an article by the author of this book, 91 N.Y. St. Bar J. 28 (Aug. 2019).

[7.0] I. INTRODUCTION

By now, most are well aware that federal anti-discrimination law includes the Americans with Disabilities Act (ADA),[1] as well as the Americans with Disabilities Act Amendments Act of 2008 (ADAAA),[2] which offer substantial protections for those with qualifying disabilities in areas including public accommodation, commercial facilities, telecommunications, and employment.[3] On July 26, 1990, President George H.W. Bush signed the ADA into law and remarked, in part:

> The Americans with Disabilities Act represents the full flowering of our democratic principles, and it gives me great pleasure to sign it into law today.
>
> In 1986, on behalf of President Reagan, I personally accepted a report from the National Council on Disability entitled "Toward Independence." In that report, the National Council recommended the enactment of comprehensive legislation to ban discrimination against per sons with disabilities. The Americans with Disabilities Act (ADA) is such legislation. It promises to open up all

---

1 104 Stat. 327, Americans with Disabilities Act of 1990; Pub. Law 101-336 (101st Congress), *see* https://www.govinfo.gov/content/pkg/STATUTE-104/pdf/STATUTE-104-Pg327.pdf; *see* https://www.govinfo.gov/app/details/STATUTE-104/STATUTE-104-Pg327/context; *see* 42 U.S.C. §§ 12101, *et seq*.

2 122 STAT. 3553; Pub. Law 110-325 (110th Congress), *see* https://www.govinfo.gov/content/pkg/PLAW-110publ325/pdf/PLAW-110publ325.pdf. Of note, President George H.W. Bush signed the original A.D.A. into law in 1990 (https://www.eeoc.gov/eeoc/history/35th/milestones/1990.html), and his son, President George W. Bush signed the A.D.A.A.A. into law in 2008 (https://adata.org/ada-timeline/ada-amendments-act-adaaa-signed).

3 "Nearly 1-in-5 people have a disability." Lynn Foley & Connal McNamara, *Why Law Firms Should Make Web Accessibility a Priority in 2018*, The Nat'l Law Rev., June 4, 2018, https://www.natlawreview.com/article/why-law-firms-should-make-web-accessibility-priority-2018 (citing U.S. Census Bureau Report (2016)). In contrast, it is reported that one-half of 1% of law firm partners and associates have disabilities. Jason Tashea, *For Law Firms on the Web, Online Accessibility for the Disabled is Good Business*, ABA Journal, May 21, 2019. This is offered as one potential reason for why the issue of law firm website accessibility is usually not a top-of-the-agenda issue in the legal profession. *Id.* However, following the emergence of the COVID-19 pandemic, this is likely to change for all in society, with life largely "lived online." Given increased online services and commerce, businesses and law firms must ensure that those with qualifying disabilities may "accomplish what they want to accomplish" the same as someone without a disability. *See* Victoria Hudgins, *Law Firms' Websites Are Violating the ADA. Why Isn't It a Bigger Deal?*, N.Y.L.J. at p. 5, Mar. 24, 2020; *see also* Eddie Ndopu, *It's Time to Rethink the Language of Accessibility. And to Imagine a More Equal World*, Time, May 21, 2020, https://time.com/5839846/rethink-the-language-accessibility-more-equal (this does not mean that we equate "equality" with "sameness", but rather equality and accessibility mean "our individual and collective differences are not deal-breakers…" when we interact with the world).

> aspects of American life to individuals with disabilities -- employment opportunities, government services, public accommodations, transportation, and telecommunications."[4]

The ADA is enforced by the U.S. Equal Employment Opportunity Commission (EEOC), although the Department of Justice and the U.S. Attorney General are responsible for creating and publishing rules and regulations concerning Title II (State and Local Governments) and Title III (Public Accommodations and Commercial Facilities).[5] Some states, such as New York, have similar protections for those with qualifying disabilities.[6] In New York, the Division of Human Rights has responsibilities very similar to the EEOC.[7]

The topic of numerous articles and cases in recent years has been the expansion of protections to envelop the accessibility of web pages and Internet resources when it comes to those with qualifying disabilities under the ADA or relevant state laws, and the growth of lawsuits seeking to enforce rights[8]—an area complicated by the fact that there is currently no uniform guidance, and no specific rules for websites promulgated by the Department of Justice.[9] This chapter collects cases and commentaries, with a particular eye toward informing attorneys, managing partners, law

---

4 *Transcript of Statement By The President July 26, 1990*, The White House, July 26, 1990, https://www.archives.gov/research/americans-with-disabilities/transcriptions/naid-6037493-statement-by-the-president-americans-with-disabilities-act-of-1990.html.

5 *See* https://www.ada.gov/2010_regs.htm.

6 *See* New York State Human Rights Law (Executive Law) §§ 290, *et seq.*

7 *See* https://dhr.ny.gov/law#HRL293.

8 Although 2019 set a record, with over 11,000 Title III lawsuits filed under the ADA, overall the number of lawsuits filed claiming inaccessible websites, and related violations, held steady from 2018. *See* Jason Grant, *2019 Sets New Records For ADA Title III Suits*, N.Y.L.J. at p. 1, Feb. 28, 2020; Jason Grant, *'Curve Flattens' for ADA Website-Accessibility Lawsuit Filings, Seyfarth Report Says*, N.Y.L.J. at p. 1, May 7, 2020. In 2019, 11,053 lawsuits under Title III of the ADA were filed across the United States, and of those 2,256 were website-accessibility suits. *Id.* For 2018, there were 2,258 website-accessibility lawsuits filed across the United States, out of 10,163 total Title III suits that year. *Id.* Furthermore, New York is the leading place for website-accessibility filings. It was reported that in 2018, there were 1,564 lawsuits filed in the federal courts of just New York State claiming that websites violated provisions of the ADA; in 2019, the number for New York's federal courts was 1,354 website-accessibility claims filed. *Id.* As a comparison, in 2017 there were 814 website-accessibility lawsuits nationwide, out of 7,663 total Title III suits in the United States. *See id.*

9 *See* Matt Stark, *Navigating the Murky Waters of ADA Compliance in the Internet Age*, N.Y. L.J. at p. 4, May 22, 2019 (with reference to 42 U.S.C. § 12181(7); 28 C.F.R. § 36.104). *See also* 28 C.F.R. § 36.302.

firm administrators and business marketing directors. The question explored: If your law firm utilizes a website, but that website is not accessible to those with a certain disability—for instance, it is not enhanced and accessible to the hearing impaired (if there is an audio component) or the visually impaired (lacking a screen-reader function)—is the firm or business, through its website, in violation of the ADA or N.Y.S. law, and potentially subject to litigation and liability?[10]

10 "To state a claim under Title III, [plaintiff] must allege (1) that she is disabled within the meaning of the ADA; (2) that defendants own, lease, or operate a place of public accommodation; and (3) that defendants discriminated against her by denying her a full and equal opportunity to enjoy the services defendants provide." *Camarillo v. Carrols Corp.*, 518 F.3d 153, 156 (2d Cir. 2008) (per curiam) (citing, *inter alia*, 42 U.S.C. § 12182(a); *Molski v. M.J. Cable, Inc.*, 481 F.3d 724, 730 (9th Cir. 2007); *Powell v. Nat'l Bd. of Med. Exam'rs*, 364 F.3d 79, 85 (2d Cir. 2004)); *see also Juscinska v. Paper Factory Hotel, LLC*, 2019 WL 2343306 at *3 (S.D.N.Y. June 3, 2019) (Carter, D.J.). Additionally, a plaintiff in these cases must plead facts with particularity, alleging deficiencies that allegedly impede navigation of the website, or how the plaintiff's disability affects utilization of the website. Failure to plead with particularity risks dismissal. *See Harty v. Nyack Motor Hotel Inc.*, 2020 WL 1140783 (S.D.N.Y. Mar. 9, 2020) (Karas, D.J.). Furthermore, "[f]or an injury to be 'particularized,' it 'must affect the plaintiff in a personal and individual way.'... To be 'concrete' an injury 'must actually exist': the injury must be 'real' and not 'abstract.'... Generally, 'even in the context of a statutory violation,' 'a bare procedural violation, divorced from any concrete harm,' does not satisfy the injury-in-fact requirement of Article III." *Laufer v. 1110 Western Albany, LLC*, 2020 WL 2309083 at *3 (N.D.N.Y. May 8, 2020) (Sannes, D.J.) (citing and quoting *Spokeo, Inc. v. Robins*, 136 S. Ct. 1540, 1547-50 (2016) (Alito, J.); *Lujan v. Defs. of Wildlife*, 504 U.S. 555, 560 n.1, 112 S.Ct. 2130 (1992) (Scalia, J.)). *See also Hernandez v. Caesars Lic. Co., LLC*, 2019 WL 4894501 (D.N.J. Oct. 4, 2019) (testers, to have standing, also must demonstrate concrete injury – that they experienced harm or differential detrimental treatment).

If Title III[11] of the ADA applies to websites in your jurisdiction, it will apply to large and small commercial websites alike, since Title III applies to places of public accommodation (businesses) of all sizes.[12]

[7.1] II. THE RELEVANT GUIDANCE— A DIVIDE IN NEED OF A BRIDGE

According to *A Guide to Disability Rights Laws*, published by the U.S. Department of Justice, Civil Rights Division, Disability Rights Section, in February 2020:

> To be protected by the ADA, one must have a disability or have a relationship or association with an individual with a disability. An individual with a disability is defined by the ADA as a person who has a physical or mental impairment that substantially limits one or more major life activities, a person who has a history or record of such an impairment, or a person who is perceived by

---

11 Note that suits related to website accessibility may also be brought under the other Titles of the ADA, such as Title II, depending on the type of entity alleged to be operating the site. *See, e.g., Gil v. City of Pensacola*, 396 F.Supp.3d 1059 (N.D. Fla. 2019) (Wetherell, D.J.) (suit under Title II of the ADA, and Section 504 of the Rehabilitation Act, alleging inaccessibility of government website); *Price v. City of Ocala*, 375 F. Supp. 3d 1264 (M.D. Fla. 2019) (same, and addressing the difference between Title II and Title III standing under the ADA). There is a slight difference between the elements necessary to state a claim under Title II versus Title III. "To state a claim under Title II, a plaintiff must allege: '(1) that he is a "qualified individual with a disability;" (2) that he was "excluded from participation in or ... denied the benefits of the services, programs, or activities of a public entity" or otherwise "discriminated [against] by such entity;" (3) "by reason of such disability."...' To state a claim under Title III, a plaintiff must establish '(1) that the plaintiff is disabled; (2) that the defendant owns, leases, or operates a place of public accommodation; and (3) that the defendant denied the plaintiff—on the basis of the disability—full and equal enjoyment of the premises.'" *Price*, 375 F.Supp.3d at 1269 (citing, *inter alia*, *Shotz v. Cates*, 256 F.3d 1077, 1079 (11th Cir. 2001); *Bell v. FTMC, LLC*, 2018 WL 4565745 at *1 (M.D. Fla. Sept. 24, 2018); 42 U.S.C. §§ 12132, 12182). Courts also look to future injury when evaluating Title II and III claims. *See Price*, 375 F.Supp.3d at 1269-1270 ("In considering the future injury element of standing in Title III cases, district courts in this Circuit apply a four-factor test that this Court will refer to as the *Houston* factors. The *Houston* factors are: '(1) the proximity of the defendant's business to the plaintiff's residence; (2) the plaintiff's past patronage of the defendant's business; (3) the definiteness of the plaintiff's plan to return; and (4) the frequency of the plaintiff's travel near the defendant's business.'") (citing, *inter alia*, *Houston v. Marod Supermarkets, Inc.*, 733 F.3d 1323, 1328 (11th Cir. 2013)).

12 *See Del-Orden v. Bonobos, Inc.*, 2017 WL 6547902 at *7–10 (S.D.N.Y. Dec. 20, 2017) (Engelmayer, D.J.). *But see Dominguez v. Taco Bell Corp.*, 2020 WL 3263258 (S.D.N.Y. June 17, 2020) (Schofield, D.J.) (distinguishing *Del-Orden*, finding gift cards are not a place of public accommodation ("a place where goods and services are provided"), but rather a way to acquire goods, and plaintiff failed to plead facts showing defendant did not offer auxiliary aids or services sufficient to permit use of the information on the gift cards; thus the court dismissed plaintiff's lawsuit alleging failure to provide gift cards in braille for blind patrons violated the ADA).

> others as having such an impairment. The ADA does not specifically name all of the impairments that are covered.
>
> . . .
>
> Title III covers businesses and nonprofit service providers that are public accommodations, privately operated entities offering certain types of courses and examinations, privately operated transportation, and commercial facilities. Public accommodations are private entities who own, lease, lease to, or operate facilities such as restaurants, retail stores, . . . [professional] offices, . . . and recreation facilities including sports stadiums and fitness clubs. Transportation services provided by private entities are also covered by title III.
>
> Public accommodations must comply with basic nondiscrimination requirements that prohibit exclusion, segregation, and unequal treatment. They also must comply with specific requirements related to architectural standards for new and altered buildings; reasonable modifications to policies, practices, and procedures; ***effective communication with people with hearing, vision, or speech disabilities***; and other access requirements. . . .[13]

Given recent caselaw, it appears that two general categories may be carved-out at the beginning of the analysis: (a) one having a business/service that is operated solely online via website/Internet, or (b) a website business/service that has some "nexus" to a brick-and-mortar location. This distinction exists because of a very real, and troublesome, Circuit split.[14] In *Haynes v. Hooters of Am., LLC*, the plaintiff, a blind business

---

13 *A Guide to Disability Rights Laws*, Civil Rights Division, U.S. Dep't of Justice, February 2020, https://www.ada.gov/cguide.htm#anchor62335 (emphasis added) (although not specifically enumerating websites).

14 *See, inter alia*, *Haynes v. Hooters of Am., LLC*, 893 F.3d 781 (11th Cir. 2018) (Ross, D.J., by designation). *Cf. Morgan v. Joint Admin. Bd., Ret. Plan of the Pillsbury Co.*, 268 F.3d 456 (7th Cir. 2001) (Posner, J.). *See also Mahoney v. Herr Foods Inc.*, 2020 WL 1979153 at *2-3 (E.D. Pa. Apr. 24, 2020) (Baylson, D.J.) (discussing Circuit split; determining that in the Third Circuit, a website must have a nexus to a physical business location in order to be considered a place of public accommodation governed by Title III of the ADA) (citing and following *Ford v. Schering-Plough Corp.*, 145 F.3d 601, 612 (3d Cir. 1998)); *Carroll v. FedFinancial Fed. Credit Union*, 324 F.Supp.3d 658, 665 (E.D. Va. 2018) (O'Grady, D.J.) (also delineating Circuit split; finding in this case that website offered services connected to physical business location, so court did not have to determine whether website, standing alone, is a place of public accommodation).

patron, attempted to utilize the website of the restaurant operator utilizing screen reader software. However, the website was not compatible with the software plaintiff used. Plaintiff thereafter brought suit, alleging violations of Title III of the ADA.[15] Defendant argued that another lawsuit had already been filed against it on nearly identical grounds, and that it was already updating its website to bring it into legal compliance. Because of that, the U.S. district court dismissed plaintiff Haynes' suit. On appeal, the 11th Circuit vacated and remanded. Not only did the Court hold that Haynes was not a party to the prior suit, and therefore could not monitor or enforce the agreement for updating of the website, there was nothing in the record showing that Hooters had updated its website. Therefore, the issues were still "live."[16] Furthermore, the 11th Circuit held that

> Haynes requested in his complaint that the district court direct Hooters to continually update and maintain its website to ensure that it remains fully accessible. Accordingly, even if Hooters' website becomes ADA compliant, Haynes seeks injunctive relief requiring Hooters to maintain the website in a compliant condition. Thus, . . . there is still a live controversy about whether Haynes can receive an injunction to force Hooters to make its website ADA compliant or to maintain it as such.[17]

In *Haynes*, the business in question had brick-and-mortar locations, supplemented by the website at issue, and plaintiff's action challenging the lack of ADA compliance by that website presented "live" questions in the opinion of the 11th Circuit.

However, in *Morgan v. Joint Admin. Bd., Ret. Plan of the Pillsbury Co.*, the lawsuit was filed under the ADA by retired disabled persons challenging a retirement plan negotiated to include differing benefits depending upon whether one retired "early" at age 55, at the "normal" retirement age of 65, *or "early" due to disability*. Among the holdings of the 7th Circuit Court of Appeals, for purposes of this chapter, was the following:

> The plaintiffs have, however, another string to their bow. They appeal to the public accommodations provisions of the Act (Title III), which forbid discriminating against

15 *See* 42 U.S.C. §§ 12181, *et seq.*; *Haynes*, 893 F.3d at 783.

16 *Haynes*, 893 at 784.

17 *Id.*

> disabled persons with respect to access to places of public accommodation. . . . The defendant asks us to interpret "public accommodation" literally, as denoting a physical site, such as a store or a hotel, but we have already rejected that interpretation. An insurance company can no more refuse to sell a policy to a disabled person over the Internet than a furniture store can refuse to sell furniture to a disabled person who enters the store. . . . The site of the sale is irrelevant to Congress's goal of granting the disabled equal access to sellers of goods and services. What matters is that the good or service be offered to the public.[18]

The 7th Circuit had previously held, in *Doe v. Mutual of Omaha*, that:

> The core meaning of [Title III, section 302(a)], plainly enough, is that the owner or operator of a store, hotel, restaurant, dentist's office, travel agency, theater, ***Web site***, or other facility (whether in physical space or in electronic space) . . . that is open to the public cannot exclude disabled persons from entering the facility and, once in, from using the facility in the same way that the nondisabled do.[19]

Similarly, in the U.S. District Court for the District of New Hampshire (in an unpublished opinion), the Court denied a defendant's motion to dismiss a challenge to its website wherein defendant argued it lacked a "nexus with a physical 'brick-and-mortar' location" and therefore did

18 *Morgan*, 268 F.3d at 459 (citing, *inter alia*, 42 U.S.C. § 12182(a); *Doe v. Mutual of Omaha Ins. Co.*, 179 F.3d 557, 558–59 (7th Cir. 1999); *Carparts Distr. Ctr., Inc. v. Auto. Wholesaler's Ass'n of New England, Inc.*, 37 F.3d 12, 19 (1st Cir. 1994)).

19 *Mutual of Omaha Ins. Co.*, 179 F.3d 557, 559 (Posner, C.J.) (citing *Carparts*) (emphasis added). *See also Nat'l Fed. of the Blind v. Scribd Inc.*, 97 F.Supp.3d 565 (D. Vt. 2015) (Sessions, D.J.); *Nat'l Ass'n of the Deaf v. Netflix, Inc.*, 869 F.Supp.2d 196 (D. Mass. 2012) (Ponsor, D.J.). *See also, generally,* 42 U.S.C. § 12812(b)(1)(A); 28 C.F.R. § 36.202(a) ("Denial of participation. A public accommodation shall not subject an individual or class of individuals on the basis of a disability or disabilities of such individual or class, directly, or through contractual, licensing, or other arrangements, to a denial of the opportunity of the individual or class to participate in or benefit from the goods, services, facilities, privileges, advantages, or accommodations of a place of public accommodation."); 28 C.F.R. § 36.202(b) ("Participation in unequal benefit. A public accommodation shall not afford an individual or class of individuals, on the basis of a disability or disabilities of such individual or class, directly, or through contractual, licensing, or other arrangements, with the opportunity to participate in or benefit from a good, service, facility, privilege, advantage, or accommodation that is not equal to that afforded to other individuals.").

"not constitute a 'public accommodation.'"[20] However, the same Court acknowledged the deepening Circuit split, between those decisions in the First and Seventh Circuits on the one hand, and those in the Third, Fifth, Sixth and Ninth Circuits on the other,[21] wherein "the majority of Courts of Appeals that have addressed this issue require a 'public accommodation' to be an actual, physical space or have a nexus to an actual, physical space, such that stand-alone websites may not be considered 'public accommodations.'"[22] The Second Circuit U.S. Court of Appeals has not, as of the time of this writing, specifically and directly addressed the application of the ADA to online services/the internet—although in one decision that court did apply the ADA to insurance services, even if those services were provided entirely online, and regardless of nexus to a physical building).[23] It is important to note, though, that *even those courts requiring the establishment of a "nexus" do thereafter hold that websites*

---

20 *Access Now, Inc. v. Blue Apron, LLC*, 2017 WL 5186354 (D.N.H. Nov. 8, 2017) (Laplante, D.J.) (unpublished) (citing *Carparts* and *Morgan*). *Cf. FedFinancial Fed. Credit Union*, 324 F.Supp.3d 658 (disagreeing with *Access Now, Inc.*).

21 Although the *Blue Apron* Court did not specifically include the Second and Eleventh Circuits in the breakdown, we know that the courts in the Second Circuit have aligned with the First and Seventh, while the courts in the Eleventh Circuit have aligned with the Third, Fifth, Sixth and Ninth. *See* J. Tashea, *supra*, ABA Journal. Furthermore, the American Bar Association House of Delegates (of which the author of this book is a former member) passed Resolution 116C at the 2018 Annual Meeting, aligning itself with the First, Second and Seventh Circuits, and "urg[ing] all courts and other appropriate government entities to interpret Titles II and III of the Americans with Disabilities Act (ADA) to apply to technology, and goods and services delivered thereby, *regardless of whether the technology exists solely in virtual space or has a nexus to a physical space*, subject to all statutory requirements, limitations, exceptions, exemptions, and defenses." Text of ABA Revised Resolution 116C (2018) (emphasis added), https://www.americanbar.org/content/dam/aba/images/abanews/2018-AM-Resolutions/116c.pdf; *see also* Amanda Roberts, *A Tangled Web*, ABA Journal at 16 (July/Aug. 2019); Lee Rawles, *House Resolutions Decry Over-Discipline in Schools, Urge Tech Access for Those with Disabilities*, ABA Journal, Aug. 7, 2018, http://www.abajournal.com/news/article/disability_rights_resolutions.

22 *Blue Apron, LLC*, 2017 WL 5186354 at *4 (citing, *inter alia*, *Magee v. Coca–Cola Refreshments USA, Inc.*, 833 F.3d 530, 534 (5th Cir. 2016); *Earll v. eBay, Inc.*, 599 Fed. Appx. 695, 696 (9th Cir. 2015) ("We have previously interpreted the term 'place of public accommodation' to require 'some connection between the good or service complained of and an actual physical place'"); *Ford v. Schering–Plough Corp.*, 145 F.3d 601, 612–14 (3d Cir. 1998) ("rejecting the reasoning in *Carparts* and holding that 'public accommodation' does not refer to non-physical access"); *Parker v. Metro. Life Ins. Co.*, 121 F.3d 1006, 1013–14 (6th Cir. 1997)).

23 *See Thorne v. Formula 1 Motorsports, Inc.*, 2019 WL 6916098 at *2 (S.D.N.Y. Dec. 19, 2019) (Oetken, D.J.); *Pallozzi v. Allstate Life Ins. Co.*, 198 F.3d 28 (2d Cir. 1999), *op. amended on denial of reh'g*, 204 F.3d 392 (2d Cir. 2000) (Leval, J.).

having such nexus must be compliant with Title III of the ADA, for use by persons with and without disabilities alike.[24]

In New York State, while there appears to be little caselaw directly on point, the cases that exist line up New York with the holdings of the federal courts in the First, Second and Seventh Circuits.[25] First, New York Courts have held that provisions of the New York State Human Rights Law "must be liberally construed to accomplish the purposes of the statute"; and indeed the provisions of both the State and New York City laws are "construed 'broadly in favor of discrimination plaintiffs, to the extent that such a construction is reasonably possible.'"[26] Furthermore, as recently as August 2017, it was stated that "[w]hether a website itself is a 'place of public accommodation' or an 'accommodation, advantage, facility or privilege' of a retail store appear[ed] to be an issue of first impression under the NYSHRL."[27] The *Andrews* Court made clear, though, that "[o]ver time, the New York State Legislature has 'repeatedly amended the statute to expand its scope,' specifying that the list of places of public accommodation 'is illustrative, not specific.'. . . 'This history provides a clear indication that the Legislature used the phrase place of public accommodation in the broad sense of providing conveniences and ser-

---

24 *See Fuller v. Smoking Anytime Two, LLC*, 2018 WL 3387692 (S.D. Fla. July 11, 2018) (Ungaro, D.J.) ("Plaintiff... adequately alleged a nexus between Defendant's website and its physical stores because the website is 'heavily integrated with' and 'operates as a gateway to' those stores", such that defendant's motion to dismiss was denied). *See also Gil v. Winn Dixie Stores, Inc.*, 242 F.Supp.3d 1315 (S.D. Fla. 2017) (Scola, D.J.).

25 Note that while under New York law damages awarded to successful plaintiffs challenging limitations to website accessibility are reportedly limited (capped at $500), there is no limit on the attorneys' fees awarded to a prevailing plaintiff. *See* Jason Grant, *ADA Website Accessibility Suits Flood NY Federal Courts, Report Says*, N.Y.L.J. at 1 (Jan. 18, 2019). As anyone involved in litigation is aware, attorneys' fees alone can embody a substantial sum. There is also the matter of equitable, injunctive relief and concomitant costs.

26 *Cahill v. Rosa*, 89 N.Y.2d 14, 20, 674 N.E.2d 274, 276 (1996) (Simons, J.) (citing, *inter alia*, Exec. Law § 300; *U.S. Power Squadrons v. State Human Rts. Appeal Bd.*, 59 N.Y.2d 401, 452 N.E.2d 1199 (1983)); *Williams v. N.Y.C. Trans. Auth.*, 171 A.D.3d 990, 992, 97 N.Y.S.3d 692, 695 (2d Dep't 2019); *see also Mohammed v. Great Atlantic & Pacific Tea Co., Inc.*, 44 Misc.3d 396, 398, 986 N.Y.S.2d 796, 798 (Sup. Ct. N.Y. Cty. 2014) (York, J.) (looking to N.Y. Exec. Law §§ 291, *et. seq.*, and N.Y.C. Admin. Code §§ 8-107, *et. seq.*). *See also* N.Y. Civil Rights Law § 40-c. Federal cases have likewise held that "[i]n general, the ADA must be broadly construed as it was designed to 'provide a clear and comprehensive national mandate for the elimination of discrimination against individuals with disabilities.'" *Juscinska*, 2019 WL 2343306 at *2 (citing *Noel v. N.Y.C. Taxi & Limousine Comm'n*, 687 F.3d 63, 68 (2d Cir. 2012)).

27 *Andrews v. Blick Art Materials, LLC*, 268 F.Supp.3d 381 (E.D.N.Y. 2017) (Weinstein, Senior D.J.). *But see Dominguez v. Banana Republic, LLC*, 2020 WL 1950496 (S.D.N.Y. Apr. 23, 2020) (Woods, D.J.) (distinguishing *Andrews*).

vices to the public and that it intended that the definition of place of accommodation should be interpreted liberally.'"[28]

The *Andrews* Court, citing to both the *U.S. Power Squadrons* case in New York and the case of *National Organization for Women, Essex County Chapter v. Little League Baseball, Inc.* in New Jersey, held that a place of "public accommodation" need not have a fixed location or real estate, such that in New York, "place" is "a 'term of convenience, not limitation.'"[29] Ultimately, in *Andrews*, the U.S. District Court for the Eastern District of New York, looking to New York law as construed and interpreted consistent with the ADA, determined that "[t]hrough plaintiff's assertion that he is unable to use the website due to his disability, he has stated a claim that [defendant]… violated the NYSHRL," and defendant's motion to dismiss the discrimination claim was denied.[30]

---

28 *Andrews*, 268 F.Supp.3d at 399 (citing *Cahill*); *Banana Republic, LLC*, 2020 WL 1950496 at *7 ("Courts in this district have already addressed the question of what constitutes a 'place' for the purpose of Title III in the context of deciding that websites are places of public accommodation…. In short, those courts have read the word 'place' broadly to include every 'sales or rental establishment' and 'service establishment.'") (citing, *inter alia, Andrews*, 268 F.Supp.3d at 393). *But see Dominguez v. Taco Bell Corp.*, 2020 WL 3263258 (S.D.N.Y. June 17, 2020) (Schofield, D.J.) (distinguishing *Banana Republic*, finding gift cards are not a place of public accommodation ("a place where goods and services are provided"), but rather a way to acquire goods, and plaintiff failed to plead facts showing defendant did not offer auxiliary aids or services sufficient to permit use of the information on the gift cards; thus the court dismissed plaintiff's lawsuit alleging failure to provide gift cards in braille for blind patrons violated the ADA). *See also* Jenna Greene, *Judge Shreds First of 200+ ADA Suits Demanding Gift Cards in Braille*, N.Y.L.J. at p. 6, May 4, 2020 (discussing the filing of more than 200 lawsuits against retailers claiming gift cards not in braille violated the ADA; and addressing that *Banana Republic* was the first of a number of cases where these claims were dismissed—both on the basis of standing (failure on the prong of intent to return), and for lack of Title III regulation/applicability (since gift cards are not "places of public accommodation")).

29 *Andrews*, 268 F.Supp.3d at 399-400 (citing *U.S. Power Squadrons*, 452 N.E.2d at 1203; *Nat'l Org. for Women, Essex Cty. Ch. v. Little League Baseball, Inc.*, 127 N.J. Super. 522, 318 A.2d 33, 37 (N.J. App. Div. 1974)).

30 *Andrews*, 268 F.Supp.3d at 400. *Cf. Price v. City of Ocala*, 375 F.Supp.3d 1264, 1269 (M.D. Fla. 2019); *Gil v. City of Pensacola*, 396 F.Supp.3d 1059, 1062-1064 (N.D. Fla. 2019) (Wetherell, D.J.) (addressing claim of inaccessibility of government website under Title II of the ADA; distinguishing *Price*; "The court identified the following factors to be considered with the totality of the relevant facts in determining whether the plaintiff has alleged a real and immediate threat of future injury in the context of a suit alleging inaccessibility of a governmental entity's website: (1) the plaintiff's connection with the defendant; (2) the type of information that is inaccessible on the website; and (3) the relation between the inaccessibility and the plaintiff's alleged future harm"; due process did not require permitting plaintiff to amend the complaint, because the *Price* decision had already been issued before the *Gil* plaintiff filed an amended complaint) (citations omitted).

[7.2] III. CONCLUSION: A "COMPLIANT" WEBSITE?

If your law firm—like virtually all 21st century law firms—utilizes a website as part of your business and marketing activities, what then can we take from the above discussion in this area that has deeply divided courts across the nation? In the opinion of this author, there are two very important points not to be ignored or minimized:

(1) If your firm or business has a brick-and-mortar physical location, as many if not most do, then the law appears clear across all jurisdictions under the ADA (and those applying New York law) that your website must be fully compliant with Title III of the ADA and the provisions of the New York State Executive Law (Human Rights Law) and Civil Rights

Law for unimpeded use by all persons regardless of disability.[31] The website must, for instance, be compatible with screen readers for the visually impaired, or with similar services and products for the hearing impaired,

---

31 In the *Juscinska* case, a plaintiff with cerebral palsy brought suit against a hotel owner/operator alleging violations of Title III of the ADA, as well as the N.Y.S. and N.Y.C. Human Rights Laws, alleging that the hotel's website did not provide room accessibility information for disabled guests, but provided full online service to the non-disabled. The Court, in denying defendant's motion to dismiss, noted: "Here, as alleged in the Complaint, Plaintiff was not able to browse Defendant's website and make a reservation with the same efficiency, immediacy, and convenience as those who do not need accessible guest rooms. . . . Plaintiff was unable to discern the accessible features of rooms that would meet her needs. . . . Defendant's website did not provide Plaintiff with the opportunity to evaluate the suitability of common areas and the amenities Defendant provides to its guests. . . . Taking the facts in the Complaint as true, it is plausible that, at the time Plaintiff visited Defendant's website, it was not compliant with the ADA as interpreted by the DOJ." *Juscinska*, 2019 WL 2343306 at *3. Furthermore, the Court disagreed with defendant that the hotel's 24/7 telephone line, to which prospective guests could pose questions, was an acceptable auxiliary aid and service that would moot plaintiff's claims. *Id.* at *4 (". . . at this stage, the mere availability of a phone service does not mean that Plaintiff has or is treated the same as other individuals. The ability and ease in which someone can research and reserve a room in a hotel is a service. In her Complaint, Plaintiff sufficiently alleges that she was denied that service based on her disability"). *See also Parks v. Richard*, 2020 WL 2523541 at *2 (M.D. Fla. May 18, 2020) (Chappell, D.J.) ("ADA website cases are somewhat tricky because courts nationwide are trying to fit the square peg of an online injury into the round hole of traditional standing analysis.... And there is little authoritative guidance to help district courts.... Fortunately, cases across the Middle and Southern Districts addressed an ADA tester's standing for this type of hotel website case. Each concluded allegations like Parks' show standing for an injury.... Here, the website failed to identify the motel's accessible features or allow booking of accessible rooms. So the Court concludes Parks alleged he suffered an injury in fact by encountering barriers that violate the ADA") (citing *Price v. Escalante - Black Diamond Golf Club LLC*, 2019 WL 1905865 (M.D. Fla. Apr. 29, 2019); *Poschmann v. Fountain TN, LLC*, 2019 WL 4540438 at *2 (M.D. Fla. Sept. 19, 2019)); 42 U.S.C. § 12182(b)(1)(A)(iii); 28 C.F.R. § 36.202(c) ("Separate benefit. A public accommodation shall not provide an individual or class of individuals, on the basis of a disability or disabilities of such individual or class, directly, or through contractual, licensing, or other arrangements with a good, service, facility, privilege, advantage, or accommodation that is different or separate from that provided to other individuals, unless such action is necessary to provide the individual or class of individuals with a good, service, facility, privilege, advantage, or accommodation, or other opportunity that is as effective as that provided to others."). *But cf.* 28 C.F.R. § 36.303 ("auxiliary aids & services", when qualifying); *Price v. Escalante - Black Diamond Golf Club LLC*, 2019 WL 1905865 at *7-*8 ("at least this much appears clear: websites themselves are not 'places of public accommodation,' and a plaintiff must allege a nexus between a website and a 'place of public accommodation.' . . . So the Court rejects without further discussion Price's argument that Black Diamond's website is a place of public accommodation. . . . Instead, the crux of this issue is whether Price alleged that the inaccessible portions of the website 'hinders the full use and enjoyment' of Black Diamond's facilities. . . . The answer to that question is no. . . . Price has not alleged how the inability to access the July 2017 newsletter in December 2018 hinders Price's full use and enjoyment of Black Diamond's facilities. Absent such allegations, the Court concludes that Price failed to state a claim.") (citations omitted).

as but one example for compliance.[32] Some would argue that the benefits to law firms extend beyond avoidance of liability: "There is a strong business case to be put forward for pursuing web accessibility for your law firm. . . . The benefits go beyond minimizing litigation risk, to include corporate social responsibility, financial returns, and benefits to the technical aspects of your firm's digital presence."[33]

(2) If your law firm or business is completely virtual, and has no "nexus" to a physical real estate or brick-and-mortar location, then you should be certain to identify the holdings of the courts (and the provisions of the state/local statutes) in your jurisdiction/Federal Circuit, such that you do not run afoul of the protections of the ADA when it comes to users qualifying for accommodations when accessing your website and web services.

The above is meant to provide food for thought and consideration, at least until some future time when Congress might act with additional legislation/amendment of current legislation, the Supreme Court of the United States might resolve the enduring Circuit split, or the Department of Justice restarts rule-making under the ADA to specifically address

---

32 There are opinions by commentators concerning how a firm might make its website compliant with the law. Some argue that there is no such thing as "ADA compliant law firm websites" because there is currently no rule or regulation under the ADA specifically speaking to ADA compliance by websites. Dan Jaffe, *Law Firm Website Accessibility and ADA Compliance*, LawLytics, https://www.lawlytics.com/blog/ada-compliance (Jan. 26, 2019). While that is technically true, the author of this chapter would at least caution readers that compliance with caselaw/common law requirements set forth in particular jurisdictions for website accessibility under state and federal law is mandatory, and failure to comply in those jurisdictions may well result in liability. Even so, it is not an insurmountable obstacle for a website to become compliant in most circumstances, and many times an easy fix may be employed, particularly because if the website is compliant with the relevant jurisdiction's caselaw guidance and the text of the ADA statute, the website owner/operator has flexibility in the specific measures taken. *Id.* (citing Sept. 25, 2018 letter from U.S. Dep't of Justice to Members of Congress).

33 L. Foley and C. McNamara, *supra*, The Nat'l Law Rev., June 4, 2018.

websites.[34] In the meantime, owners of websites may look to the Web Content Accessibility Guidelines (WCAG 2.0) provided by the World Wide Web Consortium (W3C).[35] The WCAG is purely advisory in nature, and provides four Principles of guidance for law firms, including: "WCAG Principle 3: Understandable: The information and operation of the website's user interface must be understandable. This means that the content on your site should appear in a predictable and standard way that is intuitive for readers, and readable and understandable for assistive devices."[36] Employing all of the WCAG Principles may simply not be cost effective for solo, small and medium size firms, but again the Principles are not mandatory, and, indeed, courts have held that the WCAG 2.0 can be utilized as an equitable remedy for non-compliance, but not as a basis for initial liability in the case of an alleged ADA violation; it is guidance in the absence of DOJ rule-making.[37] One may also look to the supplementary WCAG 2.1 (June 5, 2008) for further guidance (WCAG 2.1 augments, but does not replace or supersede, WCAG 2.0).[38] While advisory, the WCAG are considered by some to be the "gold standard,"[39] and perhaps may be thought of in a similar fashion to the Sedona Conference principles and best practice guidelines issued prior to the Federal Rules of

---

34 However, in the meantime, some courts have held that, as part of their inherent authority and duty as the Judicial Branch, they may interpret and apply the law given the legislation that has been crafted and passed by the Legislative Branch, and signed into law by the Executive Branch. *See Martinez v. San Diego Cty. Credit Union*, 264 Cal. Rptr. 3d 600, 618 (Cal. Ct. App. 4th Dist. 2020) (a sufficient allegation was made to show nexus of website to physical place, thus court did not reach issue of ADA applying to website with no physical nexus; however, court also stated: "we find unavailing Credit Union's legal contention that the alleged defects in its website can be remedied only by Congress's enactment of a specific website accessibility standard. The argument is inconsistent with the fundamental principle that a legislature has the authority to enact general laws and delegate enforcement issues to a regulatory body and/or to leave it to the judicial branch to interpret the law and determine whether the party has complied in the particular case.…This is particularly true with respect to the ADA, which often requires a flexible approach to enforcement") (citing *Marbury v. Madison*, 5 U.S. 137, 177, 1 Cranch 137 (1803) (Marshall, C.J.) (discussing role of the judiciary and the principle of separation of powers; "[i]t is emphatically the province and duty of the judicial department to say what the law is").

35 https://www.w3.org/TR/WCAG20.

36 D. Jaffe, *supra*, LawLytics (the article also provides guidance on 22 points of interest with which all attorneys should be familiar concerning website accessibility).

37 *See id.*; *Robles v. Domino's Pizza, LLC*, 913 F.3d 898, 904-908 (9th Cir. 2019) (Owens, J.). *cert. denied* 140 S.Ct. 122 (Mem) (Oct. 7, 2019). *See also* L. Foley & C. McNamara, *supra*, The Nat'l Law Rev.

38 *See* https://www.w3.org/TR/WCAG21; M. Stark, *supra*, N.Y. L.J.

39 *See* J. Tashea, *supra*, ABA Journal.

Civil Procedure and Federal Rules of Evidence amendments that specifically addressed eDiscovery and electronically stored information.[40]

A recent decision of the California Court of Appeal held that the trial court (which had granted summary judgment and an injunction to a blind patron of a restaurant's website) did not commit error in holding a restaurant's website—having a nexus to the physical place of business—was subject to the provisions of Title III of the ADA; and, further, that the trial court did not commit error when it conflated and referenced the Guidelines of the W3C and the requirements of the ADA.[41]

In closing, consider the following: Acting contrary to the guidance contained in (1) or (2) *supra*—resulting in discriminatory impact on some Internet users—might not only result in violations of law and concomitant civil liability, but also again in potential violations of ethical rules possibly resulting in professional discipline in those jurisdictions having adopted the language like that of ABA Model Rule 8.4(g), just as previously discussed in Chapter 3, *supra*.[42] Be forewarned, be cautious, and beware.

---

40 https://thesedonaconference.org/publications.

41 *Thurston v. Midvale Corp.*, 39 Cal.App.5th 634, 252 Cal.Rptr.3d 292 (Cal. Ct. App. 2d Dist. 2019).

42 *See, e.g.*, Am. Bar Assoc. Model Rule of Prof'l Conduct 8.4(g); N.Y. Rule of Prof'l Conduct 8.4(g), (h); Md. Atty's Rule of Prof'l Conduct 19-308.4(e) ("It is professional misconduct for an attorney to:... (e) knowingly manifest by words or conduct when acting in a professional capacity bias or prejudice based upon race, sex, religion, national origin, disability, age, sexual orientation or socioeconomic status when such action is prejudicial to the administration of justice, provided, however, that legitimate advocacy is not a violation of this section;..."). Violation of the ADA or N.Y.S./N.Y.C. Human Rights Law (in the leading state for the filing of website-accessibility lawsuits) by an attorney discriminating against users of a firm's website may very well result in breach of ethical proscriptions. Courts across jurisdictions take breaches of ethical proscriptions very seriously, and issue severe sanctions when attorneys are found to have acted in a discriminatory manner in their professional activities. *See, e.g. Atty Grievance Comm'n of Maryland v. Markey*, 469 Md. 485, 230 A.3d 942 (2020).

CHAPTER EIGHT

SCENARIOS AND HYPOTHETICALS FOR ANALYSIS

[8.0] I. HYPOTHETICAL #1 – RACE DISCRIMINATION IN THE WORKPLACE

A business operates in Plattsburgh, New York, and has had 150 employees for the better part of two years. One employee is Latino, and is the only Latino employee. One of the "supervisors" makes jokes about Latinos and insults this employee's Latino heritage on a daily basis. The employee has lodged a complaint with the human resources office. Following the complaint, the supervisor of the Latino employee, powerless to do anything on his own, falsely wrote up the employee for violations of company policy and reported that to a higher supervisor who thereafter fired the Latino employee. What are the issues that are raised in this scenario? What laws are potentially involved?

Analysis: Consider the information contained in Chapter 1 of this book. First, under New York law including the Amendments Act of 2019, this is a covered employer under New York Law. Further, given that the employer clearly has more than 15 employees for the requisite time under Title VII, federal law applies as well. Additionally, the initial supervisor was not a *Vance* supervisor; however, the supervisor who accepted the false write-up and terminated the employee was a *Vance* supervisor. The improper and discriminatory comments of the supervisor in this case were absolutely continuing and pervasive, creating a hostile work environment permeated by discrimination against the employee's race and/or national origin. We have no information about whether or not the workplace had a policy in place concerning employee reports of claims or complaints (in New York, such is now required under law), for analysis of the application of the *Faragher-Ellerth* defense to this racial harassment situation. We know that the employee did make an internal complaint to human resources, regardless of whether a formal policy existed. However, *Faragher-Ellerth* would likely not be applicable in this matter because the employee was fired, in an act of retaliation. Additionally, following the Amendments Act of 2019, the *Faragher-Ellerth* defense is not available under New York law.

The employer in this circumstance should be familiar with federal and New York State laws on discrimination, harassment and retaliation. There will likely be proceedings in the EEOC or Division of Human Rights (*see* Chapter 5), and thereafter proceedings in federal court for the Northern District of New York (unless plaintiff employee seeks relief entirely in NYS DHR).

[8.1] II. HYPOTHETICAL #2 – SEXUAL ORIENTATION DISCRIMINATION IN THE WORKPLACE

Imagine you are the managing member of a New York domestic LLC, with 19 employees, all of whom have worked for the business full-time for three years. The business operates three locations: one in Goshen, New York; one in Binghamton, New York; and one in Matamoras, Pennsylvania. The regional manager, a *Vance* supervisor who has the authority to hire and fire employees, is overheard making jokes about the sexual orientation of two employees, one in the Goshen location and one in the Matamoras location. The employee in the Matamoras location is a Pennsylvania resident. Over time, the jokes become more frequent and offensive, and the regional manager also begins assigning the homosexual employees the least desirable job duties, and thereafter makes the working conditions so unbearable that both resign (constructive termination). The abusive conduct in question took place at each of the employee's work locations, and the Pennsylvania employee never worked at a New York location. What potential legal liability do you face?

Analysis: Consider the information contained in Chapters 1 and 2. First, the business has enough employees to be covered under both federal and New York State law (this text does not evaluate Pennsylvania state law, thus the reader should analyze that separately). Next, we know that the New York State Human Rights Law contains a protected class provision for sexual orientation; and following the *Bostock* decision of the U.S. Supreme Court in June of 2020, sexual orientation and gender identity are protected classes under Title VII federally. Therefore, the New York resident employee would have a claim under both the New York State Human Rights Law and Title VII of the Civil Rights Act of 1964.

The Pennsylvania employee is also now covered by Title VII federally; therefore, the Pennsylvania resident employee would have a federal law claim. Again, this text does not delve into Pennsylvania law, thus the employer would have to analyze the protections, if any, under Pennsylvania state law with legal counsel.

As far as application of New York law to the activities of this New York domestic LLC doing business in Pennsylvania, the discussion in Chapter 1 makes clear that the provisions of New York's Human Rights Law (§ 298-a(1),(2)) do not apply if the offense is not *against* a New York resident or New York corporation. Here, the one employee is a Pennsylvania resident, thus it appears through analysis of the law that the Pennsylvania resident employee could not assert a claim under New York law.

[8.2] III. HYPOTHETICAL #3 – EQUAL PAY WHEN EMPLOYEE REQUESTS LESS?

A restaurant chain in New York's Hudson Valley has locations in Port Jervis and Newburgh in Orange County, Poughkeepsie in Dutchess County, and White Plains in Westchester County. The four restaurants have a combined staff (front end and kitchen) of 140 employees. When hiring for new waitstaff, the owner is careful not to ask about prior salary of the interviewee. However, during discussion with the leading applicant about the job and job requirements, the applicant specifically states, "That all sounds great. As long as I earn $15.00 per hour, I'm your person if you hire me! But I want $15.00 per hour and will accept nothing less." It is apparently not well known, but the business actually believes in paying staff in excess of minimum wage, and it pays all employees (even those earning tips) $20.00 per hour. Can the business pay the applicant only $15.00 upon hire because that is what they requested?

Before you answer, let's complicate the scenario further. For purposes of our hypothetical analysis assume the following: the applicant is a female; at her prior job she earned $10.00 per hour, and so she believes demanding $15.00 per hour would be a nice raise; the other waitstaff are all men, of different races, all of whom earn $20.00 per hour; the business owner was prepared to pay the applicant $20.00 per hour until she voiced her willingness, unknowingly, to accept less; as a businessperson, the owner of the restaurant is always on the lookout for cost savings.

Now what say you?

Analysis: The employer should be very cautious in this scenario. Consider the information from Chapter 3. First, the employer was careful not to seek or ask about any information that would violate New York's new provisions of law preventing an employer from justifying pay differentials based on prior salaries when it comes to gender gaps. However, the employee voluntarily provided information about the pay rate she sought. The employer can consider the information voluntarily provided. Perhaps this new hire also has much less experience than any of the currently employed waitstaff. The employer might have potential legitimate, non-discriminatory reasons to pay the new hire $15.00 per hour rather than the $20.00 per hour paid to the other waitstaff; and the employer would still be paying higher than restaurant minimum wage, while not basing the decision on any improper information.

In this circumstance, though, the employer should still take care. If the applicant were a male, would the employer say, "Well, it is fine that you would accept $15.00 but we pay $20.00"? That may be a question raised in any future equal pay lawsuit. Further, if the employee finds out that the employer is paying all other waitstaff $20.00 per hour, will plaintiff have a claim that on its face looks like a gender discriminatory pay gap? The employer, already willing to pay all other waitstaff $20.00 per hour, and in an effort to be non-discriminatory and inclusive of diversity, may want to consider paying the new hire the same rate as the other similarly situated employees. If there are distinctions that could legitimately justify a lower rate of pay, those should be analyzed with legal counsel.

[8.3] IV. HYPOTHETICAL #4 – EEOC AND/OR COURT FILING?

Employer has a New York State domestic corporation, doing business with locations in Rochester, Troy, Peekskill, and Long Island City. There are 42 employees, most of whom have worked for the company for at least the last 18 months. A male supervisor is making sexual advances toward and comments to a female subordinate on a weekly basis for four months. The company has a clear sexual harassment and non-discrimination policy, modeled after the New York DOL/DHR policies, and publicized to all employees per the law. The employee, however, does not lodge a complaint, and there is thus no investigation conducted by the company. The male supervisor leaves the company, and the female employee suffers no further sexual harassment. The female employee thereafter, 299 days after the last instance of sexual harassment by the former male supervisor, files a charge with the EEOC. Not long after, though, the female employee changes her strategy, withdraws her EEOC charge, and instead files a complaint in New York State Supreme Court (a New York trial court), alleging claims under Title VII of the Civil Rights Act of 1964 and the New York State Human Rights Law.

Note that the company's policies also contain a pre-dispute mandatory arbitration provision, applying to complaints such as those of the female employee.

What are the issues that are raised in this scenario? What laws are potentially involved?

Analysis: Recall the information from Chapters 1 and 5. The employee in this situation appears to have claims for discrimination and hostile work environment under both federal and New York State law. Under federal law, because the complaint falls under Title VII, the plaintiff employee was required to exhaust administrative remedies, meaning a filing first with the EEOC, and receipt of a probable cause determination (or the passing of 180 days or existence of futility) before she could proceed to any court. Furthermore, she had 300 days to file with the EEOC— 300 days from the date of the last incident complained of. Here, plaintiff employee filed within 300 days, just making it at day 299. However, plaintiff thereafter withdrew the charge, effectively ending the matter. Once 300 days passed, any federal claim she had was untimely and no longer viable. By withdrawing the charge from EEOC, employee effectively allowed the clock to run past 300 days—remember that the clock had stopped at 299 days upon filing of the charge and restarted when the charge was withdrawn from EEOC. Once 300 days passed from the incident in question, the employee no longer had timely federal claims.

Under New York State law, following the Amendments Act of 2019, it no longer matters if the employer has a policy that is not followed by the employee in reporting allegations of harassment or discrimination, because the *Faragher-Ellerth* defense is not applicable under State or City law. Furthermore, we know that the employee cannot circumvent federal exhaustion requirements by "electing remedies" to proceed to state court. That "election of remedies" only exists under New York State law. Federal claims, even if brought under concurrent jurisdiction in state court, must first exhaust administrative remedies through the EEOC or DHR processes.

The plaintiff employee's New York State law claims filed in state court do appear viable in this scenario, given a three-year statute of limitation under state law, and thus the employer would likely seek to analyze and address the concerns with legal counsel. Finally, the employer may challenge the court filing, arguing that the pre-dispute arbitration clause compels arbitration, but CPLR 7515 versus federal FAA preemption and the federal court decision in *Latif* clouds that application.

[8.4] V. HYPOTHETICAL #5 – MEDICAL MARIJUANA USE

Employer operates a New York Domestic LLC in Latham, New York (in Albany County). Employer has 19 employees, and one employee is particularly well-liked and performs his job admirably, such that he is promoted to a management position. The promotion requires a standard drug test, and the employee submits to the test. When the results come back, the employee tests positive for component parts of marijuana. The employer terminates the employee, but the employee argues that the marijuana is utilized pursuant to New York's Compassionate Care Act,[1] because employee is HIV-positive. The employer argues that federal law does not require accommodation of drug use deemed illegal by federal drug policy. What result?

Analysis: One may think that marijuana use is an automatic strike against an employee. However, that is not necessarily the case. In this area, we find ourselves squarely in the realm of federalism—the conflict between states' rights and states' laws and federal authority and federal laws. The federal government has asserted that federal drug policy is the primary authority in this scenario. States, meanwhile, have argued that drug policies and medical use fall under state power, and notions of health/safety/welfare. Under federal law, marijuana possession, even if used for medical purposes, is still viewed as a crime. The federal government and agencies will not acknowledge any medical benefit. However, New York and a number of other states now permit medical use of marijuana by statute.

Under federal law, if any employee requests, under the ADA, an accommodation whereby they be permitted to use a narcotic that is deemed illegal under federal law, the requested accommodation is unreasonable and need not be provided, and if the employee tests positive for the narcotic, the employer can terminate them.[2]

There has been a shift in some jurisdictions, though, with some employee-friendly rulings on this issue.[3] In *Barbuto*, the plaintiff, suffer-

1 *See* N.Y. Pub. Health Law § 3360, *et seq.*

2 *See Garcia v. Tractor Supply Co.*, 154 F.Supp.3d 1225 (D.N.M. 2016), *appeal dismissed*, Case No. 16-2020 (10th Cir. Mar. 25, 2016). "This case turns on whether New Mexico's Compassionate Use Act ('CUA') combined with the New Mexico Human Rights Act provides a cause of action for Mr. Garcia. Everpresent in the background of this case is whether the [federal] Controlled Substances Act preempts New Mexico state law." The *Garcia* court evaluated cases from other states on the same or similar issues, and while state laws may exempt medical marijuana users from state prosecution, they do not protect users from federal prosecution, nor can they require that employers accommodate something that federal law expressly prohibits. *See also Lambdin v. Marriott Resorts Hospitality Corp.*, 2017 WL 4079718 (D. Haw. Sept. 14, 2017) (on appeal No. 17-17053 (9th Cir.) as of September 2, 2019) (citing *Garcia*; granting defendant summary judgment under both the ADA and Hawaii state law because Hawaii had also adopted *McDonnell Douglas* burden shifting under state law).

3 *See Barbuto v. Advantage Sales & Mkting., LLC*, 477 Mass. 456 (2017).

ing from Crohn's Disease and irritable bowel syndrome, was told that her medical use of marijuana at home would not be an issue. She did not use at work and did not come to work under the influence. The court found that if the medication prescribed is against an employer's policy, the employer has a duty to engage in the interactive process to identify reasonable alternative terms and conditions of employment. If there is no equally effective reasonable alternative, the employer has the burden of showing the employee's use of the medication creates an undue hardship to the business to justify refusal of an exception to the policy. For instance, employees cannot be impaired at work, or hampered in the execution of their job functions. Although the employer in *Barbuto* argued that marijuana was illegal under federal law, the Massachusetts Supreme Judicial Court held that did not make it *per se* unreasonable as an accommodation. Failing to engage in the interactive process might run afoul of that state's act.

In Connecticut, we find the federal court case of *Noffsinger v. SSC Niantic Operating Co., LLC.*[4] State law in Connecticut included the Palliative Use of Marijuana Act. The law contained a provision prohibiting employers from discriminating against authorized users, and the court upheld the law. The state law was not preempted by any federal law, including the Controlled Substances Act and Americans with Disabilities Act. The employer's motion to dismiss was denied in large part, and the employee or prospective employee using marijuana in accordance with state law could maintain an action against an employer for discrimination.

Is there a matter of semantics here? Are courts splitting hairs to make a distinction between state laws that permit dispensing and use of medical marijuana, and the federal Controlled Substances Act that prohibits marijuana possession and use for any reason? There is a distinction between state laws that permit such use and distribution, thereby prohibiting prosecution under state criminal laws, and state anti-discrimination laws that require employers to accommodate medical marijuana use even if that use violates the federal law. But, now, with the shifting decisions, employers must take care depending on the wording of the state statutes, and the case-specific circumstances of use and the workplace needs.[5]

---

4 273 F. Supp. 3d 526 (D. Conn. 2017).

5 *See and compare White Mountain Health Ctr., Inc. v. Maricopa County*, 386 P.3d 416, 241 Ariz. 230 (Ariz. Ct. Apps. 2016), *with Emerald Steel Fabricators, Inc. v. Bureau of Labor & Industries*, 348 Or. 159, 230 P.3d 518 (2010).

In New York, the Compassionate Care Act specifically grants protections for certified patients, under the Human Rights Law, as those having a disability. Under the CCA, New York employers with four or more employees may not discharge or discipline an employee who is a certified marijuana use patient. This is an evolving area. If an employer has an employee who is a certified patient, and uses medical marijuana, and tests positive for it, an accommodation may be necessary under the State Human Rights Law (and New York City Human Rights Law), unless same would jeopardize a federal contract, or violate federal regulations that govern the business. There are also some other questions: i.e., is the employee needing to use the marijuana while on the job? What are the job duties—driver, forklift operator, surgeon, litigator, police officer? Perhaps an interactive process discussion will be needed to determine if there are other jobs the person is qualified for, where the marijuana use will not inhibit their abilities to safely complete the essential functions.

As is clear from this brief discussion, medical marijuana and the divide between state and federal law is experiencing an ongoing sea-change, which requires careful analysis with legal counsel. See Chapter 6 for more discussion concerning the ADA, disability protections and policies, and the interactive process.

[8.5] VI. HYPOTHETICAL #6 – THE MOVIE THEATRE PATRON WITH A DISABILITY

Entrepreneur owns a movie theatre in a small city/large town. A patron comes to the theater requesting a tactile interpreter—using American Sign Language—because the patron is both blind and deaf, and the interpreter would allow the disabled patron to experience what sighted and hearing customers could experience. Is the theatre required to provide the interpreter under the Americans with Disabilities Act?

Analysis: Recall the material in Chapter 6. We begin with two important questions. (1) Is the theatre a place of public accommodation? Answer: Yes. (2) Does the theatre need to consider the accommodation? Answer: Yes. Then we come to the third question on which the case may hinge: (3) Is the accommodation reasonable? Answer: According to the Third Circuit U.S. Court of Appeals, yes, subject to defenses such as "undue hardship" or "undue burden."

This was the scenario in *McGann v. Cinemark USA, Inc.*,[6] which is cited in Chapter 6. The plaintiff movie patron was both deaf and blind. Prior to his wife's passing, she interpreted for him. After that, a particular theater that plaintiff had attended provided a tactile interpreter. The defendant movie theater in this particular case at issue was showing a movie that plaintiff's regular theater was no longer showing.

The defendant theater chain (having 335 theaters and 4,499 screens across 41 states) was not a small business. It did offer services for those with disabilities, but none that could accommodate this particular plaintiff's needs. The theater argued that it had never received a request for a tactile interpreter like plaintiff's before, and because of the complexity of the movie (*Gone Girl*), two interpreters would be required from the service provider for a minimum of two hours each, at a cost of $50–$65 an hour, and the request was denied.

The plaintiff, claiming a violation of Title III of the ADA, brought suit in U.S. district court. After a bench trial, the chief magistrate judge ruled for the theatre. Thereafter, the Third Circuit stated that: "Title III begins with a '[g]eneral rule' that '[n]o individual shall be discriminated against on the basis of disability in the full and equal enjoyment of the goods, services, facilities, privileges, advantages, or accommodations of any place of public accommodation.' . . . These general prohibitions include, inter alia, denying an individual on the basis of a disability 'the opportunity . . . to participate in or benefit from the goods [or] services' of a public accommodation."[7] There was no dispute that plaintiff was disabled as per the ADA. Furthermore, an ASL tactile interpreter is an auxiliary aid or service, and the tactile interpreter was a qualified interpreter.

The Third Circuit then provided detailed analysis regarding how denial of the interpreter denied plaintiff or excluded plaintiff from defendant's services. Although the Circuit reversed the district court, the case was remanded so that the district court could consider one of defendant's defenses: "'undue burden' under Title III 'mean[ing] significant difficulty or expense.'"[8] If defendant theatre could establish a defense of undue burden, that would allow the theatre to prevail in defending itself in the case and denying the accommodation as unreasonable. The reader should also

6 873 F.3d 218 (3d Cir. 2017).

7 *McGann*, 873 F.3d at 222 (citing 42 U.S.C. § 12182(b)(1)(A)(i)).

8 *Id.* at 231 (citing 28 C.F.R. § 36.104.).

look to the case of *Washington State Communication Access Project v. Regal Cinemas, Inc.*[9]

[8.6] VII. HYPOTHETICAL #7 – INACCESSIBLE WEBSITE

XYZ, Inc. is a business operating in Manhattan, with a leased storefront located on the ground level of a midtown building. XYZ decides to utilize a website to attract further business and customers. Finding success, XYZ opens a second location in Hoboken, New Jersey and a third location in Cocoa Beach, Florida. Thereafter, a potential customer contacts XYZ to complain that they are a blind patron, and are unable to use XYZ's website because the site is not compatible with any software or technology that the patron otherwise uses to surf the web and access the sites of other businesses. XYZ responds that it is a small business and is sorry it cannot help the customer online. XYZ recommends the customer try another store or visit the brick-and-mortar locations for assistance from a sales associate. What result?

Analysis: This scenario is addressed in Chapter 7. Here, the business appears to be in violation of both New York State Human Rights Law/ Civil Rights Law provisions and Title III of the Americans with Disabilities Act (neither New Jersey nor Florida state law is addressed in this book, and thus would require separate analysis with legal counsel to determine if the business is likewise violating any New Jersey or Florida laws).

Keep in mind that in contrast to "reasonable accommodations" for disabilities discussed in Chapter 6, a "place of public accommodation" is a business—it means the "business" itself. For this hypothetical, recall that the size of the business does not matter, all places of public accommodation must comply with Title III of the ADA, and thus this business is subject to the ADA. Furthermore, the business has a brick-and-mortar location. Although the courts are split as to whether a website alone qualifies as a place of public accommodation, as discussed in Chapter 7, the courts are in agreement that if a business with a physical location also operates a website tangential to or augmenting the business itself, that website must be compliant with the ADA and state law for accessibility by those with disabilities. It is also of no moment, given the caselaw addressed in Chapter 7, that XYZ offers for the patron to come to the

9 173 Wash. App. 174, 293 P.3d 413 (Wash. Ct. Apps. Div. 1 2013) (issue of movie patron access under state law).

business' physical location for assistance. That is not providing the visually impaired patron the same services as provided to those not having the same impairment.[10]

In this hypothetical, the website should be compatible with screen readers for the visually impaired, allowing the disabled patron to be similarly situated to, and have equal access to the same information as, non-disabled patrons. The benefits are multiple. Avoiding lawsuits is one reason. Others? Being inclusive, welcoming, open to diversity, and opposed to bias in society.

10 *See Juscinska v. Paper Factory Hotel, LLC*, 2019 WL 2343306 at *4 (S.D.N.Y. June 3, 2019) (a 24/7 phone line accessible to those with disabilities who are unable to access certain information online is not the same as a website allowing both disabled and non-disabled patrons to access all necessary information about hotel rooms online).

APPENDIX A

Sexual Harassment Policy for All Employers in New York State

Introduction

[*Employer Name*] is committed to maintaining a workplace free from sexual harassment. Sexual harassment is a form of workplace discrimination. All employees are required to work in a manner that prevents sexual harassment in the workplace. This Policy is one component of [*Employer Name's*] commitment to a discrimination-free work environment. Sexual harassment is against the law[1] and all employees have a legal right to a workplace free from sexual harassment and employees are urged to report sexual harassment by filing a complaint internally with [*Employer Name*]. Employees can also file a complaint with a government agency or in court under federal, state or local antidiscrimination laws.

Policy:

1. [*Employer Name's*] policy applies to all employees, applicants for employment, interns, whether paid or unpaid, contractors and persons conducting business, regardless of immigration status, with [*Employer Name*]. In the remainder of this document, the term "employees" refers to this collective group.

2. Sexual harassment will not be tolerated. Any employee or individual covered by this policy who engages in sexual harassment or retaliation will be subject to remedial and/or disciplinary action (e.g., counseling, suspension, termination).

3. Retaliation Prohibition: No person covered by this Policy shall be subject to adverse action because the employee reports an incident of sexual harassment, provides information, or otherwise assists in any investigation of a sexual harassment complaint. [*Employer Name*] will not tolerate such retaliation against anyone who, in good faith, reports or provides information about suspected sexual harassment. Any employee of [*Employer Name*] who retaliates against anyone involved in a sexual harassment investigation will be subjected to disciplinary action, up to and including termination. All employees, paid or unpaid interns, or non-employees[2] working in the workplace who believe they have been subject to such retaliation should inform a supervisor, manager, or [*name of appropriate person*]. All employees, paid or unpaid interns or non-employees who believe they have been a target of such retaliation may also seek relief in other available forums, as explained below in the section on Legal Protections.

[1] While this policy specifically addresses sexual harassment, harassment because of and discrimination against persons of all protected classes is prohibited. In New York State, such classes include age, race, creed, color, national origin, sexual orientation, military status, sex, disability, marital status, domestic violence victim status, gender identity or expression, familial status, predisposing genetic characteristics, and criminal history.

[2] A non-employee is someone who is (or is employed by) a contractor, subcontractor, vendor, consultant, or anyone providing services in the workplace. Protected non-employees include persons commonly referred to as independent contractors, "gig" workers and temporary workers. Also included are persons providing equipment repair, cleaning services or any other services provided pursuant to a contract with the employer.

Adoption of this policy does not constitute a conclusive defense to charges of unlawful sexual harassment. Each claim of sexual harassment will be determined in accordance with existing legal standards, with due consideration of the particular facts and circumstances of the claim, including but not limited to the existence of an effective anti-harassment policy and procedure.

4. Sexual harassment is offensive, is a violation of our policies, is unlawful, and may subject [*Employer Name*] to liability for harm to targets of sexual harassment. Harassers may also be individually subject to liability. Employees of every level who engage in sexual harassment, including managers and supervisors who engage in sexual harassment or who allow such behavior to continue, will be penalized for such misconduct.

5. [*Employer Name*] will conduct a prompt and thorough investigation that ensures due process for all parties, whenever management receives a complaint about sexual harassment, or otherwise knows of possible sexual harassment occurring. [*Employer Name*] will keep the investigation confidential to the extent possible. Effective corrective action will be taken whenever sexual harassment is found to have occurred. All employees, including managers and supervisors, are required to cooperate with any internal investigation of sexual harassment.

6. All employees are encouraged to report any harassment or behaviors that violate this policy. [*Employer Name*] will provide all employees a complaint form for employees to report harassment and file complaints.

7. Managers and supervisors are **required** to report any complaint that they receive, or any harassment that they observe or become aware of, to [*person or office designated*].

8. This policy applies to all employees, paid or unpaid interns, and non-employees, such as contractors, subcontractors, vendors, consultants or anyone providing services in the workplace, and all must follow and uphold this policy. This policy must be provided to all employees and should be posted prominently in all work locations to the extent practicable (for example, in a main office, not an offsite work location) and be provided to employees upon hiring.

What Is "Sexual Harassment"?

Sexual harassment is a form of sex discrimination and is unlawful under federal, state, and (where applicable) local law. Sexual harassment includes harassment on the basis of sex, sexual orientation, self-identified or perceived sex, gender expression, gender identity and the status of being transgender.

Sexual harassment is unlawful when it subjects an individual to inferior terms, conditions, or privileges of employment. Harassment need not be severe or pervasive to be unlawful, and can be any harassing conduct that consists of more than petty slights or trivial inconveniences. Sexual harassment includes unwelcome conduct which is either of a sexual nature, or which is directed at an individual because of that individual's sex when:

- Such conduct has the purpose or effect of unreasonably interfering with an individual's work performance or creating an intimidating, hostile or offensive work environment, even if the reporting individual is not the intended target of the sexual harassment;

- Such conduct is made either explicitly or implicitly a term or condition of employment; or

- Submission to or rejection of such conduct is used as the basis for employment decisions affecting an individual's employment.

A sexually harassing hostile work environment includes, but is not limited to, words, signs, jokes, pranks, intimidation or physical violence which are of a sexual nature, or which are directed at an individual because of that individual's sex. Sexual harassment also consists of any unwanted verbal or physical advances, sexually explicit derogatory statements or sexually discriminatory remarks made by someone which are offensive or objectionable to the recipient, which cause the recipient discomfort or humiliation, which interfere with the recipient's job performance.

Sexual harassment also occurs when a person in authority tries to trade job benefits for sexual favors. This can include hiring, promotion, continued employment or any other terms, conditions or privileges of employment. This is also called "quid pro quo" harassment.

Any employee who feels harassed should report so that any violation of this policy can be corrected promptly. Any harassing conduct, even a single incident, can be addressed under this policy.

Examples of sexual harassment

The following describes some of the types of acts that may be unlawful sexual harassment and that are strictly prohibited:

- Physical acts of a sexual nature, such as:
  - Touching, pinching, patting, kissing, hugging, grabbing, brushing against another employee's body or poking another employee's body;
  - Rape, sexual battery, molestation or attempts to commit these assaults.

- Unwanted sexual advances or propositions, such as:
  - Requests for sexual favors accompanied by implied or overt threats concerning the target's job performance evaluation, a promotion or other job benefits or detriments;
  - Subtle or obvious pressure for unwelcome sexual activities.

- Sexually oriented gestures, noises, remarks or jokes, or comments about a person's sexuality or sexual experience, which create a hostile work environment.

- Sex stereotyping occurs when conduct or personality traits are considered inappropriate simply because they may not conform to other people's ideas or perceptions about how individuals of a particular sex should act or look.

- Sexual or discriminatory displays or publications anywhere in the workplace, such as:
  - Displaying pictures, posters, calendars, graffiti, objects, promotional material, reading materials or other materials that are sexually demeaning or pornographic. This includes such sexual displays on workplace computers or cell phones and sharing such displays while in the workplace.

- Hostile actions taken against an individual because of that individual's sex, sexual orientation, gender identity and the status of being transgender, such as:
  - Interfering with, destroying or damaging a person's workstation, tools or equipment, or otherwise interfering with the individual's ability to perform the job;
  - Sabotaging an individual's work;
  - Bullying, yelling, name-calling.

Who can be a target of sexual harassment?

Sexual harassment can occur between any individuals, regardless of their sex or gender. New York Law protects employees, paid or unpaid interns, and non-employees, including independent contractors, and those employed by companies contracting to provide services in the workplace. Harassers can be a superior, a subordinate, a coworker or anyone in the workplace including an independent contractor, contract worker, vendor, client, customer or visitor.

Where can sexual harassment occur?

Unlawful sexual harassment is not limited to the physical workplace itself. It can occur while employees are traveling for business or at employer sponsored events or parties. Calls, texts, emails, and social media usage by employees can constitute unlawful workplace harassment, even if they occur away from the workplace premises, on personal devices or during non-work hours.

Retaliation

Unlawful retaliation can be any action that could discourage a worker from coming forward to make or support a sexual harassment claim. Adverse action need not be job-related or occur in the workplace to constitute unlawful retaliation (e.g., threats of physical violence outside of work hours).

Such retaliation is unlawful under federal, state, and (where applicable) local law. The New York State Human Rights Law protects any individual who has engaged in "protected activity." Protected activity occurs when a person has:

- made a complaint of sexual harassment, either internally or with any anti-discrimination agency;
- testified or assisted in a proceeding involving sexual harassment under the Human Rights Law or other anti-discrimination law;
- opposed sexual harassment by making a verbal or informal complaint to management, or by simply informing a supervisor or manager of harassment;
- reported that another employee has been sexually harassed; or
- encouraged a fellow employee to report harassment.

Even if the alleged harassment does not turn out to rise to the level of a violation of law, the individual is protected from retaliation if the person had a good faith belief that the practices were unlawful. However, the retaliation provision is not intended to protect persons making intentionally false charges of harassment.

Reporting Sexual Harassment

Preventing sexual harassment is everyone's responsibility. [*Employer Name*] cannot prevent or remedy sexual harassment unless it knows about it. Any employee, paid or unpaid intern or non-employee who has been subjected to behavior that may constitute sexual harassment is encouraged to report such behavior to a supervisor, manager or [*person or office designated*]. Anyone who witnesses or becomes aware of potential instances of sexual harassment should report such behavior to a supervisor, manager or [*person or office designated*].

Reports of sexual harassment may be made verbally or in writing. A form for submission of a written complaint is attached to this Policy, and all employees are encouraged to use this complaint form. Employees who are reporting sexual harassment on behalf of other employees should use the complaint form and note that it is on another employee's behalf.

Employees, paid or unpaid interns or non-employees who believe they have been a target of sexual harassment may also seek assistance in other available forums, as explained below in the section on Legal Protections.

Supervisory Responsibilities

All supervisors and managers who receive a complaint or information about suspected sexual harassment, observe what may be sexually harassing behavior or for any reason suspect that sexual harassment is occurring, **are required** to report such suspected sexual harassment to [*person or office designated*].

In addition to being subject to discipline if they engaged in sexually harassing conduct themselves, supervisors and managers will be subject to discipline for failing to report suspected sexual harassment or otherwise knowingly allowing sexual harassment to continue.

Supervisors and managers will also be subject to discipline for engaging in any retaliation.

Complaint and Investigation of Sexual Harassment

All complaints or information about sexual harassment will be investigated, whether that information was reported in verbal or written form. Investigations will be conducted in a timely manner, and will be confidential to the extent possible.

An investigation of any complaint, information or knowledge of suspected sexual harassment will be prompt and thorough, commenced immediately and completed as soon as possible. The investigation will be kept confidential to the extent possible. All persons involved, including complainants, witnesses and alleged harassers will be accorded due process, as outlined below, to protect their rights to a fair and impartial investigation.

Any employee may be required to cooperate as needed in an investigation of suspected sexual harassment. [*Employer Name*] will not tolerate retaliation against employees who file complaints, support another's complaint or participate in an investigation regarding a violation of this policy.

While the process may vary from case to case, investigations should be done in accordance with the following steps:

- Upon receipt of complaint, [*person or office designated*] will conduct an immediate review of the allegations, and take any interim actions (e.g., instructing the respondent to refrain from communications with the complainant), as appropriate. If complaint is verbal, encourage the individual to complete the "Complaint Form" in writing. If he or she refuses, prepare a Complaint Form based on the verbal reporting.

- If documents, emails or phone records are relevant to the investigation, take steps to obtain and preserve them.

- Request and review all relevant documents, including all electronic communications.

- Interview all parties involved, including any relevant witnesses;

- Create a written documentation of the investigation (such as a letter, memo or email), which contains the following:
    - A list of all documents reviewed, along with a detailed summary of relevant documents;
    - A list of names of those interviewed, along with a detailed summary of their statements;
    - A timeline of events;
    - A summary of prior relevant incidents, reported or unreported; and
    - The basis for the decision and final resolution of the complaint, together with any corrective action(s).

- Keep the written documentation and associated documents in a secure and confidential location.

- Promptly notify the individual who reported and the individual(s) about whom the complaint was made of the final determination and implement any corrective actions identified in the written document.

- Inform the individual who reported of the right to file a complaint or charge externally as outlined in the next section.

Legal Protections And External Remedies

Sexual harassment is not only prohibited by [*Employer Name*] but is also prohibited by state, federal, and, where applicable, local law.

Aside from the internal process at [*Employer Name*], employees may also choose to pursue legal remedies with the following governmental entities. While a private attorney is not required to file a complaint with a governmental agency, you may seek the legal advice of an attorney.

In addition to those outlined below, employees in certain industries may have additional legal protections.

State Human Rights Law (HRL)

The Human Rights Law (HRL), codified as N.Y. Executive Law, art. 15, § 290 et seq., applies to all employers in New York State with regard to sexual harassment, and protects employees, paid or unpaid interns and non-employees, regardless of immigration status. A complaint alleging violation of the Human Rights Law may be filed either with the Division of Human Rights (DHR) or in New York State Supreme Court.

Complaints with DHR may be filed any time **within one year (three years beginning Aug. 12, 2020)** of the harassment. If an individual did not file at DHR, they can sue directly in state court under the HRL, **within three years** of the alleged sexual harassment. An individual may not file with DHR if they have already filed a HRL complaint in state court.

Complaining internally to [*Employer Name*] does not extend your time to file with DHR or in court. The one year or three years is counted from date of the most recent incident of harassment.

You do not need an attorney to file a complaint with DHR, and there is no cost to file with DHR.

DHR will investigate your complaint and determine whether there is probable cause to believe that sexual harassment has occurred. Probable cause cases are forwarded to a public hearing before an administrative law judge. If sexual harassment is found after a hearing, DHR has the power to award relief, which varies but may include requiring your employer to take action to stop the harassment, or redress the damage caused, including paying of monetary damages, attorney's fees and civil fines.

DHR's main office contact information is: NYS Division of Human Rights, One Fordham Plaza, Fourth Floor, Bronx, New York 10458. You may call (718) 741-8400 or visit: www.dhr.ny.gov.

Contact DHR at (888) 392-3644 or visit dhr.ny.gov/complaint for more information about filing a complaint. The website has a complaint form that can be downloaded, filled out, notarized and mailed to DHR. The website also contains contact information for DHR's regional offices across New York State.

Civil Rights Act of 1964

The United States Equal Employment Opportunity Commission (EEOC) enforces federal anti-discrimination laws, including Title VII of the 1964 federal Civil Rights Act (codified as 42 U.S.C. § 2000e et seq.). An individual can file a complaint with the EEOC anytime within 300 days from the harassment. There is no cost to file a complaint with the EEOC. The EEOC will investigate the complaint, and determine whether there is reasonable cause to believe that discrimination has occurred, at which point the EEOC will issue a Right to Sue letter permitting the individual to file a complaint in federal court.

The EEOC does not hold hearings or award relief, but may take other action including pursuing cases in federal court on behalf of complaining parties. Federal courts may award remedies if discrimination is found to have occurred. In general, private employers must have at least 15 employees to come within the jurisdiction of the EEOC.

An employee alleging discrimination at work can file a "Charge of Discrimination." The EEOC has district, area, and field offices where complaints can be filed. Contact the EEOC by calling 1-800-669-4000 (TTY: 1-800-669-6820), visiting their website at www.eeoc.gov or via email at info@eeoc.gov.

If an individual filed an administrative complaint with DHR, DHR will file the complaint with the EEOC to preserve the right to proceed in federal court.

Local Protections

Many localities enforce laws protecting individuals from sexual harassment and discrimination. An individual should contact the county, city or town in which they live to find out if such a law exists. For example, employees who work in New York City may file complaints of sexual harassment with the New York City Commission on Human Rights. Contact their main office at Law Enforcement Bureau of the NYC Commission on Human Rights, 22 Reade Street, 1st Floor, New York, New York; call 311 or (212) 306-7450; or visit www.nyc.gov/html/cchr/html/home/home.shtml.

Contact the Local Police Department

If the harassment involves unwanted physical touching, coerced physical confinement or coerced sex acts, the conduct may constitute a crime. Contact the local police department.

APPENDIX B

Minimum Standards For Sexual Harassment Prevention Policies

Every employer in the State of New York is required to adopt a sexual harassment prevention policy pursuant to Section 201-g of the Labor Law. An employer that does not adopt the model policy must ensure that the policy that they adopt meets or exceeds the following minimum standards. The policy must:

i) prohibit sexual harassment consistent with guidance issued by the Department of Labor in consultation with the Division of Human Rights;

ii) provide examples of prohibited conduct that would constitute unlawful sexual harassment;

iii) include information concerning the federal and state statutory provisions concerning sexual harassment, remedies available to victims of sexual harassment, and a statement that there may be applicable local laws;

iv) include a complaint form;

v) include a procedure for the timely and confidential investigation of complaints that ensures due process for all parties;

vi) inform employees of their rights of redress and all available forums for adjudicating sexual harassment complaints administratively and judicially;

vii) clearly state that sexual harassment is considered a form of employee misconduct and that sanctions will be enforced against individuals engaging in sexual harassment and against supervisory and managerial personnel who knowingly allow such behavior to continue; and

viii) clearly state that retaliation against individuals who complain of sexual harassment or who testify or assist in any investigation or proceeding involving sexual harassment is unlawful.

Employers must provide each employee with a copy of its policy in writing. Employers should provide employees with the policy in the language that is spoken by their employees.

* * *

The adoption of a policy does not constitute a conclusive defense to charges of unlawful sexual harassment. Each claim of sexual harassment will be determined in accordance with existing legal standards, with due consideration of the particular facts and circumstances of the claim, including but not limited to the existence of an effective anti-harassment policy and procedure.

APPENDIX C

Sexual Harassment Prevention Employer Toolkit

NEW YORK STATE | Combating Sexual Harassment

Introduction

New York State is a national leader in the fight against sexual harassment and is partnering with employers across the state to further our commitment to ending sexual harassment in the workplace.

This toolkit will provide you step-by-step guidance to implementing the required training and sexual harassment policy, directing you to resources available through New York State and the relevant state agencies.

These resources are all available on the State's Combating Sexual Harassment in the Workplace website: **www.ny.gov/programs/combating-sexual-harassment-workplace**.

What are the Requirements?

Notice to Employees

Every employee in New York State must receive a sexual harassment prevention notice at the time of hiring and during their annual sexual harassment training. This notice must contain: 1) your sexual harassment policy and 2) the information presented at the sexual harassment prevention training. You must provide employees with this notice, policy and training information in English and in an employee's primary language if it is Spanish, Chinese, Korean, Polish, Russian, Haitian-Creole, Bengali, or Italian. Model templates are available online.

Policy (see pages 2-4)

Under the new law, every employer in New York State is **required to establish a sexual harassment prevention policy**. The Department of Labor in consultation with the Division of Human Rights has established a model sexual harassment prevention policy for employers to adopt, available at www.ny.gov/programs/combating-sexual-harassment-workplace. Or, employers may adopt a similar policy that meets or exceeds the minimum standards of the model policy (www.ny.gov/combating-sexual-harassment-workplace/employers#model-sexual-harassment-policy).

Training (see pages 5-6)

In addition, every employer in New York State is **required to provide employees with sexual harassment prevention training**. The Department of Labor in consultation with the Division of Human Rights has established this model training for employers to use. Or, employers may use a training program that meets or exceeds the minimum standards of the model training (www.ny.gov/combating-sexual-harassment-workplace/employers#training-requirements).

Policy

All employers must adopt and provide employees with their sexual harassment prevention policy.

If you want to adopt the State Model Policy:

- Download the model policy, available online: www.ny.gov/combating-sexual-harassment-workplace/employers#model-sexual-harassment-policy
- The State Model Policy contains fields for you to list your business name and the name/contact information for the individual(s) you have designated to receive sexual harassment complaints. Fill in those fields and apply whatever branding (e.g., logos, etc.) you like.
- You may choose to modify the policy to reflect the work of your organization and industry specific scenarios or best practices.
- Distribute the policy to all employees in writing or electronically.
- Employers are also encouraged to have employees acknowledge receipt of the policy, and to post a copy of the policy where employees can easily access it. You are also encouraged to provide the policy and training to any non-employees providing services in the workplace.

If you already have a policy and do NOT want to adopt the State Model Policy:

- Use the checklist on the next page to ensure your policy meets or exceeds the required minimum standards.
- New employees must receive this policy at the time of hiring.
- Ensure your complaint form and process are up to date and that employees are made aware of them as part of the policy.
- If you do not have a complaint form, a model is available online: www.ny.gov/combating-sexual-harassment-workplace/employers#model-complaint-form
- Review the online FAQs, which outline numerous common questions that may arise: www.ny.gov/combating-sexual-harassment-workplace/combating-sexual-harassment-frequently-asked-questions
- Distribute a copy of your finalized policy to all employees in writing. This may be done electronically, for example, by email. Employers are also encouraged to have employees acknowledge receipt of the policy, and to post a copy of the policy where employees can easily access it.
- You are also encouraged to provide the policy and training to any non-employees providing services in the workplace.

Policy: Minimum Standards Checklist

An employer that does not use the State model policy -- developed by the State Department of Labor and State Division of Human Rights -- must ensure their policy meets or exceeds the following minimum standards.

The policy **must**:

- ☐ Prohibit sexual harassment consistent with guidance issued by the Department of Labor in consultation with the Division of Human Rights;
- ☐ Provide examples of prohibited conduct;
- ☐ Include information concerning the federal and state statutory provisions concerning sexual harassment, remedies available to victims of sexual harassment, and a statement that there may be applicable local laws;
- ☐ Include a complaint form;
- ☐ Include a procedure for the timely and confidential investigation of complaints that ensures due process for all parties;
- ☐ Inform employees of their rights of redress and all available forums for adjudicating sexual harassment complaints administratively and judicially;
- ☐ Clearly state that sexual harassment is considered a form of employee misconduct and that sanctions will be enforced against individuals engaging in sexual harassment and against supervisory and managerial personnel who knowingly allow such behavior to continue; and
- ☐ Clearly state that retaliation against individuals who complain of sexual harassment or who testify or assist in any investigation or proceeding involving sexual harassment is unlawful;
- ☐ Be provided to employees, in writing, at the time of hiring and at every annual training; and
- ☐ Be provided in English <u>and</u> in an employee's primary language if it is Spanish, Chinese, Korean, Polish, Russian, Haitian-Creole, Bengali, or Italian. Model templates are available online.

Training: Instructions for Employers

All employees must complete sexual harassment prevention training at least once per year. This may be based on calendar year, anniversary of each employee's start date or any other date the employer chooses. New employees should be trained as quickly as possible.

If you already have a training:

- Use the checklist on the next page to ensure your training meets or exceeds the required minimum standards.
- If your existing training does not, it should be updated to include all the listed elements. You may also provide supplemental training to employers who have already completed the training to ensure they have received training that meets or exceeds the minimum standards.
- Review the online FAQs, which outline numerous common questions that may arise: www.ny.gov/combating-sexual-harassment-workplace/combating-sexual-harassment-frequently-asked-questions

If you want to adopt the State Model Training:

- Download the model training, available online: www.ny.gov/combating-sexual-harassment-workplace/employers#training-requirements.
  - You may execute this training in a variety of ways, including live in person, via webinar or on an individual basis, with feedback as outlined in the training guidance document.
  - Depending on how you choose to present your training, you may utilize different available resources. For example, if you do a live presentation, you should download the PowerPoint and read the script that appears in the "Notes" of each slide.
  - If you choose to train employees with the video, you may direct them to watch it online or download it and show to a group, after which you would provide them a mechanism for feedback, as outlined in the training guidance document.
- Customize the training document(s) and modify them to reflect the work of your organization, including industry specific scenarios or best practices.
- The training should detail any internal process employees are encouraged to use to complain and include the contact Information for the specific name(s) and office(s) with which employees alleging harassment should file their complaints.
- You may wish to include additional interactive activities as part of the training, including an opening activity, role playing or group discussion(s).
- Review the online FAQs, which outline numerous common questions that may arise: www.ny.gov/combating-sexual-harassment-workplace/combating-sexual-harassment-frequently-asked-questions

Training: Minimum Standards Checklist

An employer that does not use this model training -- developed by the State Department of Labor and State Division of Human Rights -- must ensure their training meets or exceeds the following minimum standards.

The training **must**:

- ☐ Be interactive (*see the model training guidance document for specific recommendations*);
- ☐ Include an explanation of sexual harassment consistent with guidance issued by the Department of Labor in consultation with the Division of Human Rights;
- ☐ Include examples of unlawful sexual harassment;
- ☐ Include information concerning the federal and state statutory provisions concerning sexual harassment and remedies available to targets of sexual harassment;
- ☐ Include information concerning employees' rights of redress and all available forums for adjudicating complaints; and
- ☐ Include information addressing conduct by supervisors and additional responsibilities for supervisors.

Every employee must receive sexual harassment prevention training annually. During this annual training, **employers must also provide employees a notice** that contains:

(i) the employer's sexual harassment policy; and

(ii) a copy of the information presented at the sexual harassment prevention training.

Employers must provide employees with this notice, policy and training information in English <u>and</u> in an employee's primary language if it is Spanish, Chinese, Korean, Polish, Russian, Haitian-Creole, Bengali, or Italian. Model templates are available online.

Sexual Harassment Prevention Notice

Sexual harassment is against the law.

All employees have a legal right to a workplace free from sexual harassment, and [*Employer Name*] is committed to maintaining a workplace free from sexual harassment.

Per New York State Law, [*Employer Name*] has a sexual harassment prevention policy in place that protects you. This policy applies to all employees, paid or unpaid interns and non-employees in our workplace, regardless of immigration status. You are receiving this notice, as required by law, either at the time of hiring or during your annual sexual harassment prevention training.

If you believe you have been subjected to or witnessed sexual harassment, you are encouraged to report the harassment to a supervisor, manager or [other person designated] so we can take action.

Our complete policy ☐ is enclosed/attached ☐ may be found at the link below:

____

Our training materials ☐ are enclosed/attached ☐ may be found at the link below:

____

Our Complaint Form ☐ is enclosed/attached ☐ may be found at the link below:

____

If you have questions or to make a complaint, please contact:

[Person or office designated]

[Contact information for designee or office]

For more information and additional resources, please visit:
www.ny.gov/programs/combating-sexual-harassment-workplace

10/19 Version

APPENDIX D

No. 204

EXECUTIVE ORDER

DECLARING JUNETEENTH A HOLIDAY FOR NEW YORK STATE EMPLOYEES

WHEREAS, the news of liberation of slaves came to Texas more than two years after President Abraham Lincoln's Emancipation Proclamation went into effect on January 1, 1863; African Americans across the state were made aware of their right to freedom on June 19, 1865, when Major General Gordon Granger arrived in Galveston with federal troops to read General Order No. 3 announcing the end of the Civil War and that all enslaved people were now free, as well as to maintain a presence in Texas for the purpose of enforcement of emancipation among slave-owners throughout the state; and

WHEREAS, the Empire State has a tradition of acknowledging significant milestones in advancing the cause of freedom, and New Yorkers, some of whom descend directly from those brave men and women that gained freedom on that day, join in celebrating the 155th anniversary of Juneteenth, an observance that commemorates the official announcement made in the State of Texas regarding the abolition of slavery and the freeing of some quarter-million African Americans; and

WHEREAS, the observance of Juneteenth honors the history, perseverance, and achievements of African Americans, and celebrates America's progress and continuing commitment to realizing the principles of liberty and equality upon which our nation was founded; and

WHEREAS, this observance is a reminder of the hardships and losses suffered by African Americans in their struggle to attain freedom, and we pay tribute to the memory of those who made the ultimate sacrifice in this quest; through their experiences and those of others who were successful in achieving victory, we find among the most poignant and valuable lessons of humankind that continue to resonate with people of all backgrounds; and

WHEREAS, the official emancipation of African Americans throughout the United States literally and figuratively opened doors of opportunity that enabled following generations to contribute immeasurably to our nation's richness, equality of citizens, and global leadership, and today communities across our state – from Brooklyn to Buffalo – mark the anniversary of Juneteenth with appropriate commemoration; and

WHEREAS, it is fitting that all New Yorkers join to commemorate such an important day in our nation's history, as we take this opportunity to reflect upon and rejoice in the freedom and civil rights that we all share as Americans;

NOW, THEREFORE, I, Andrew M. Cuomo, Governor of the State of New York, by virtue of the Constitution of the State of New York, specifically Article IV, section one, and the laws of the state of New York do hereby recognize June 19, 2020 as Juneteenth, which shall be a holiday for state employees, who if not required to work, shall be entitled to leave at full pay without charge to existing accruals and for those employees who are required to work, they shall receive one day of compensatory time.

G I V E N under my hand and the Privy Seal of the State in the City of Albany this seventeenth day of June in the year two thousand twenty.

BY THE GOVERNOR

Secretary to the Governor

APPENDIX E

NEWS ADVISORY

New York State
Unified Court System

Hon. Lawrence K. Marks
Chief Administrative Judge

Contact:
Lucian Chalfen
Public Information Director
Arlene Hackel, Deputy Director
(212) 428-2500

www.nycourts.gov/press

Date: June 29, 2020

Revised Guidelines Aim to Facilitate Swifter Provision of Appropriate Accommodations for Court Users with Special Needs

NEW YORK–As part of the court system's ongoing efforts to enhance access to justice for New Yorkers with visual, hearing, communication, mobility, cognitive and other disabilities, Chief Administrative Judge Lawrence K. Marks has approved the implementation of new guidelines to simplify the handling of requests for accommodations of disabilities made by parties, attorneys, witnesses and other court visitors in the New York State trial courts.

The revised guidelines were developed at the recommendation of the Advisory Committee on Access for People with Disabilities, formed in 2017 to examine and advise the Chief Judge and Chief Administrative Judge on a broad scope of issues to ensure best practices in providing access for individuals with disabilities.

The guidelines, which will serve to expedite the provision of appropriate accommodations for those with special needs, are summarized as follows:

- Accommodation requests may be made orally or in writing.
- All accommodation requests made in advance of a court appearance in New York City should be directed to the Chief Clerk of the Court.
- All accommodation requests made in advance of a court appearance outside New York City should be directed to the District Executive.

- The Chief Clerk/District Executive will assess whether the request involves a judicial accommodation, such as an adjournment, additional time to submit papers, phone appearance, trial breaks etc.; or an administrative accommodation, such as the provision of assistive listening devices, use of a Sign language interpreter etc.

- If the request solely concerns a judicial accommodation (which can only be granted or denied by the judge presiding over the proceeding), it will be immediately forwarded to the judge's chambers for a determination and the requestor so notified.

- If the request is solely administrative in nature, it will be handled by the Chief Clerk/District Executive or a designee.

- Sometimes non-judicial personnel are the first to receive the request, while other times the request is not made until the person appears in court. Requests involving accommodations of an administrative nature will be referred to the Chief Clerk/District Executive; requests made directly to a judge for purely judicial accommodations will be determined by the presiding judge without referring it to the Chief Clerk/District Executive.

- Any aspect of a request made directly to a judge in New York City that involves an administrative accommodation will be referred to the Chief Clerk of the Court; outside New York City, such administrative accommodation requests will be forwarded by the judge to the District Executive.

- Chief Clerks and District Executives must consult with the courts' Statewide ADA Coordinator before denying an accommodation request. If a request is denied, the Chief Clerk/District Executive must issue a written Denial of Accommodation Form and give it to the requestor, with a copy to the State ADA Coordinator. An administrative denial is subject to review, within 10 days, by the State ADA Coordinator.

Further information regarding these guidelines, along with information about the court system's commitment to assuring access to all, is available at: http://ww2.nycourts.gov/accessibility/index.shtml.

# # #

CASES

STATUTES, RULES AND REGULATIONS

FEDERAL

United States Code

Code of Federal Regulations

STATE

Civil Practice Law and Rules

Civil Rights Law

Corrections Law

Education Law

New York City

N.Y.C. Administrative Code

Michael L. Fox is Assistant Professor of Business Law in the School of Business at Mount Saint Mary College, in Orange County, New York. He teaches in the undergraduate business program and Masters of Business Administration program. He also serves as the Coordinator of the Business Graduate (MBA) Program, and as the College's Pre-Law Advisor. In addition, he is Assistant Adjunct Professor of Law in Professional Responsibility at Columbia University School of Law in New York City. Before this book, he authored the book *Primer for an Evolving eWorld* (Kendall Hunt Publ. Co. 2019, 2d Ed. 2020).

Professor Fox received his Bachelor of Arts degree, Phi Beta Kappa and *summa cum laude*, from Bucknell University, with a major in Economics and minor in Biology. He was elected to Phi Beta Kappa in his junior year. At graduation, he received the award for highest standing among those in the major field of Economics. Professor Fox received his Doctor of Law degree from Columbia University School of Law, where he was a Harlan Fiske Stone Scholar and an Articles Editor on the *Columbia Business Law Review*.

Professor Fox is a former law clerk to Hon. Lawrence E. Kahn, U.S. District Judge, Northern District of New York, in Albany. He has been rated AV-Preeminent by Martindale-Hubbell since 2015, and was selected to the Upstate New York Super Lawyers list from 2013 through 2016, when he was engaged in the active practice of law. He is admitted to practice in New York State, as well as the U.S. District Courts for the Southern, Eastern and Northern Districts of New York (*N.D.N.Y. is currently inactive*), the Second Circuit U.S. Court of Appeals, and the Supreme Court of the United States. He has been a litigation associate with Stroock & Stroock & Lavan LLP, in Manhattan; and, sequentially, an associate, senior counsel, and partner and litigation managing attorney at Jacobowitz & Gubits, LLP, in New York's Hudson Valley. At Jacobowitz & Gubits his primary practice areas included Federal Practice, Electronic Discovery, Estates Litigation, Employment and Discrimination Law, and Business Entity Disputes. From February 2014 to November 2016, he served as Deputy Corporation Counsel and special labor counsel for the City of Port Jervis. Just prior to entering full-time academia, he was special counsel with the Hudson Valley law firm Catania, Mahon, Milligram & Rider, PLLC.

Professor Fox is a former Vice President for the Ninth Judicial District of the New York State Bar Association, and former member of the NYSBA Executive Committee. He previously served as a Delegate in the American Bar Association House of Delegates from 2008 through 2014, and as a Delegate in the NYSBA House of Delegates from 2008 to 2014. He is currently again serving in the NYSBA House of Delegates, 2015 to present. He is a member of the Commercial and Federal Litigation Section, and a past Chairperson of the Young Lawyers Section (one of NYSBA's largest Sections). He also serves on the NYSBA Committee on Professional Discipline and Committee on Legal Education and Admission to the Bar, among others; and Chairs NYSBA's Standing Committee on Communications and Publications. Involved with the NYSBA YLS Trial Academy program, held at Cornell Law School, since its inception in 2010, Professor Fox served as a member of critique faculty and co-chair of the Committee on the NYSBA YLS Trial Academy from 2013 through 2019. In 2017 and 2018 he served as a team leader and lecturer at Trial Academy; and in 2019, he served as a lecturer and critique faculty at the 10th Anniversary Trial Academy. Professor Fox serves on the Board of Directors of the Orange County Bar Association and the Advisory Board of the Food Bank of the Hudson Valley.

Professor Fox is co-host of *Gold/Fox: Non-Billable,* a podcast of the New York State Bar Association, available on Spotify, Google Play, Apple iTunes/Podcast App, iHeart Radio App, or wherever podcasts are available. He has authored or co-authored numerous articles and CLE materials, and has spoken at more than 100 conferences, programs and symposia, concerning federal civil procedure, attorney-client privilege and work product, electronic discovery and social media, evidence, professional ethics, employment/anti-discrimination law, and pre-law advice.